I HAVEN'T UNDERSTOOD ANYTHING SINCE 1962 AND OTHER NEKKID TRUTHS

Lewis Grizzard

BALLANTINE BOOKS • NEW YORK

Library of Congress Catalog Card Number: 92-53653

ISBN 0-345-38597-7

This edition published by arrangement with Villard Books, a division of Random House, Inc. Villard Books is a registered trademark of Random House, Inc.

Manufactured in the United States of America

First Ballantine Books Edition: January 1994

Contents

One of the Few Introductions in Literature That's Worth Reading

I HAD A HANDLE ON THINGS IN 1962. IT WAS THE YEAR I turned sixteen and got my driver's license. It was the year I lettered in basketball and baseball in high school. I'd never heard of Vietnam in 1962. I didn't know that eating fried foods was bad for me. Arnold Palmer was still winning golf tournaments. Sandy Koufax was still pitching for the Dodgers.

Whenever I wanted French fries in 1962, Mama would cut potatoes by hand and cook them for me. Movies hadn't become "films," most of them still made sense, and nobody in them—unless they were made in Sweden—got naked. I had a large collection of Elvis records in 1962 and hung out at my home-town truck stop that had an all-country jukebox featuring Hank Williams, Faron Young, Jim Reeves, Ernest Tubb, Kitty Wells, and Patsy Cline.

I had a pretty blond girlfriend. The best thing on television was *Gunsmoke*. Miss Kitty was a good businessperson, but she wasn't pushy and could accept a compliment from a man without charging him with sexual harassment.

I slept well in 1962.

But the very next year, somebody shot the president. I was changing classes in high school when the principal announced it on the public-address system. Soon after, I saw the alleged assassin shot dead on live television.

Then the Beatles came.

Then all hell broke loose.

And changes began to unravel my simple, neat world. What once was good became bad. What once was unthinkable became acceptable. Somebody introduced Lite beer, forerunner to nonalcoholic beer. The national television news went from fifteen minutes to a half hour, because there was more bad news to announce. A lot more.

People—American people—got completely naked on the movie screen, the free-agent system was introduced into professional sports, and a fat kid named Jack Nicklaus replaced Arnold Palmer as the world's best golfer.

Sandy Koufax got arthritis and retired.

And it didn't stop there. It began to steamroll over me. So much of what I had been taught was right, suddenly was wrong. Girls wanted to be in the Boy Scouts. Later, homosexuals wanted to be in the Boy Scouts.

The "isms" came. Racism, sexism. The phobias came. Homophobia, xenophobia. Causes sprang up faster than I could keep up with them. Save the Whales. Nuke the Whales for Jesus.

Hippies. Drugs. Punk rock.

Northern sportswriters complained because Southern colleges wouldn't recruit black athletes, so

Southern colleges recruited black athletes in droves. Then Northern sportswriters said all Southern college athletic departments had "plantation mentalities" and were exploiting the black athletes.

They started advertising feminine-hygiene products on television. People began paying two dollars for a bottle of water.

I had three friends killed in Vietnam.

Phil Donahue got his own television show.

My second wife made me go to see a psychiatrist. We were living in Chicago. The psychiatrist wanted to know if my mother had ever held me and read to me as a child.

I said, "Probably." He asked if I would mind if he held me and read to me. What did I know about psychiatry?

The man held me and read to me from some kid's book about a rabbit and a turtle, as I recall. I lasted about four minutes before I burst out of his apartment. My second wife and I got a divorce.

My grandfather had been a Democrat. All my forebears had been Democrats. Then the liberals took over the Democratic party and spent all our money, so I became a Republican, the party of Dwight Eisenhower, whom my grandfather hated for spending so much time playing golf at Augusta National when he was president. I felt guilty for that.

Watergate. The older I get, the more I think it was much ado about nothing other than a new breed of journalists running amok instead of covering fires. Journalists wanted to bring down presidents. So they did.

I managed three divorces by 1982, and then began going out with women who looked at me like I was crazy when I asked them to fry hand-cut French fries for me.

AIDS, OPEC, the sushi eaters, PMS, VCR, ICBM, CD, and what happened to TLC? "The Arabs are trying to buy America," somebody said. Somebody else replied, "Don't worry. The Japs won't sell it to them."

I wrote the word "Japs" in a column. An editor replaced it with "Japanese" and told me I was insensitive.

The American League adopted the designated-hitter rule.

The privately owned American passenger-train system collapsed. I had to remember my seat cushion could be used for flotation in case my plane crashed into a body of water.

Miami was lost to the Cubans. San Francisco was lost, first to the hippies, and then to the homosexuals. New York was lost, because it became ungovernable. Washington became a crime capital, gangs in Los Angeles got their hands on nuclear weapons, and a hole in the ozone layer is going to burn us all to a crisp one day anyway, if radon or cholesterol doesn't get us first.

The Berlin Wall fell. When can we expect a unified Germany to attack Poland again? The Soviet Union crumbled. We'll have to use our tax money to feed its citizens.

We won the war in the Gulf, but we didn't have George Patton or Douglas MacArthur around to tell the president to stick to it and then go ahead and take care of Saddam Hussein once and for all.

The Atlanta Braves finally went to the World Series, and the Native Americans (aka The People Who Were Here First) screamed racism because the team used a Native American name and its fans dressed up like Cochise and brought tomahawks to games. Atlanta won all three outdoor games of the

World Series. Unfortunately, it lost all four played indoors under a Teflon roof in Minneapolis.

I went out with a woman who got mad at me because I told her I was too tired to have sex.

"Besides," I told her, "we've only known each other for three hours."

She got up, dressed, and went home. I never saw her again.

A lot of good people got assassinated. A lot of bad people got off too easy.

Del Shannon committed suicide.

I was switching through the cable one day and came upon MTV. Good God.

Somebody introduced instant grits.

Masters and Johnson decided to get a divorce.

I was reading one day and came upon the name of some sort of rock-music group called the Butthole Surfers.

Do what?

It's been thirty years since 1962. I'm forty-six, haven't forgiven the Japs for Pearl Harbor, have tired of all of the movements that just won't go away, still don't want to be around homosexuals, remain convinced Bernie Goetz did the right thing when he shot those punks in the New York subway, can quit smoking for a time but can't seem to kick it for good, have never drunk Perrier, still write on a manual typewriter, can't figure out telephones anymore, put too much vodka in my screwdrivers, despise computers, and I still don't have a clue what it is women really want.

This book is dedicated to everyone just like me, the Lord have mercy upon us.

The Speech Police

I KEEP THINKING ABOUT EARL BUTZ. POOR OL' EARL. HE was the first victim of the Speech Police, or at least the first I can remember.

Earl Butz, for those who don't or can't remember, was secretary of agriculture under Gerald Ford. Earl told a joke one day in 1976. He probably didn't think much about it, because he told it in public, which is where jokes are usually told. He probably had been telling jokes for years, and he had never gotten into trouble before.

But somebody overheard Earl tell this particular joke, and they told somebody else, and somebody else told somebody else, until it was in the papers and on television, and Earl Butz lost his job as secretary of agriculture because he told a joke.

It was a racial joke. I'm not going to repeat it here because it's not that funny, and I want to make all the wimpy pansy-asses who are going to faint when they read some of the things I'm going to say later in this book read a little more before they faint.

Racial humor is easy humor. And anybody holding a position like the one Earl Butz had should have been smarter than to tell a joke like that in public.

But that's not the point. The point is Earl Butz was the first victim of the modern-day Speech Police.

Jimmy Carter was second. He got nailed in the same year as Earl.

Jimmy Carter was running for the presidency in 1976. In front of representatives of the media, he put the following two words together:

"Ethnic" and "purity."

Mountains trembled. Foundations shook.

"Did you hear what Jimmy Carter said?"

"No, what?"

"He said, 'ethnic purity.' "

"He didn't!"

"Yes, he did."

"Is that good or bad?"

"That's bad."

"Why?"

"Because it sounds like something Hitler might have said."

"So that makes Jimmy Carter a . . ."

"You're absolutely correct. It makes him a bigot."

"And a racist."

"And a Nazi."

So all of a sudden we had a bigoted, racist Nazi running for president of the United States.

"But do we know that for sure?"

"Sure we do. He's a Southerner, isn't he?"

If Jimmy Carter had run for president in 1992 and had said "ethnic purity," he not only wouldn't have been elected, as he was in '76, but he also would have been forced out of the race, been berated by African-Americans, Italian-Americans, Polish-Americans, Native Americans, Jewish-Americans, Hispanic-Americans, Asian-Americans, Arab-Americans, Whatever-Americans, and Abe Rosenthal of *The New York Times*.

Even David Duke, who really *was* a Nazi and a KKK'er, knew better than to say "ethnic purity." So did Pat Buchanan, who said (and caught all kinds of hell about it) if you dropped a million Englishmen into Virginia one day, they would be able to blend with the culture faster than a million Zulus. But he never said "ethnic purity."

What Jimmy Carter meant by "ethnic purity" was that it wasn't such a horrible thing to have neighborhoods and regions where the same sort of people lived.

Most every American city includes such areas. There's usually a Chinatown and a Little Italy and a Harlem and a barrio. The immediate thought that comes to mind today is huddled masses of homeless and have-nots living in squalor. And, in some areas, that certainly is the case. But it can also mean a nice neighborhood where people of the same cultural background live because people of the same cultural background seem to be drawn together. Human nature, they call it.

Jimmy Carter didn't see anything wrong with any of this. He simply wasn't for rounding everybody up and then reestablishing them into neighborhoods by some pre-set quota whereby each area had to be a perfectly balanced cultural mix.

It didn't mean Jimmy Carter didn't want African-Americans moving into all-white neighborhoods. It didn't mean he wanted to resegregate the schools.

But Jimmy Carter had used "ethnic" and "purity" together. The Führer wanted a pure German race where everybody had fair skin, blond hair, and blue eyes. He thought it would make his country stronger. Hitler was also a madman. Nobody in his or her right mind would have thought Jimmy Carter with his smile and his born-againness would be for anything like that.

But the media are no longer in their right mind. When *The New York Times* and *The Washington Post* brought down Richard Nixon, they started an entirely new sort of journalism in this country, which goes something like this: "Sooner or later, that son of a bitch is going to say something we can nail him to the cross with, so don't let him out of your sight."

Thus, I believe, were born the Speech Police.

Jimmy Carter managed to get elected in 1976 because the Speech Police were still in their embryonic stage. And at least he hadn't told a racial joke about tight vaginas, loose tennis shoes, and a warm place to do No. 2 (that's absolutely as far as I'm going), like Earl Butz did.

But the Speech Police had, in fact, been established, and they began to grow bigger and bigger and stronger. Joseph McCarthy should have been so vigilant.

How many have fallen since to these watchdogs of people who have thoughts and then have the audacity to speak them?

Jimmy (the Greek) Snyder, the legendary bookmaker, mentioned "breeding" when he was speaking of the African-American professional athlete. The Speech Police got him fired from his job with CBS sports.

Poor old Andy Rooney said something the homosexuals didn't like, and CBS suspended him.

ipanis, general manager of the Los Angeles
s baseball team, said African-Americans
ed buoyancy. He lost his job overnight.

immy Breslin, renowned New York columnist,
called an Asian-American female colleague a "yellow cur." He was suspended.

And let's look at more recent instances that have
occurred as the Speech Police have grown to mon-
strous proportions.

Vice President Dan Quayle was speaking of New
York governor Mario Cuomo, who was touted as a
Democratic presidential candidate in 1992. As he
spoke, Quayle never used the governor's last name.
He referred to him only as "Mario."

The Speech Police jumped on that one. By using
only "Mario," they concluded, Quayle was trying to
point out the governor was an Italian and what he
was really saying was that Governor Cuomo was a
member of the Mafia, and if he were to be elected
president, he'd probably appoint John Gotti to a high
Cabinet post.

When Japanese officials said American workers
were lazy, the Speech Police didn't make a move.
But when Senator Ernest Hollings of South Carolina pointed out it was the American worker who
developed the two atomic bombs the United States
dropped on the Japanese to end World War II, the SP
got its panties into a terrible wad.

Pat Buchanan also called the Chinese leader a
"dwarf." That made him insensitive to Asian-
Americans *and* short people. He also said Congress
was an Israeli-occupied territory, the anti-Semitic
little pit bull.

You don't even have to say anything to get in
trouble with the Speech Police and their small, but
ferocious, corps. Barbara Bush was asked to do the

commencement address at all-female Welle.
lege. But the little snippets who go to schoc
refused to have any of that, despite the fact i.
older sister was first lady of the United States.

The female student body, or a good part of it, said
they didn't want to listen to a woman who had accomplished nothing more in her life than marry a
future president, and they didn't want to waste their
time on her since they were all going to become lawyers.

The fact that Barbara Bush raised a family, ran a
home, and probably had more influence on the leader
of the free world than anybody else alive was lost on
them. If I'd been Barbara Bush, I'd have said, "Tell
the little shits to go to hell." Ninety-nine percent, at
least, of the American population would have
thought that was great. The Speech Police, on the
other hand, would have called for her tongue to be
cut out, and a feminist terrorist group probably
would have sneaked into the White House and killed
her dog.

Before going any further, allow me to explain just
who the Speech Police are.

At the top are *The New York Times* and *The
Washington Post*. They have tapped the telephones
and tongues of everybody in the United States who
is anybody. Everything that anybody who is anybody says is recorded in the *Times*'s and *Post*'s news-
rooms. Editors listen to these recordings, and if
anybody who is anybody says anything they regard
as racist, sexist, gay-bashing, or any kind of bash-
ing, they carry large stories about it.

Just under the *Times* and the *Post* are the television networks. Most of the time, they find out who
the Speech Police's victims are by reading the *Times*

and the *Post*. Then they do stories on the nightly news. Not everybody reads the *Times* or the *Post*, of course. But everybody watches television.

Under the television networks are the editors of other newspapers around the country. If it was in the *Times* or the *Post*, they will put it in their papers and display it prominently, because they wish they worked for the *Times* or the *Post*. Then somebody writes an editorial that is basically a rewrite of what the *Times* and the *Post* editorials said.

Next comes spokespersons for whatever or whomever the *Times* or *Post* has said has been bashed. The president of the National Association for the Advancement of Left-handed Lesbian Cross-dressers Who Want to Marry Each Other and Adopt Pet Squirrels calls a press conference, which the *Times* and the *Post* cover. He or she expresses outrage and calls for the head of whoever has been collared by the Speech Police.

The spokespersons also call for boycotts and protests. The networks cover the press conferences and follow that up with coverage of the boycotts and protests. People boycotting and protesting with signs and chants have made more television appearances in the last several years than Vanna White.

Other newspapers carry stories about the press conferences and cover the boycotts and protests, as well. Readers and viewers are inundated with all this and say, "Damn, I'm sick of this crap," but nobody pays much attention to what people who *aren't* anybody say or think, so it goes on and on.

Next on the list come liberal thinkers, leaders in the fields of religion and education. They are always interviewing on television some minister of some religious sect you never heard of, or Dr. So-and-so, head of the sociology department at some large, liberal-thinking college or university like Harvard or Stanford or Pussy Willow A&M, who says a lot of things you don't understand. And for good reason. What people like that say rarely makes sense.

After these people come activists, people who have a lot of time on their hands and go around looking for things to be offended by. This group normally doesn't work in factories, gasoline stations, Waffle House restaurants, lumberyards, or on police departments or farms. You can't go around trying to be offended if you have to work so you can eat and sleep out of the rain.

A lot of activists have beards. Even female activists. Most of them have educations, but many of them have been educated beyond their intelligence.

Add all these people together, and they amount to a minuscule percentage of the entire population, but that doesn't matter. Since they control all the newspapers and television networks, they also have the floor at all times, and the rest of us never get a chance to be recognized.

But one might ask, "What about conservative politicians? Can't and don't they ever speak out?" Oh, one might slip and say he or she doesn't believe in racial quotas and suggest the welfare system needs changing, but the *Times* et al. will scream, and an aide to the politician will say, "I don't care if that's the way you feel. You just can't say things like that anymore."

That's what the Speech Police finally have done. They have made the American tradition of speaking one's mind almost a hanging offense.

"But what if one speaks his mind and it happens to be the truth?"

The *truth?* What's the truth got to do with anything? We know damn well a million Englishmen could be dropped into Virginia and the only problem they would have is finding warm beer. A million Zulus wouldn't have a chance. It's not that there's anything wrong with a million Zulus. As a matter of fact, I pulled for the Zulus in the movie *Zulu Dawn,* when that same million came over the hill and wiped out all those snotty, overconfident English soldiers.

But could a Zulu walk into a brokerage house in Richmond and get a job? Of course not. Could a Zulu adapt quickly to the strange Western customs? Sure—they would all be running around in their loincloths trying to get a membership in a health club.

But by saying what he did, despite the fact that it was true, Pat Buchanan was labeled a racist because he said Zulus, and Zulus are from Africa, where African-Americans are from, and he probably thinks African-Americans aren't buoyant just like Al Campanis.

How the Speech Police managed to deal with truth is they started something called *political correctness,* which is fairly simple to define. It means *keep your mouth shut, even if it is true, because we don't care about truth anymore.* What if somebody asks you, "What do you think of welfare mothers who continue to have babies out of wedlock because they can get more benefits that way?" The truthful way to answer is by saying, "To hell with 'em. The welfare system is completely out of control, and although I certainly believe in helping people if they really need it, I also believe there are many instances of welfare cheating, and as long as welfare is available, it will, in fact, zap the ambition for some to go out and see if they can find a job. Plus, the government is going broke trying to pay for it."

That's the truth, but it's not politically correct.

The best way to answer is first to ask a question: "How many babies are we talking about a welfare mother having out of wedlock?"

And let's say the answer is, "Oh, about seventeen."

The politically correct answer would be, then, "The government should buy her a roomier Cadillac."

Here are some other things you can't say if you want to be politically correct, regardless of whether or not they are true.

—"If male homosexuals would stop having unprotected anal sex with one another, it probably would go a long way in helping stem the rising tide of AIDS cases."

—"The Rev. Al Sharpton is an opportunist who looks like Fats Domino with a Prince Valiant haircut."

—"I pulled for Clarence Thomas."

—"I wouldn't pee on Ted Kennedy's leg if he was on fire."

—"I think women who don't shave their legs aren't sexy."

—"Look at where all the racial strife is now—New York. People have learned to get along in Mississippi."

—"Goddamn sneaky Japs. I still don't trust 'em."

—"Is Pat Schroeder a pain in the ass, or what?"

—"Just because one group happened to do poorer on a test than another group, I don't think we should make the test easier for the group that did the poorest. Why don't we keep the test the same and figure out a way to smarten up the group that came in second?"

—"I thought *Grand Canyon* sucked."

—"Jesus, I'm tired of hearing about the plight of the black athlete. How much does Michael Jordan make a year anyway?"

—"My wife found some old *Amos and Andy* tapes and gave them to me for Christmas. Boy, I'd forgotten just how funny that was. I don't understand why they can't bring them back. What's the difference between Fred Sanford and Kingfish?"

—"Why don't they make golf courses just for women? They could take all day playing, and nobody would give a damn."

—"If they can pick a black (African-American) All-American team, why can't they pick a white All-American team?"

—"Damn, I'm sick of the federal government telling me I've got to hire some idiot who doesn't know his ass from third base just because he's [fill in the blank]."

—"I worked sixteen hours a day, seven days a week, for years until I finally made it. Why should the government take my hard-earned money to pay some son of a bitch who is too lazy to work?"

—"You know, a lot of the things David Duke said made sense."

—"Crank up the *Enola Gay*."

Say anything like any of that, and you are politically incorrect, which also means you are racist, sexist, homophobic, etc., and you also probably are for giving drug traffickers the death penalty.

Political correctness also means changing a few ideas about history. Christopher Columbus is no longer a brave explorer, for instance. He's a rotten white guy who introduced all sorts of disease to the New World he discovered, and he should be erased from the history books and more attention should be given to Afrocentrism, which is about civilization beginning in Africa, where it was later introduced to the Greeks by soul singer James Brown, who was wrongly incarcerated several thousand years later by racist South Carolina law-enforcement officers who didn't realize the reason James was doing all that dope and trying to outrun them at 110 miles per hour was to protest there aren't any African-Americans in the National Hockey League.

That's basically a politically correct history of the world, except you need to throw in that Plato and Socrates were homosexual lovers, God is a black woman, and the Devil is a white guy who belonged to the all-white Kappa Alpha fraternity when he was an undergraduate at the University of Alabama.

In order to be politically correct, it is also necessary to know the correct term to use when referring to certain groups who are very touchy about things like that.

If you're still saying "black," you're wrong. It's African-American now, and don't dare mention that the *C* in NAACP still stands for you know what.

Indians are not Indians anymore. They are Native Americans, despite the fact America got its name from an Italian.

"Gay" and "homosexual" may even be on the way out. Soon, one might be asked to say "individuals exercising their right to engage in an alternative lifestyle."

Then, you get into your other So-and-so-Americans like Italians, Hispanic, etc., except you never refer to anybody whose forebears came from say, England, because English-Americans are all a bunch of rich Protestant white people who have all the money and good jobs and got them by kicking around everybody else.

Where a white guy gets into trouble the most often is when he refers to the gender that isn't male. That gender used to be called "female." But "female" is out, because the word "male" is in there, so how about "feperson"? How about "women"? No, that has "men" in it. Some members of the Speech Police are saying it's okay to say that word, as long as you spell it "wo-myn." So is a "hysterectomy" a "herterectomy" now? If you read about Catherine the Great are you reading about Russian herstory?

To be completely politically correct, should men say, instead of "Look at that womyn over there"; "Look at the individual who is certainly my equal in each and every way over there"?

We've gone way beyond the old "Miss," "Ms.," and "Mrs." debate. I found out something else, too. Never call a trumpet player a "lady." Here's what happened to me:

The Atlanta Braves, woeful since back when you still said you were "shacked up with your main squeeze" instead of today's politically correct "cohabitating with your significant other," won the 1992 National League Baseball Pennant. The Braves hosted their first World Series in mid-October, and I was there on assignment for my newspaper, to columnize about what I saw and felt on this historic (herstoric) occasion.

When it came time for the national anthem, the stadium announcer said a trumpet player from the St. Louis Symphony would do the honors.

I began to think, which I shouldn't have. Start thinking in these times and you simply don't know where it could lead.

My first thought was, "Why is a trumpet player from the St. Louis Symphony doing the national anthem at the first World Series game ever played in Atlanta?"

Wasn't there anybody from Atlanta who could have played the national anthem? I felt bringing in an outsider was both inappropriate and an affront. This was Atlanta's finest hour. The person from St. Louis who played the anthem happened to be a *womyn*. The reason I knew that was because the stadium announcer had called her name, and it was something like "Delores." Also, I could see her on the field.

After the game, I wrote something like, "At 8:42, a trumpet player from the St. Louis Symphony, a lady, played the national anthem. I'm not sure why."

I admit it was a lazy paragraph. In the first place, I should have asked somebody who might have known why somebody from St. Louis was playing the national anthem at Atlanta's first home World Series game. I would have found out, as I did later, Major League Baseball, not the Braves, decides who's going to play the national anthem at World Series games, and perhaps somebody in on that decision-making arm owed something to said trumpet player.

Where I made my big mistake, however, was identifying the trumpet player as "a lady." Local feminist members of the Speech Police barraged me the next few days with letters and telephone calls, and threatened the continued health of my testicles.

I was berated and called a Neanderthal because these women said it was a dirty, rotten sexist thing to do to identify the gender of the trumpet player.

Some of the letters and calls also said I was being patronizing for using the term "lady."

I didn't understand. Weren't we taught at journalism school about giving all the details in a story? The trumpet player had, in fact, been a womyn. I was simply stating a fact. A *truth*, that pesky word again.

According to the letters and calls, however, here was why I was politically incorrect for identifying the gender of the trumpet player. Wrote one irate "individual who is [my] equal, etc.":

"If the trumpet player had been a male, would you have written 'A trumpet player, etc., a gentleman, . . . ?' Of course you wouldn't. But you found it somehow strange a woman would be playing the trumpet at a baseball game, and by using the term 'lady' you expressed that feeling. The fact is, women can play a trumpet just as well as men."

I certainly never meant to imply such a thing, although if there would have even been a Battle of the Sexes in trumpet playing back when Louis Armstrong was still alive, I'd have taken him over any trumpet player the National Organization of Women might have entered.

I actually went as far as to call a spokes-Ms. at *Ms.* magazine for further enlightenment. I was told basically the same thing the letter-writers and callers said. I was politically incorrect for identifying the gender of the trumpet player. I was also told "lady" is no longer an operable term, as when a womyn drives into a mechanic shop with a broken muffler, and Leroy, the head mechanic, greets her by saying, "What can I do for you, little lady?"

I wrote somewhat of an apology in a subsequent column, pleading ignorance to all the rules of political correctness. After that, I got an equal amount of calls and letters from men saying I had betrayed them by apologizing. I also got a few calls and letters from the other gender (and I'm not implying anything by saying "the other gender," I just couldn't think of any other way to say it) indicating they still liked to be called "a lady." But these women likely still make the coffee for their male bosses each morning.

Perhaps some sort of disclaimer is necessary at this point. I know if this book is reviewed by anybody for the *Times* or the *Post* they will skip right over this, but I'm going to say it anyway:

1. I don't want to put black people in the back of the bus again. The civil-rights movement was the right thing to do, and the courage of those involved set an example for all humanity.

But I'm tired of racism as an excuse. More black men are in jail than in college. Black leaders blame white people for that, and as long as there is somebody else to blame, nothing gets done about a problem.

Black politicians get caught stealing. It's a racist plot, somebody cries. And there's a subsequent rally at the First Ebenezer Baptist Church, where supporters of the politicians get together and shout racism in unison. They also wind up on the news and in the papers the next day.

Marion Barry? It was white people who put that cocaine in his pipe. Richard Arrington, mayor of Birmingham? He didn't do anything wrong. Because we're talking about Birmingham, as in Alabama, Selma, the South, the fire hoses, dogs, Rosa Parks, and Bull Connor. Another racist scheme to bring down black leaders.

Hosea Williams, an old civil-rights war-horse, has been a one-man traffic hazard in Atlanta for years. We're talking everything from DUI to hit-and-run. Hosea said a lot of his problems with the Atlanta police dated back to the time he tried to get a white police chief thrown out. Another racist plot.

And does the fact there hasn't *been* a white police

chief in Atlanta in decades muddy Hosea's credibility? It does with me.

Racism is such a convenient excuse. Get caught and you can always explain it away. The truth is, some black politicians steal, just like some white politicians.

I used to play a lot of tennis, but my right arm fell off as a result, so I had to quit. Several years ago, I was playing in a tournament and drew an opponent who happened to be black. At the end of one rally, he hit a ball that was wide by a good five feet. I called it out.

He called me a racist.

Racism will never die, indeed, until it ceases to be used.

2. If a womyn, or whatever I'm supposed to call them, can do the job of a man, she should be given an equal chance to get that job and receive the same pay as a man would receive if he held the position. I still have a little problem with women on the golf course who will keep hitting the ball until they get it into the hole, instead of picking up and moving to the next hole when they reach double or triple bogey, as golf's handicap system provides, but that's a minor thing compared to the larger question of women's rights in the workplace.

3. Homosexuality really doesn't bother me until it spills into the streets or is flaunted at me. I sort of feel the same way about heterosexuality, although not as strongly. God gave us the motel room so we wouldn't do things like that.

But political correctness has gotten out of hand. The Speech Police have gotten out of hand. They are stifling expression. It used to take me, say, an hour to write a newspaper column, once I settled on the idea and decided not to be embarrassed about it.

Today, I must search deep for any insensitivities in each sentence, each word. Politicians have to be wary of each statement they utter, lest some group become aroused and they have to go on the nightly news and say, "I regret referring to [name it] as [name it]." Politicians were sidesteppers nonpareil as it was.

Lord knows, there is such a thing as good taste and manners. And there is also such a thing as individuals holding lofty positions using some judgment. As much as I abhor the Speech Police, I certainly don't want the president of the United States opening his press conferences by telling divisive racial jokes.

Don Rickles is the only white person who can still get away with using racial humor, for some reason I don't understand. The president can't do it. Unless we have a black president one day. Then, he or she can make fun of white people drinking Tab and wearing weird clothes when they play golf. It's okay to stereotype the majority.

Let's take the classic example of the freedom of speech. It doesn't give somebody the right to yell "Fire!" in a crowded theater, true, but it's still a great way to get a seat when you arrive late for *Fried Green Tomatoes,* and the place is packed. I'd rather a few folks get away with remarks better left unsaid than to make it frightening to open one's mouth for fear the words that come out are going to offend the 10 million minority and special-interest groups whose antennae are always up to find an offending tongue.

Allow me, if you will, a couple of personal experiences with the Speech Police, whose Written-Word Division has had its way with me on a number of occasions.

The New York Times Sunday Magazine once did a profile on me. I knew I didn't have a chance going in, because *The New York Times,* when it does anything on anything Southern, is going to get racism in there somewhere.

The *Times* assigned a writer to me. He attended a speech I gave to a Memphis real estate group visiting Atlanta for a national convention.

I did an hour for the group. Not once—not *once*—did I do racial humor. I never have. It's suicide, for one thing. For another thing, I don't need it.

Yet, when the article appeared, the writer did make the point that mine was an all-white audience. I didn't invite the audience. I was hired to do a job, and I don't tell the people who write me a check who should be in the audience.

The writer wanted to accompany me to my hometown of Moreland, Georgia. I gave him the three-cent tour—Moreland rarely gets a mention on even the most detailed maps. We drove by where I attended school from the second through the eighth grades. I mentioned I'd had some good friends and some good times, like when somebody lit a cherry bomb and flushed it down one of the toilets in the boys' bathroom. Cherry-bomb fuses will burn under water. What will they think of next? Water and porcelain went everywhere.

I showed him where we used to play baseball and told him Dudley Stamps once hit a ball all the way from home plate up to the monkey bars where the young kids played. It didn't seem near as far a distance looking at it then than when Dudley delivered his Ruthian swing back in 1959, but time shrinks a lot of things.

The reporter had one question for me after I had finished my reminiscing.

"Were there any black children in school with you back then?"

He knew better than to ask that. He knew I was talking about the rural South in the '50s. But he just had to ask me the question anyway. I could see a passage in his story already, "Lewis Grizzard, who gave the speech to an all-white audience, went to an all-white school where students practiced for racial bombings of churches that came later by destroying the school plumbing system with powerful fire-works, likely supplied by the Ku Klux Klan."

The article that appeared was entitled "Is It True What He Says About Dixie?" I knew they'd get "Dix-ie" in there somewhere.

A photographer came to Atlanta and wanted to take a picture of me in front of a house with a lot of columns for that same article.

"You know," he said, "like Tara."

Yeah, I knew. I suggested we go back to my old home place where my Great-Great-Great-Grand-daddy Simon LeGree Grizzard had all those slaves he used to gather before him on the front porch at night and say, "Sing, you happy Negroes."

He actually went for it before I told him I was making fun of the Speech Police's idea that every-body from the South still carried a whip and raised cotton.

What we finally did was go to a friend's house in Newnan, Georgia, county seat of my native Coweta, six miles north of Moreland. He didn't have a house anywhere near something like the mythical Tara, but he did have a couple of modest columns.

I leaned up against one of the columns, and the photographer got his shot. I was surprised they hadn't asked me to bring a Confederate sword to the shoot.

The thoroughness of the Speech Police is often incredible. Here's what else the *Times* article did:

It dealt with a column I'd written from Oxford, Mississippi, a couple of years earlier concerning my attendance at an Ole Miss–Georgia football game. Ole Miss/James Meredith. Ole Miss/Governor Ross Barnett. Ole Miss/*Mississippi Burning*. Georgia/fat sheriffs. Georgia/chain gangs. Georgia/"You ain't eyeballin' me are you, boy?"

Ole Miss won the game. Ole Miss's nickname is the Rebels. At Ole Miss, the band still plays "Dixie." At Ole Miss, the fans still wave the Confederate flag.

I asked a guy after the game, "How do y'all get away with that?"

"Well," he said, "we ain't supposed to do it, but we do it anyway."

At Ole Miss, they still bring bottles of bourbon into football games. At Ole Miss, the fraternity boys still dress in Weejuns, khakis, button-down white shirts, ties, and blue blazers. Their dates dress like they're going to dinner at the Peabody in Memphis. The men give their dates corsages for the game.

At Ole Miss, somebody still prays before kickoff, and usually mentions "the game of life" and "please protect these fine young men from both schools."

At Georgia games, the whiskey Nazis, made up of campus security police individuals, search pocketbooks and coats of fans entering the game to make certain they don't bring in any alcoholic beverages and mix them into Coca-Cola like Georgia fans did for about four hundred years.

Of course, the determined still manage to slip into the game with a Ziploc bag filled with booze they stash in their underwear, and a few spies and loyalists manage to slip past the gestapo on occasion, too.

The Georgia band used to play "Dixie," but doesn't

anymore. Dixie got too tangled up in hate, and if the band did play "Dixie," the governor probably would call out the National Guard in the state to make it stop.

As a matter of fact, the Georgia band once had Dixie in its name. It was known for years as the Dixie Redcoat Band. But there was a lot of screaming, so it became, simply, the Redcoat Band.

My stepbrother, Ludlow Porch, radio star, author, and letters-to-the-editor writer, wrote a letter to the editor when that happened and said this:

"I wholeheartedly agree with the decision to drop the term 'Dixie' from the name of the University of Georgia band. I dated an ol' girl named Dixie once and she stole $200 out of my wallet.

"But should we stop there? Nay, nay. So, now it's just the Redcoat Band. We shouldn't use the word 'red' at a publically funded university. 'Red' as everybody knows means 'Commie.'

"And the entire word, 'redcoat.'

"What an affront to all who fought and died during the Revolutionary War when we won our independence from Britain by whooping up on its army, the Redcoats.

"So Dixie and Redcoat is out, leaving the Band. But 'band.' Did somebody say, 'band'? Doesn't that bring to mind Pancho Villa and his band of Mexican desperadoes? What an affront to U.S. General Black Jack Pershing who had to take his troops into Mexico to stop Villa. 'Band' has got to go, too.

"So that leaves us with 'The,' what a stupid name for a musical group. So we drop that and we don't call the former University of Georgia Dixie Redcoat Band anything. We'll be a better people for it."

A student athlete, like a gymnast, used to say a

prayer over the public-address system before Georgia football games. That was before the ACLU decided that was a violation of church and state, like having prayer in school, and threatened to sue the university if the practice of praying before football games didn't stop. It stopped.

So, in the column from Oxford, I mentioned a lot of this. I said a football game at Ole Miss reminded me of the early '60's when I was a student at Georgia.

Ole Miss beating Georgia wasn't a rarity years ago when Ole Miss was a national power. But on this occasion, it had been a long time between Rebel victories over my beloved Bulldogs.

The Ole Miss fans went a little bonkers. There is a lovely spot on the Ole Miss campus called the Grove. It's like a park. It's where the Ole Miss faithful engage in the wonderful sport of tailgaiting before and after each Ole Miss home game.

I walked through the Grove after the game. People stopped me and welcomed me to the campus. "Sorry about having to ruin it by beatin' you," a fan said. "But we don't do it very often."

Nice people, I was thinking.

Then I saw something I couldn't believe. I saw part of Ole Miss's band, maybe fifteen members, together in the Grove, serenading the fans a good two hours after the game had ended.

Ole Miss has black football players. Ole Miss has black members of the band. Of the fifteen playing in the grove, I'd guess at least five were black.

They were playing "Dixie." Over and over, they played "Dixie."

I looked at what I saw. True, the crowd was overwhelmingly white. But there were black people in the Grove. And there were those black band members joining in "Dixie."

So, in the column, I wrote about the fact the state of Mississippi has been ripped up one side and down for so long. The racist Mississippi. The ignorant Mississippi. The racially motivated murdering Mississippi.

But, I wrote, maybe the people in Mississippi actually have come further than any of the rest of us in looking past old symbols of hate. Maybe they had learned to understand the differences in the white and black cultures and each become comfortable with the other's. I saw a peaceful scene that afternoon, one far removed from the pit of racial violence that is New York City, for instance.

The *Times* found the column. The *Times* found that one out of more than a decade worth of others, and used it to continue to flirt with the idea that somewhere inside me—deep, perhaps, but still there—Jim Crow lived on.

For the record, however, I received over five thousand letters from Mississippians thanking me for that column.

One citizen wrote, "It's the first time anybody's said anything nice about Mississippi in thirty years. It made me cry."

The Washington Post had its way with me once, too. I was in town on a publicity tour for a new book, and I was interviewed by a reporter from the Style section. Nice interview.

The next morning, there I was pictured atop the section with an accompanying article. The first paragraph said there were a lot of things I didn't like. Bossy women were mentioned. So were homosexuals. And "blacks"—after that word came three words in parenthesis—"(especially poor ones)."

The Washington Post said I didn't like poor black people.

I read the lead paragraph several times to make sure I was reading what I thought I was reading. I was.

I was horrified. Where had that come from? I certainly hadn't said to the interviewer, "If there's one thing I can't stand, it's poor black people." I was positive I'd never written anything that would imply that, either.

Even if I had, no editor in his right mind would have allowed it. I tried to think, where on earth could that have come from? Was it perhaps something I had said about the welfare system? I personally think the welfare system needs some serious revamping. I got that idea from watching squirrels in my backyard.

Squirrels never stop working. Squirrels are relentless in their pursuit to store food. Squirrels know if they don't go out and hunt their food, nobody else is going to do it for them.

I look at squirrels, and then I look at my dog, Catfish, the black Lab. Catfish spends a lot of time sleeping on my living-room couch. He never goes outside and looks for food. That's because he doesn't have to. He knows he can lie right there on the sofa, and I'll provide his food for him. He's on a welfare scholarship.

But simply because I think the public teat goes out to too many who are undeserving, does it necessarily follow I don't like poor black people?

I don't like Jesse Jackson, but he isn't poor. I don't know who writes his checks, but I know he wears expensive suits and somehow is able to show up anywhere in the world where he thinks there's a TV or photo opportunity for him. I don't like Jesse Jackson because I think he's a bombastic fraud who, deep down, would like to be king of America, and he thinks he deserves it.

I don't like Rev. Al Sharpton, either. He had to know Tawana Brawley was lying the whole time, but he needed to use her to advance himself. I also want Wilt Chamberlain to prove he had sex with twenty thousand women by naming each of them. I wonder why soul singer James Brown got all that attention at the 1992 Emmy Awards when his most recent accomplishment was serving a prison sentence, and I think the jury did right in finding Mike Tyson guilty of rape. Stop this man before he fondles, and does worse, again.

But poor black people? With whom did *The Washington Post* get me confused? I've never worn a sheet.

Naturally, I read the entire article in the *Post* Style section. If a reporter makes a broad statement in the beginning of an article (Lewis Grizzard doesn't like poor black people), he or she is supposed to support the statement by giving specific examples of why later. Journalism 101.

There was nothing in the article to back up the statement in the first paragraph. Nothing. In fact, the article even had its moments of flattery.

But we're talking the Great *Washington Post* here. *The* newspaper of record when it comes to the doings of our federal government. And an editor never noticed a reporter had made a rather serious charge about somebody and then had nothing to support the charge?! Didn't the *Post* lose a Pulitzer Prize when it was discovered the reporter who did the winning work made up the whole thing? Who really *was* Deep Throat? Woodward or Bernstein's Harvey?

Speech Police brutality is what I call it. Guilt by geography.

The *Times* and the *Post* and the other members of the SP won't like this book because it will set new heights for political incorrectness.

My only purpose, however, is to say: "Let's relax all this New Sensitivity a little before we all have to get our jaws wired shut because we're afraid that no matter what we might say, some son of a bitch is going to take offense."

There is also something else I wanted to say: Do you realize there is only one group of citizens it is okay to stereotype and make fun of, and be able to get away with it and not bring down the wrath of the Speech Police?

This group is known as rednecks. Bubbas. Good ol' boys. You can say or write anything about them.

"Rednecks are a bunch of dumb Southerners who marry their cousins, stay drunk most of the time, are ignorant, filthy, and basically worthless."

Nobody is going to beat over your head with a verbal billy stick for saying that. "You might be a redneck if you go to a family reunion looking for your next wife," wrote the Atlanta-native comedian Jeff Foxworthy, who writes books filled with one-liner redneck stereotyping.

But what if somebody wrote, "You might be a homosexual if you wear more eye shadow than your sister?"

That's "gay-bashing." That's verboten. But to hell with the rednecks. They're all illiterate and members of the Ku Klux Klan.

All that is, in fact, a load of cow manure large enough to cover up all the pickup trucks the famous daredevil Awful (Bubba) Knawful could jump over in his souped-up Moon Pie delivery truck. Jump over a few cars on a motorcycle, and they make you an American hero. Awful needed a mile and a half to get his truck going at full speed before he could make the jump, but a Moon Pie truck weighs fifty times as much as a motorcycle, and if Awful hadn't been looked down upon because he happened to be Southern and tended to end a lot of his sentences with prepositions, he might have made it to ABC's *Wide World of Sports*.

The fact is, the so-called redneck, with whom I will deal in great detail later, is the only acceptable target for stereotyping and derogatory humor.

I've been called a redneck. That, and its cousin, "good ol' boy." It doesn't bother me, and I much prefer it to "liberal," "snob," "intellectual," "gay activist," "spokesperson for Mr. Dukakis," or "President of the National Association of Weenies and Wimps."

What I would like to be known as, and how I would prefer being referred to, is a rather new label in this age of the label. Oddly enough, it was an African-American who came up with the one I, and many like me, prefer.

Andrew Young, former U.S. congressman, civil-rights leader, ambassador to the United Nations under President Carter, mayor of Atlanta, and an intelligent, thoughtful, hell of a nice guy despite all that, was asked in 1984 what he thought Walter Mondale's chances were of defeating Ronald Reagan in the presidential election.

Another thing that always impressed me about Andy was he wasn't afraid to speak his mind, hang the consequences. He once referred to fellow civil-rights activist Hosea Williams as a "turd-tapping nigger," whatever that is, and he was always getting in trouble as a member of the Carter administration with his thoughts on everybody and anything from Abe Lincoln to the PLO. He was nicer to the PLO than he was to Lincoln.

Anyway, then Mayor Young answered that Mondale didn't have a chance. The reason?

"His campaign is being run by a bunch of smart-ass white boys."

There it was. I knew it the minute I saw it in print. *Smart-ass white boys.* That's me. That's a lot of us. We are the Speech Police's worst nightmare.

Watch Out For Me, I'm A S.A.W.B.

I remember an earlier book review by a New York (I can't say if she was a lady or not, but her name was Wanda) critic, who said, "Lewis Grizzard has got to be an act. Nobody can still be this backwards, not even a white Southerner."

Well, I'm probably just as bad as some people think I am in at least some areas. I'm more antipompous, anti–rock music and anti–the idea of eating raw fish than I am a racist, sexist, and all that other stuff, but, yes, I do wonder who pays Jesse Jackson, I don't trust women with hyphenated last names wearing suits, and I attempt to avoid restaurants with homosexual waiters.

I also remember being told by an editor, after I had attacked someone like Ted Kennedy or Jane Fonda, that I was "currying to the worst instincts of the right wing." Hell, I *am* the worst instincts of the right wing, in a lot of ways. I'm against luxury taxes, for instance. The liberals wanted a luxury tax on such items as expensive boats in an effort to get the rich guys. So the rich didn't buy any boats, and the people who build, paint, and sell boats all lost their jobs. Yes, I'm a trickle-downer, and proud to be one! I also agree with the great statesman, the late Nor-

man Van Brocklin, who was also coach of the Atlanta Falcons professional football team. After some
soccer-style kicker from Hungary or some place
missed a chip-shot field goal on the last play of the
game, and the Falcons lost, Van Brocklin was asked
his thoughts on the defeat.

"They ought to tighten the goddamn immigration
laws in this country," he said.

I'm a Pat Buchanan conservative, not a George
Bush conservative or a David Duke conservative.
Bush wiggles and waffles too much for me, and David
Duke is stupid. You don't seek a career in politics by
starting out as a Nazi and a Klansman.

And this is no act. It's real. It's me. And know
what else? I think there are a lot of other people like
me, sick of the Speech Police, sick of being afraid to
speak the truth, sick of groups like the Queer Nation, the ACLU, and the National Association of
Women Who Would Just Like to Beat the Hell Out
of Every Man They See.

Sick of whining, more than anything else. Whine,
whine, bitch, bitch. It's become the national pastime.

Read on, if you dare.

••• 2 •••

Straight Southern Male Seeks Anyone Who Understands What the Hell Is Going On

Once, I put an ad in the Personals section of the newspaper. I had never done such a thing before, but I was desperate. I couldn't get a date.

I was between relationships at the time, which is to say my girlfriend had run off to join a cult that worshiped plastic, the kind that comes in the form of a wallet-sized card with raised letters and numbers on it. I had a couple of those cards, but my girlfriend had worn them down to slick, and they were no good to her anymore. She had accomplished this on a trip to London, where she bought a sizable interest in Harrods.

When I checked out of our London hotel, the Dorchester, the cashier took my plastic and returned a few seconds later to tell me I would not be able to use it to settle my account.

"And why not?" I asked.

"Because, sir," I was told, "we cannot make an

imprint of it. Your name and account number have been worn off completely, I'm afraid."

Luckily, I had enough traveler's checks with which to settle with the hotel.

My girlfriend, however, had overheard the conversation with the hotel cashier and, sensing the ramifications of being with a man with no writing on his plastic, left me a few days after we returned to the United States to join the cult. The last I heard of her, she had received the American Express Distinguished Service Cross for accumulating over two thousand dollars in charges in one afternoon at a store that sold only pantyhose and garden fertilizer.

So there I was, alone. That situation certainly wasn't new to me. I had already lost three wives and countless other girlfriends, but I remained convinced if I continued to persevere, I at last would find a woman with whom I could have a relationship that lasted longer than a commercial for a treatment for yeast infections.

A couple of friends tried to fix me up with blind dates. One such date had a tattoo on her forearm that said, "Castrate First, Ask Questions Later," and another began our date by asking the eternal question, "Do you think rasslin's fake?"

Then, one day I was looking through the classifieds and came upon the Personals section, where people advertise for other people. "Why not?" I asked myself. I could take out an ad that asked for exactly what I wanted, and I might get lucky.

First, of course, I had to decide exactly what I wanted. I didn't want a woman my own age. Women my own age usually had been divorced a couple of times and hated men. That didn't mean they didn't want to find a man. What they wanted was to find a man they could make absolutely miserable to get even with for those first two bastards.

Women my own age tended to be difficult to impress as well. Let's say you are in Paris and you say to a woman your own age, "Dear, I have reservations for two at Maxim's tonight."

Often as not, they will reply, "I hope the service is better than it was last time I was there."

Younger women, on the other hand, might reply, "Really? Gosh, if you'll take me there, I'll put on that outfit you bought me when we get back to the hotel, the one with all the feathers."

Something else, too. I pride myself on knowing all fifty of the state capitals. Try me:

Missouri? It's the one most often missed. Most people think it's St. Louis. No way. It's Jefferson City.

Young women tend to be impressed by a man who knows his state capitals. He reminds them of their fathers, who knew which numbers to invert when they asked him to help them learn how to divide fractions.

I was out with a woman my age once, and in an effort to impress her, I went to my hole card, the state capitals.

"I know all the state capitals," I told her.

"Me, too," she replied. "As a matter of fact, I married my first husband in Jefferson City, the son of a bitch."

So what I decided I wanted was a woman, say, between twenty-three and twenty-eight. I wanted her attractive, of course, with no tattoos, with no previous acting experience in porno films, but with an active sexual imagination. She didn't have to be Betty Crocker, but I wanted her at least to be able to fry a chicken and make hand-cut french fries. I didn't care whether or not she came from a wealthy background. Actually, I would be thrilled if her father owned downtown Dallas, but I'd previously been married to a daughter of a wealthy man. Unfortunately, she wouldn't get any money from Daddy until he crossed the river Jordan. And he was a health nut.

I decided if I was going to go to all the trouble and expense of taking out an ad in the personals, I might as well go for it all. I might as well ask for everything I ever wanted in a woman. I probably wouldn't get it, since that woman probably didn't exist, probably *never* existed, but Marvin R. of Keokuk probably never thought he'd win the Publishers Clearing House Sweepstakes, either.

Okay, young. And how about this? A home-economics major in college. Fry that chicken and those potatoes, and "Darling, how would you like to have a slice of the apple pie I baked this afternoon?"

"Can you serve it à la mode?"

"Of course, sweetheart. And how about some ice cream on it, too?"

Be still, my heart.

Young, attractive, home-ec major. No porno experience, but will wear things at night with feathers on them and has no earthly idea male sex organs come in different sizes.

And where had she become a home-ec major? This was very important. I am a graduate of the University of Georgia. I really don't care much for anybody who isn't, but I normally can deal with them if they at least are graduates of a Southeastern Conference school, unless it's Vanderbilt, where even the majorettes know Springfield, not Chicago, is the capital of Illinois.

So my first choice would be a young, attractive,

willing-to-be-kinky, home-ec major from the University of Georgia.

We could go to all the Georgia football games together, and she wouldn't think getting down on one's knees and barking at a Clemson fan was odd behavior or the result of staying for too many years at the school of veterinary medicine. We *do* bark at Georgia football games. We are the Bulldogs, pronounced either "Bulldawgs" or, the preferred, "Dawgs," and when there is a kickoff, we stand and scream, as the kicker approaches the ball, "Gooooooooooooooooo . . ."

When the ball is kicked, we add, "Dawgs!" followed by five barks: "Woof, woof, woof, woof, woof!"

Okay, it's a Georgia thing. You wouldn't understand.

But I'd settle for an Alabama girl, say. I'd been out with a few Auburn girls already. They were hard to wean off their Plainsmen background, but if you took them to a cattle auction occasionally, you eventually could win them over.

I decided this was what I would say I wanted in my personals ad:

"Young (23–28), attractive, willing female. SEC (preferable UGA, no Vanderbilts need apply) home-ec major who has never experienced Maxim's and doesn't even know there exists such a place as Montpelier, Vt."

That part was fairly easy. But then I looked closely at the personals and realized I also would have to describe myself in the ad. It didn't take me long to figure out what the coded initials in each ad meant:

M: Male
F: Female
W: White

B: Black
A: Asian
NA: Native American
NAC: Native American (Cherokee)

I suppose there are codes for Eskimos, Kiwanians, and people from Tasmania, too, but no such individuals had placed an ad in the newspaper I was checking that day.

There's more:

S: Straight
G: Gay
BI: Whatever

(Nobody who liked to do it with goats was mentioned, either.)

There were religious references, of course:

C: Catholic
P: Protestant
J: Jewish
M: Muslim
S: Person who goes to those churches where they pass around rattlesnakes to prove their faith.
RBS: Recently bitten person who goes to those churches where they pass around rattlesnakes to prove their faith would like to meet a nurse with background in poison control.

What I didn't find, however, were any codes for an individual's geographic background as it pertained to regions. Hispanic, sure. But Mexican? Spaniard? Asian. North Korean or South Korean? Native American? Would a Cherokee want to go out with a Crow?

I'm straight. I'm white. I'm male. But I'm also Southern, and it was very important I get that across in my ad. I didn't want some lovely child recently graduated with a master's in home ec from the University of Tennessee to think she might be getting hooked up with some guy who majored in Staying Warm at the University of Minnesota.

So here is what I would call myself in my personals ad:

"SSWM (whose great-great-great-grandfather fought for the losing side at Gettysburg): Seeks young (23–28), attractive and willing female. SEC (UGA, preferable; no Vanderbilts need apply) home-ec major who has never experienced Maxim's (famous restaurant in Paris, France, where I might take you once they reinstate my Amex, MC, etc.) and doesn't even know there is such a place as Montpelier, Vt."

I also realized I needed to put my own age (mid-'40's with a little zip still remaining on fastball); whether or not I dug ditches for a living (I don't. You put "prof." in that case) and whether or not I smoked. People are really picky about smoking these days. I smoke. I didn't want to get hooked up with some young woman who had anything against second-hand smoke. If she also smoked, that would be great, but if she didn't, I still would want her to pick up a carton of Vantage when she was grocery shopping and not bitch about it and try to send me to a stop-smoking clinic where they made you sleep with a eucalyptus plant for a week.

I also have an occasional social cocktail, but I don't do drugs. It would be necessary to point that out, as well. I figured I also ought to put in something about preferring country music and detesting hard rock, heavy metal, punk rap, Prince, MTV, the B-52's, and asparagus. (Not to be confused with Bean Sprouts, the rock group with the recent hit "Let's Do It in the Ranch Dressing.")

Then there was my political bent. Pat Buchanan, compared to me, is a bed-wetting liberal. Except when deer hunters say to me, "If we don't kill deer, they'll all starve to death," I reply, "Well, why don't you just take them some food?"

I also own a red truck—I thought I ought to mention that. And I'm a golfer. I have a four iron, instead of a rifle that would blow a deer to kingdom come (or kingdom went), in the gun rack of my truck.

I also don't wear socks, read the Sports section first, hate Northern actors and actresses who try to fake Southern accents, prefer white bread, love barbecue, think Meryl Streep is a dog, order World War II tapes off television, suffer from xenophobia (the fear of anybody named "Xeno," especially if he's from a foreign country), homophobia (the fear of being out of town and wandering into a gay bar by mistake), and claustrophobia (the fear of having to buy a lot of expensive female jewelry every Christmas).

My ad finally was ready. I phoned the Classified-ad department of the newspaper.

"Classified-ad department of the newspaper," a female voice said.

"I would like to take out a personal ad," I said.

"Can't get a date, huh?" the voice replied.

"Well," I answered, "it's just that I, uh . . ."

"You don't have to explain, dear. I've been doing personals for twenty years, and I've dealt with all kinds in my career," the voice went on.

"Let's see, you're in your mid-forties, been divorced several times—three?"

"Three," I said.

"And there have been lots of girlfriends, but none of them have worked out. They spend all your money and are ungrateful to you, and what you want now is some twenty-three-year-old bimbette who has never heard of Montpelier, Vermont. Am I right?"

This was uncanny.

"Time is running out on me," I said, "and I'm afraid if I finally don't find a woman with whom I can have a long-standing relationship, I'm going to wind up alone in a nursing home."

"With a lot of hair growing out of your ears, and you'll drool a lot," said the woman. "I had a brother like that, the poor soul. He kept wanting to meet a woman who had been a home-ec major in college, because he liked to eat. He never found one, developed an ulcer in the process, and is now in a nursing home, and all he can eat is saltine crackers soaked in milk."

What a revolting picture. I had to find the right woman.

"So tell me what you want to say in your ad," the woman said.

I told her.

"Oh, no," said my personals-ad counselor when I had finished.

"What's the matter?" I asked.

"Everything is the matter," she answered. "You're a SSWM, a straight Southern white male." The words came out of her mouth like she was spitting out rodent hairs.

"What's wrong with being one of those?" I asked her.

"Everything is wrong with being one of those," she said. "Straight Southern white males are the most politically incorrect individuals we have in nineties society. They are racists and sexists and gay-bashers. They are one step out of the Stone Age. They are fossils. They are obsolete. They just don't wash anymore. I wouldn't wish one on my worst enemy.

"They like football and country music and they

drive trucks. They are Nazis politically, have no appreciation of great art, such as the acting of the most lovely Meryl Streep, their preferred diet is atrocious, and they are deathly afraid of guys named 'Xeno,' especially if they are from a foreign country."

"Are you saying you aren't going to accept my ad?" I asked.

"Listen, you redneck," said the woman, her voice now dripping with venom, "if you've got the money, I'll run your ad, but you're wasting your time. No woman in her right mind would answer an ad to meet Slim Pickens. Why don't you just forget about this and save your money so you can go to a tractor pull with those other good ol' boys you hang around with."

I was shocked beyond words. I was suddenly some sort of monster, some outcast? I always had been proud of my Southern heritage. My great-great-great-grandfather, whom I mentioned earlier, was the famous Confederate general Beauregard Grizzard, who had three horses and four Red Cross nurses shot out from under him during the Civil War and had lived through it all. After the war was over, he had opened a bait-and-beer store and sold more Pabst Blue Ribbon, red wigglers, and Louisiana pinks than any other bait-and-beer store in an eight-county area.

And, sure, I'm straight. I didn't even enjoy taking showers with other members of my basketball team when I was in high school. What could be wrong with that? Gay-basher? Me? At least I had learned to say "gay," rather than those other, more descriptive words we once used.

Then there was the racist thing. Just because you're a straight Southern white male, it doesn't necessarily mean you're racist, does it? My boyhood friend and idol, Weyman C. Wannamaker, Jr., was asked once if he was a member of the Klan.

"That's the rumor going around," he was told.

"You misunderstood," said Weyman. "Nobody said I was a member of the Klan. What they said was I'm a booger under the sheets."

I've never been a member of the Ku Klux Klan or any other racist group either, and I wouldn't even know where to go to buy one of those pointy-headed hats the Klansmen wear. The KKK mart? That would be my best guess.

And sexist. Just because I wanted a home-ec major so she can prepare me good things to eat? I would cook for myself, but I majored in journalism. The only thing they taught journalism students to cook up was a good angle to a story. I could still respect a woman who cooked dinner for me the next morning.

And allow me to say this: If a woman can do the same job as a man, she should be allowed to do it and receive equal pay. **DID YOU SEE THAT?** I'm not for keeping women barefoot and pregnant. I've been married three times, and not a single one of my wives ever got pregnant. I also happened to have bought my third wife a pair of five-hundred-dollar leather boots in the Gucci store in Florence, Italy, in 1980. A man who wanted to keep his wife barefoot certainly wouldn't shell out that kind of cash for a pair of boots. Most all women suffer from Imelda Marcus syndrome anyway—the desire to own, or at least try on, every pair of women's shoes on earth. Is that a sexist remark? If it is, I apologize, but I buy a pair of shoes and I wear them every day until they wear out. Then I go and buy another pair of shoes.

It has been my experience with women, however, that a closet without 416 pairs of shoes in it is like a necklace with no earrings to match.

But back to the barefoot thing for a moment, I must admit I don't see anything wrong with a woman taking off her shoes and feeling the terra firma on the bare underside of her feet, occasionally. It even can be a turn-on, an earthy sort of thing, like seeing a woman run naked through the forest. I've never seen a woman run naked through the forest, but it sounds like a lot more fun than going out there with a rifle, waiting for some poor unsuspecting deer to come along so I can shoot it and keep it from starving to death.

Kathy Sue Loudermilk, the sexiest girl in my school, didn't even start wearing shoes until she was in high school, when the health teacher wrote a note to Kathy Sue's parents demanding they put shoes on her before she either got ringworm or stepped on a rusty nail and came down with lockjaw.

Kathy Sue didn't want to wear any shoes. She was one of the first let's-get-close-to-nature individuals I ever knew. She liked to feel the comforting red Georgia clay under her feet. She didn't even mind going to the henhouse to collect eggs for her mother and stepping in a neat pile of chicken leavings either.

I come from a rural, agricultural background myself, and I've known the feeling of stepping into chicken leavings, green with a touch of white right on top, while barefoot. While others might think such a thing was disgusting, the sensation actually is like stepping onto a pile of cool Jell-O pudding. It feels quite good to the area between the toes and makes a nice little squiggly sound, as in "Squiiiirg-lup," which is a combination of the words "Squirp" and "Squiggle." I actually once knew twin girls whose parents had named them Squirp and Squiggle, both of whom had a toe-sucking fetish, and there is nothing wrong with that. They later turned pro and opened a toe-sucking clinic, as a matter of fact, and were guests on a recent *Donahue* show where they discussed toe-sucking at length and even demonstrated their technique on Phil, who admitted he always had wanted his wife, Marlo, to suck his toes, but he had always been afraid to ask her.

"I want to thank Squirp and Squiggle," Phil closed his show, "for today's enlightening program. Tomorrow, our topic will be left-handed Lesbian crossdressers with rotten teeth."

Regardless of all that, however, I still had the problem of no woman in my life at the moment and the fact my personals counselor thought I, and my kind, were worse than a howling case of herpes.

Still, she had said if I had the money, she would run the ad, and I wasn't convinced I was some sort of social leper, despite what she had said.

So I told the woman, "Regardless of what you might think of straight Southern white males, my dear woman, I still want you to put the ad in the newspaper. I will pay for every inch of it, and we'll see just who can flush something out of the bushes and who can't."

"Such lovely phraseology," she replied, sarcastically. "The man thinks he's out with his dog, Ol' Gator, hunting prey."

I meant nothing by that. It was just the way I had learned to phrase certain things. I have already mentioned my lack of interest in going into the woods and shooting animals, but there shouldn't be anything wrong with an occasional allusion to the quest of game.

I'll never forget the time in the eighth grade when by boyhood friend and idol, Weyman C. Wannamaker, Jr., a great American, and I were watching Kathy Sue Loudermilk clean the chicken leavings

from between her toes as she sat on the front steps
of the schoolhouse before her first class one morning. The teachers insisted all barefoot children not
track in any smells that would distract the other
students.

Kathy Sue developed early as a child and, by the
eighth grade, already had the wheels off her training bra. There she sat in a lovely dress her mother
had made her from a Martha White flour sack. It
seemed to cling to all the strategic positions. As
Kathy Sue's lovely fingers caressed and cleaned between her darling little toes, her flour-sack dress
had ridden up to her thighs. Her hair had fallen
down into her eyes, and she was holding her mouth
in that pouty little way of hers. It was hard not to
believe in God looking at Kathy Sue that morning.

Weyman, spellbound for a moment, finally said,
"I've been to three county fairs, two square dances,
and a Shriner parade. I've seen a chicken play the
piano, a baboon that knew his ABC's, and a duck
fart under water. But," he went on nodding toward
Kathy Sue, "I ain't never seen a dog that'll hunt like
that."

I finished the rather harrowing experience with
the woman in classifieds at the newspaper who said
my ad, as much as she despised it, would run two
days hence. The first day crawled by. The anticipation was building in me with every minute that
passed. This could change my life. As soon as my ad
appeared, I was certain the letters would come pouring in, and I would have the opportunity to choose
from dozens of women who were dying to meet me.
And I wouldn't have to buy a single dinner or drink.
Why hadn't I thought of this earlier?

The morning of the day my personals ad was to
appear, I was up early waiting for the newspaper. I

sat on my front porch pouring down coffee in the black of predawn. Then, around the corner came a set of headlights. This is it. This was my newspaper carrier. He slowed in front of my house, and from the driver's side, he threw a perfect strike into the hedges in front of my house.

I have some rather large hedges in front of my house, and that's always where my carrier throws the newspaper. Sometimes, as was the case this particular morning, the paper would fall down into the hedges, out of sight. My lawn was a lot bigger target than my hedges, but newspaper carriers, I decided, are a sadistic lot. If they had to get up at that time of the day to deliver newspapers, they seemed to want their customers to be just as miserable, trying to disencumber their newspapers from remote and dangerous places such as inside large hedges or directly in front of the neighbor's sleeping pit bull named Attila.

It was still dark outside as the upper half of my torso disappeared into the hedges. I received multiple cuts to my face and hands, but after fifteen minutes of searching, I finally had my newspaper in hand.

I went inside, poured myself another cup of coffee. I glanced at the front page. The lead headline said:

ALIENS LAND IN NEW YORK CITY, ARE MUGGED BY STREET GANGS

Another slow news day. I turned to the personals and began to search for mine. I found it. The ad directly above mine said:

"GWM: Seeking partner for fun and games. Must be physically fit, able to endure intense pain, and willing to experiment. Knowledge of power tools and animal husbandry helpful. Nonsmokers and Christians only."

The ad directly below mine said:

"BBIF: Fit, 30's bi-female truck driver seeks progressive guys and gals who enjoy travel and eating at truck stops. Big smokestacks and well-built rigs important. See what truckers really mean when they say they are going to 'blow the horn.' Carrying a heavy load, I'm waiting for you."

I got four responses the first day. The newspaper forwarded them from the P.O. box that ran in the ad.

One said, "Hey, trucker, I'm southbound and down. My CB handle is 'Big'un' and I love watered-down chili. Meet me at the bus station mornings 9–11 and afternoons 4–6. My leather lathers with anticipation."

Another read:

"I'm 6-2, 190, and if you're looking for a power tool, you've come to the right place. Black and Decker doesn't have anything on this nail driver. Pain's my game and I know chickens. Yours in Christ . . ."

Obviously, both these individuals had mistakenly written to the wrong P.O. box. A third letter wanted to sell me aluminum siding, and the fourth was a pyramid scheme to sell and breed llamas from South America.

It had to get better. It didn't. I ran that stupid ad for ten days, and I received only one more letter after the initial four. It was from Jimmy Swaggart, asking me for a donation.

Naturally, I was devastated. What had happened here? I hadn't advertised for anything weird. I didn't want to do anything that involved a farm animal or staple gun. I just wanted to meet that special lady who could take me out of the love nadir in which I presently found myself.

When I called the lady at the newspaper to tell her to cancel my ad, she obviously had something smart to say:

"What did I tell you, pig?" she began. "No woman in her right mind would answer an ad from an SSWM. They are afraid you'd ask them to do something sick, like go to a country-western bar. You rednecks are all alike. Your idea of foreplay is, 'Get in the truck, bitch.' "

What could I say? She was right. If this had been a hunting expedition, all I would have gotten would've been chigger bites. If this had been a baseball game, I wouldn't have gotten a runner to first base. If it had been a war, I'd have been Iraq. If it had been a county fair, I'd have suffered whiplash on the Tilt-a-Whirl.

My ego had crashed. Even the black box with the cabin recorder had burned in the wreckage.

Here I was alone, and middle-aged, and a hair on a bar of soap. An Arab and a B'nai B'rith meeting. A one-legged man at an ass-kicking contest. Ford Pinto in a Rolls-Royce showroom. A smoker at a jogger's picnic. A green fly in a bowl of soup. A piece of porcelain at a Tupperware party. Ernest Tubb at a Guns N' Roses concert.

I'd brought a knife to a gunfight. A date to a Ducks Unlimited banquet. A mule to the Kentucky Derby. A voice of reason to a congressional debate. A cane pole to a deep-sea fishing trip. Hitler to a meeting of the American Civil Liberties Union.

I was the epitome of politically incorrect. A redneck. A good ol' boy. My name was Bubba. I drove a truck with a lot of bumper stickers. One said, AMER-

ICA: LOVE IT OR LEAVE IT. Another said, I'LL GIVE UP MY GUN
WHEN THEY PRY AWAY MY COLD, DEAD FINGERS. A third read,
I BRAKE FOR BLONDES.

I wore a baseball cap with the name of a farm-
implement company on the front.

I went around saying things like, "Anybody who
don't like Hank Williams can kiss my ass" and "Hey,
little lady, can I buy you a beer?" I enjoyed football
more than long walks and baseball more than wine-
and-cheese-tasting parties, and I lost interest in professional basketball when Bob Cousy retired.

I feared and despised welfare cheaters, rap, mushrooms, anything that had to do with the Ivy League,
fast-talking Yankees, married women who still went
by their maiden names, biscuits that come in a can,
men wearing earrings and/or ponytails, San Francisco and New York City, liberal newspaper columnists, Dan Rather, bikini underwear for men, and
photography shows that feature a picture of a naked
man with a bullwhip in his rectum.

With apologies to Jesse Helms, if that's art, my
ass is a typewriter.

But what could I do about all this? I was too old,
too set in my ways, and too stubborn in my beliefs to
change. What are straight Southern white males
supposed to do now that we've been cast aside like
an old sofa? We're still a part of this society. I like to
think we are still contributing to it. Who would
change your oil and clean out your carburetor if it
weren't for straight Southern white males?

Who would write country songs like a friend of
mine is writing, with the title, "I Can't Get Over
You Until You Get Out from Under Him"?

Who would coach football at the University of Mississippi? Who would eat all the pork pig-barbecue

sandwiches and drain all those longneck bottles of Bud? Who would be governor of Alabama? Who would love—with a nod to Tom T. Hall—old dogs, children, and watermelon wine? Who would put a car up on cement blocks in his backyard, go to stock-car races, and keep bait-and-beer stores in business, thus helping to stimulate the economy? Who would buy a pickled egg from the jar on the bar? Who would love truck stops and beer-joint waitresses and give them change to play Alan Jackson's "Don't Rock the Juke Box" on the jukebox?

Who would love and take care of sorry old dogs who sleep under trucks and get motor oil on their backs? Who would name bird dogs "Jim" and "Jesse" and own a decanter of bourbon in the shape of Elvis?

Who would say, "I heard dat" and "Now, that's a nice 'un there, a real nice 'un," on televised fishing shows? Who would chew tobacco and carry around a paper spit cup with a napkin in it?

Who would still say "tote" for "carry"; "sal-mun" for "sa-mon"; and "bull-sheeyet" for "you don't say?"

Who? Tell me who?

Us. Straight Southern white males. We need love and understanding, too, and, once you get to know us, we aren't what the cat drug in from the garbage. We're people, too. We have feelings just like everybody else, and we're damn tired of being looked down upon and having our political ballots called "the Bubba Vote."

I press onward.

Most of us work for our living. Some of us work very hard. We fly airplanes, sell used cars, heal the sick, build and design large buildings, change tires and pump gas, sing and play guitar, fight in wars, write books and plays, just to name a few of our occupations.

We also pay our bills and our taxes and provide for our families. In my case, I don't have a family, but I do take care of my dog, Catfish, the black Lab.

We normally are nice to our children, don't cheat on the golf course, give to charities, provide jobs for others, honor our parents, and give blood. Lest we forget, the father of our country, George Washington, was a straight white Southern male. And so is Dr. Billy Graham.

Certainly, we have a share of goofballs and ne'er-do-wells. What group, ethnic or otherwise, doesn't?

But we have one distinct, unifying factor. We don't know what's happened to the world, and there are a lot of things of which we are all sick and tired. I've mentioned whining and bitching. I'll mention it some more.

We're also tired of what we consider to be the chirping of little sparrows who don't have anything better to do than be disruptive and devious. I don't care if you're gay, just don't bother me with it. And what black millionaires get into what formerly all-white country clubs doesn't concern us in the least, and so you're suffering from PMS and are mad because Geraldine Ferraro never got elected vice president. We've got problems, too.

Like having a deal with the idiots in Congress who want to take and take from the productive in order to give and give to the unproductive, and having to be afraid of saying to a female employee "Good morning," and having her take it as sexual harassment and filing a lawsuit.

In a few words, we are confused and angry.

Damn right, I'm a straight Southern white male, and I got to be that way honestly, which is to say I'm proud of my heritage. It's politically incorrect by now to say such a thing, but I've already said what I thought about political correctness. I said it sucks the big one, if you don't recall, and if you think I'm enjoying speaking my mind here and telling the Speech Police to go to hell, you're right. This is more fun than playing with a pet chicken.

••• 3 •••

I Did Eat Mud, But I Always Buttoned Both Galluses

How I became a white Southern male is rather simple. My father was one. His name was Lewis McDonald Grizzard, same as mine. Quite a coincidence, I'd say.

He was born in Gwinnett County, Georgia, which is as Southern as a tater pie, which I just threw in here to say we don't talk like that very much in the South anymore. Tater pies are now sweet-potato, low-cal soufflés.

Gwinnett County is now a bedroom community to Atlanta. The Kroger store in my father's hometown, Snellville, even sells live lobsters, located in a tank back where the dead fish are. But Gwinnett County and Snellville were rural outposts when my father was born there in 1912. His father was a white Southern male, too, only his name was Adolphus Augustus Grizzard, and he was a farmer.

My father attended a small, rural Methodist church during his boyhood where he became an accomplished piano player and singer of hymns. He also plowed a mule, picked cotton, and slopped the hogs on my grandfather's farm. Although I never discussed it with my late father, I am certain he also knew the sensation of stepping onto a pile of chicken leavings with his bare feet.

This may be startling to those whose knowledge about the South has come only from the movie *Gone With the Wind*.

My grandfather didn't own any slaves, except for his twelve children, all of whom were white like him and my dad.

"Not a one?"

Not a single, solitary happy Negro slave with a cotton sack on his back saying "Massa, you want me to saddle yo' hoss now?"

As a matter of fact, I have dug deep into the Grizzard family, and I have found no evidence that any of my forebears ever lived on a plantation, drank a mint julep, danced with Scarlett O'Hara, or owned a bullwhip or a slave.

I've attempted to tell individuals from outside the South that, but they never seem to believe me.

"Come on," they say. "We know how you Southerners are. All of you grew up with slaves doing all the work and mammies cooking and changing your diapers. We've seen *Gone With the Wind* and *Mississippi Burning*. We know the drill."

Absolutely not. It is true I had some relatives who fought for the South in the Civil War (see Beauregard Grizzard, Chapter 2), but they weren't fighting to save slavery. They were fighting to make Yankee men dress better when they visited Southern beaches. They desperately wanted Yankee men to stop wearing black socks with their sandals and Bermuda shorts.

And they lost, which is why you can go to Hilton Head or any other Southern beach today and find Yankee men still walking around wearing black, over-the-calf socks with their sandals and Bermuda shorts. Lots of guys named Herb or Artie from New Jersey. You can tell them by the third-degree burns on what skin was left uncovered between the top of their socks and the bottom of their Bermuda shorts.

From what I have gathered from my father and other parental relatives, it has become clear that the A. A. Grizzard family not only didn't own any slaves, they also allowed their chickens to walk around in the yard, and they did not have indoor plumbing. There certainly is nothing wrong with either one of those things, but it does say again I came not from the landed gentry of the South, those of huge plantations, given to such practices as holding slaves and putting on great balls where courtly ladies and gentlemen such as Scarlett and Ashley did those stupid dances you always see in movies that feature plantation balls.

There are two ways to deal with chickens. One way is to build a chicken coop. You select a small area and put a chicken-wire fence around it. I don't know if the sort of wire you use in this instance has the official name of "chicken wire," but that's always what we called it. It is wire through which nothing as large as a chicken can crawl.

After the fence is erected, then it becomes necessary to build a henhouse. That's a place where the hens can get out of the elements and lay their eggs in communal warmth and peace. I'm certain Tara had a chicken coop and a henhouse. Scarlett, of course, never went to gather the eggs. There was a slave to do that. Therefore, Scarlett never knew the joy of getting chicken leavings between her toes, and I remain firmly convinced that's why she was the bitchy little twerp she most certainly was. If I'd been Rhett Butler, the first time she went into one of those pouting episodes is when I would have done the famous *Gone With the Wind* farewell scene. Frankly, I don't give a damn about a whiny, pouting woman, and after having seen *GWTW* over four hundred times, I also remain convinced Scarlett didn't have very big boobs, either. The only thing worse than a whiny, pouting woman is a whiny, pouting woman with a flat chest, which is probably a sexist remark, but you're not reading *Ms.* magazine here.

A lot of Southern people who didn't live on plantations and didn't have any slaves didn't really see the necessity of going to the expense of putting up a chicken coop and a henhouse.

They looked at the chicken question like this: What did chickens do before there were such things as coops and henhouses? They fended for themselves, that's what. Not that long ago, I was in a restaurant, and the menu featured something called "free-range chickens." I asked the waiter if a free-range chicken was the same as a regular chicken.

"The chickens we serve," he explained, "are not raised in the artificial environment of chicken farms. They roam free on the range and are much healthier chickens. That makes them more healthy for you to eat."

I ordered a free-range chicken, fried. To be honest about it, it didn't taste any different from any other chicken I'd ever eaten, but because I knew my forebears had free-yard chickens, I did feel a lot closer to my roots.

There is, however, a little situation that can arise when a family allows its chickens to walk around in its yard with no coop or henhouse.

It's easier to become attached to chickens like that. They can become pets. You walk out of the house in the morning, and there are the dogs with the oil on their backs, and there's a couple of chickens. You pet the dogs, of course, and the chickens get jealous of the attention, and you have to scratch them on their breasts. The next thing you know, you have named the chickens.

I grew up with my mother's parents, Willie and C. B. Word of Moreland, Georgia. They were white and Southern too, originally from the counties of Heard and Carroll in Georgia. They also raised free-yard chickens, which I became attached to as a mere lad, still in his single figures.

I don't know if you've ever tried to name a chicken, but it's more difficult than naming a pet like a dog. If a dog is solid black, then it's pretty simple to call it Blackie. White dogs are Whitey, and then there was Spot of Dick-and-Jane fame. Dick and Jane apparently were too busy going up and down that damn hill to get water to come up with a better name than Spot.

You don't see many chickens with characteristics that are different from any other chicken. Chickens, like alligators and boiled eggs, have a tendency to all look alike. I've never known anybody to name a chicken Blackie, and certainly not Spot.

I named three chickens when I was growing up. I named them after ladies in the community. I had a chicken named Inez after Miss Inez Puckett, who is best remembered for the night she was healed by a traveling tent evangelist, Brother Roy Dodd Hembree.

Miss Inez had been bothered by bad kidneys for years. When people referred to Miss Inez, they almost always would say "poor, pitiful Miss Inez."

Miss Inez had gone to doctors, chiropractors, and people who rubbed roots to ward off injury and sickness for years, but she still hadn't gotten relief.

So one night, she went up onstage with Brother Roy Dodd. He laid hands on her, broke out in tongues, and then said, "You're healed, praise the Lord!"

Miss Inez felt the spirit inside her and began to jump around on the stage in celebration of her healed kidneys. She became so ecstatic, however, she fell off the stage and broke her leg.

Several men from the audience rushed to her aid. One suggested an ambulance be called.

Another said, however, "Why would we do that? We'll just get Brother Roy Dodd to heal her leg."

Brother Roy Dodd said, "I think you'd better call the ambulance. I don't do broken bones, just vital organs."

Inez turned out to be a good chicken, who would peck corn out of my hand and learned her name in a matter of days. That's how I could tell the chickens I named apart. They would learn their names, and when I called out, "Come here, Inez," the chicken that responded was the chicken with that particular name. I think. They could have, I decided later, all been in this together and simply took turns coming when I called.

I named the other two chickens Ernestine, after Miss Ernestine Turnipseed, who always brought simply marvelous deviled eggs to the Methodist church dinners-on-the-ground, and Pearl after Miss Pearl Hainey, a teacher at my school who once hit the school bully, Frankie Garfield, on the top of the head with a rather large world-geography book to make him stop beating up a boy named Marcus Teal who Frankie made a habit of beating up. Marcus was a world-class bleeder. This made Frankie feel even more powerful and fearsome.

Miss Pearl was a frail woman in her early sixties, but she managed to land a fierce blow on top of Frankie's head. He not only stopped beating up Marcus, he was so stunned, his eyes crossed, and they stayed that way all the way through the rest of school. Frankie's sight was severely impaired by this, and it became much easier to run away and hide from him when he decided to beat you up.

I was impressed by, and thankful for, Miss Pearl's bonker to Frankie's head. I said right then and there, "I'm going to name a chicken after this brave lady," and I did.

I asked my father once if chickens who walked around in his yard had names like mine did, some forty years later.

"Had an ol' Domineckeer hen named Annabelle Lee once," he said.

"After the poem by Poe?" I asked.

"No," said my father, "after Annabelle Whitlock, the Snellville town whore when I was growing up. Lord, if it hadn't been for Annabelle, practically every man from Snellville would have gone to World War II a virgin, with nothing to look forward to when they got back home but a mule and a plow."

There was something else about having chickens that were allowed full access to the yard and who had names. Scarlett's mom, who likely never cooked but who directed a slave girl to handle that function at Tara, could simply say to the slave girl—we'll call her Missy—"Missy, go out to the chicken coop and kill a chicken for dinner."

Plantation-owning, slave-holding Southerners with chicken coops and henhouses never became attached to their chickens, and it was a simple matter of sending one of the help out to kill a chicken for a family meal.

Not so with families like the A. A. Grizzards of Snellville or mine in Moreland. When somebody killed a chicken for dinner, it was like a death in the family. My father used to talk about the difficulty that was involved when the family finally sat down to eat Annabelle Lee.

"It broke my heart," said my father. "Especially since I was the baby of the family, and all I got was a neck bone."

The same thing happened to all three of the chickens I named. We ate Inez for Thanksgiving one year. Christmas Day, we ate Ernestine.

Then the preacher was invited over for Sunday lunch on Easter, and Pearl's number came up.

"We can't eat Pearl," I said to my grandmother.

"You shouldn't get attached to chickens," she said, and quoted a Bible verse that didn't have anything to do with eating chickens with names, but my grandmother was always quoting Bible verses even when you said, "Looks like rain today, Mama Willie."

"The Lord said, 'Never go out in the rain without galoshes,'" my grandmother would reply, "Deuteronomy, Chapter Twelve, sixteenth verse."

My grandfather was the person who killed the chickens we ate. I was for lethal injections, but my grandfather stuck with cutting the chickens' heads off with an ax. I watched him kill Pearl, and I still have nightmares about headless chickens.

There was a tree stump in my grandparents' backyard, and when my grandfather killed a chicken, he would hold it down on the tree stump, then whack its head off with an ax.

"Do you think Pearl will know you're going to cut her head off when you take her to the stump?" I asked my grandfather.

"I know Pearl has been like a pet to you," my grandfather said, "but the preacher is coming for Sunday lunch, and Pearl is a fine specimen of a chicken. I'd say her breast will go a hand-and-a-half, and you know how preachers enjoy a big breast."

Later in life, I would follow the careers of television preachers like Jim Bakker and Jimmy Swaggart and come to realize another connection between men of the cloth and big breasts, but that's another story.

My grandfather picked up Pearl and carried her over to the stump. I didn't know about Henry VIII at the time, but I later learned he had people taken to a stump in the London Tower where their heads were whacked off.

My grandfather put Pearl's head down on the stump and held it there with his left hand. With his right hand, he came down with the ax and cut off Pearl's head. Then the damndest thing occurred.

When Pearl's head came off, he let go of the rest of Pearl, and she started to run around the vicinity of the stump, willy-nilly. What a sight to behold, a chicken with no head, able to move about for at least a few seconds before falling over and becoming Sunday dinner.

This, of course, is where the phrase, "running around like a chicken with its head cut off" emerged. It was even a *Wheel of Fortune* puzzle one evening, and I solved it with only six consonants and two vowels showing.

As far as Henry VIII is concerned, he never became attached to any person, much less any chickens, and I visited London Tower once, and the guide showed me where individuals who had the misfortune to appear on Henry's shit list were beheaded.

"Did they run around a few minutes after their heads were cut off like chickens do?" I asked the guide.

"History tells us," he answered, "that once one of Henry the Eighth's subjects had his or her head cut off, the rest of the body had a tendency to lie very still."

But here I am pecking on about chickens, and I haven't dealt with outdoor plumbing. Wasps (pronounced "waw-stez" in the South) often build nests under outdoor toilet benches. As my father told it, his Great-Aunt Rowena came to visit in Snellville from her home in Between, Georgia, named because it is located between Snellville and the next community east, Loganville.

Great-Aunt Rowena had to go to the outhouse to do a rather pressing No. 2. Things were going along fine until one of the wasps flew off the nest, which was located a few inches to the left of the hole on top of where Great-Aunt Rowena was perched, and stung her on her taint. If you're not certain what a taint is, it tain't your butt and it tain't your little thing. It's the area between the two.

"Great-Aunt Rowena," my father explained, "come out of that outhouse like a turnip truck coming down a mountain with no brakes. Unfortunately, she still had on her pink step-ins, which she had dropped to her ankles.

"When she came out of the outhouse a heartbeat after getting stung, she was doing about forty-five, even though she had to take little-bitty steps due to her pink step-ins being around her ankles.

"She came out of that outhouse screaming, 'Lord, God, I've been bit by a shit snake,' " my father said. "She made it about fifty yards before her pink step-ins around her ankles tripped her. She rolled the rest of the way to the back porch.

"Great-Aunt Rowena was a stout girl, and it took us thirty minutes to convince her she wasn't suffering from a snakebite to her taint, but had been stung by a wasp."

Great-Aunt Rowena, my father explained, never visited again, and as soon as she returned to Between, she convinced her husband, Mason, to build an indoor toilet, thus becoming the first member of my father's family to have such a convenience. Rumor had it, however, that even with indoor plumbing, Great-Aunt Rowena never went to the toilet again without a snakebite kit.

Some might say to me at this point, "Reading about your ancestors allowing their chickens to walk around in the yard and the fact they had no indoor plumbing, I see it's obvious you sprang right out of *God's Little Acre*. How much intermarriage took place, and who made the moonshine?"

God's Little Acre, of course, was a novel by Erskine Caldwell who, believe or not, was born in Moreland. As a matter of fact, a few members of Moreland's small citizenry (four hundred and change), recently had Erskine Caldwell's wooden birthplace brought into the town square with plans to restore it. I have my reservations about the plan. First, Erskine Caldwell portrayed Southerners as a human garbage heap, made up of moonshine-swilling people with no brains whatsoever and precious few teeth, who married their cousins and produced slow children who did nothing but sit in the corner and play in the dust.

There might have been a few cases of such individuals, but not every Southern family fell into such a category, and certainly not my father's or mother's.

The second reason I am against the Erskine Caldwell idea is, throughout my career as a columnist and author, I have tried to defend and glorify the South and have often made mention of my hometown and how much I still love it, for its people and for its character.

So get this: A lady from Moreland went before the three-member city council a few years ago and said she thought it would be a nice idea to put a sign at the city limits that said, HOME OF LEWIS GRIZZARD. The measure was canned, 2–1. Even after I offered to pay for the sign myself and even dig the hole for the post on which the sign would rest, the city council still wanted no part of any such thing. Naturally, I was— and still am—quite hurt by all this, and I presently am considering changing the portion of my will that leaves enough money to Moreland to erect the Lewis Grizzard Memorial Traffic Light, since my hometown still doesn't have one. I would want to put it on the highway that cuts through the heart of town where it intersects with Camp Street, which was my street growing up.

I lost a dog at that intersection once. My dog was on the way to Cureton Cole's General Store, where people eating canned Vienna sausages and saltine crackers often would share with him, due to the fact my dog—Duke Snider was his name, for my favorite baseball player at the time—was one of the great canine beggars of all time. Duke Snider could whine and wrinkle his brow and look at you with those sad eyes in such an effective way, one often would even part with a pork chop.

Anyway, Duke was crossing the highway when he was struck by an oncoming pulpwood truck driven by Gaylord Vick, who always drove flat-out and had no use for a brake pedal whatsoever.

Gaylord apologized and said, "I shore did make a mess of the little scoundrel, didn't I?"

Quite. Duke lay in the road very still and flat until my grandfather scooped his remains into a wheelbarrow with a shovel. We couldn't allow Duke to remain there and become a sail-dog. Sail-dogs are like sail-cats and sail-possums. Often, when one of these animals was run over by a turnip truck, Greyhound bus, or somebody's Packard, and allowed to remain on the highway, they wasted away to nothing more than a flat piece of fur that would harden with time.

Because the Frisbee had not been invented at that point, these flat, hardened carcasses would be taken from the highway and used as Frisbees are today, if you learned how to let one go with a lot of wrist and arm extended toward the target.

Weyman C. Wannamaker held the Moreland carcass-sailing record that probably yet stands. Old lady Bearnice Simpkins had a cat named Harley after her late husband, a local pool shark and dog breeder who had been shot in an argument over who had the best bird dog in town.

Harley said his bird dog, Ol' Fetchit, could point circles around R.L. Flournoy's Biscuit Boy. The argument occurred in the back of Bohannon's service station in Moreland, where the only pool table in town was located.

R.L. said Ol' Fetchit wouldn't point to anything but a piece of fatback, and Harley countered by saying Biscuit Boy wasn't anything but a sorry-assed leg hound that had rather hump than hunt.

R.L. went home, got his shotgun, and put a blast right into Harley's midsection. Harley was pronounced dead on arrival at the hospital in the county seat. They charged R.L. with manslaughter because he was only defending the honor of his dog, and he got out of prison after only four years due to good behavior and the fact his uncle was on the parole board.

Anyway, Miss Bearnice Simpkin's cat, Harley, was trying to cross the same intersection where Duke Snider bought the cotton gin and got run over by the 8:45 Greyhound on its way to Montgomery. A Montgomery-bound Greyhound can render a cat unrecognizable. The only way anybody knew the cat in question was Harley was because Little Bug Pierce, Big Bug Pierce's eleven-year-old boy, had seen Harley get it.

"I was waitin' to cross the highway," Little Bug explained, "and Harley was standing next to me. I seen the bus comin', but Harley didn't and ran right out in front of it. I seen one of his eyeballs squirt out from under that bus when it hit him."

Miss Bearnice was told the dreadful news about her cat, but she couldn't bear to go scrape it off the highway, so Harley just lay there for several days and got run over several more times, and was molded into the perfect sail-cat. Weyman was crossing the highway and saw it. He picked it up and brought it over to Cureton Cole's store and bet anybody who wanted the action—an orange bellywasher—he could sail Harley all the way to the front steps of the Methodist church, which was a hundred yards from the store.

Three people took the bet. What they didn't know was Weyman already had tested the wind and knew it would be behind him. Weyman, standing in front of the store with an audience of at least eight, got a running start like a discus thrower and heaved Harley toward the steps of the church.

The sail-cat rose majestically in the wind with a slight fade, due to the outside-in toss, and landed fifteen yards past the church steps, coming to rest only a few feet from the front door. Weyman drank all three of the orange bellywashers he won in the bet in celebration of his accomplishment, and there was even talk of putting a small marker at the spot where Harley landed, but the preacher said it wouldn't be the right thing to do because the Lord loved little animals just as much as He did people, and a marker would be nothing more than a glorification of how Harley came to be smushed by the bus.

I have attempted here, with heavy anecdotal backgrounding, to explain my Southern heritage. But just as I fiercely want to explain I sprang not from Tara, I also want to point out I don't fall into the category of white trash, either. Perhaps I should explain "white trash" before I go any further.

"White trash" in my youth were looked down upon. Their work ethic wasn't too strong, and their personal hygiene was questionable. White trash had other very distinct characteristics. If they lived in rotting houses with discarded sofas and chairs on the front porch with the springs and cotton stuffing coming out at various spots, it likely meant they were, in fact, white trash.

Fourteen kids all over the porch and yard, half of whom were naked, was a distinct white-trash characteristic, too. Even if a child wasn't completely naked, if he was wearing a diaper that resembled an Iraqi soldier's head garb after he'd been facedown in a desert trench for three days, hiding from Allied firepower, that was also a surefire sign some heavy WT was going on.

The males of white-trash households were normally what my grandfather called "sorry," as in they wouldn't work, shave, bathe, attend church, or button up both galluses on their overalls.

Not everybody who wore overalls was white trash, either. A lot of good, churchgoing white Southern men wore overalls when I was growing up, but they buttoned both galluses and always wore a shirt underneath.

Not so white trash. They were too lazy—or "sorry" —to button but one gallus, and they often didn't wear anything underneath their overalls, not even underdrawers, much less a shirt.

These were the people Erskine Caldwell wrote about in his portrayals of rural Southern life. Erskine's problem, and sin, was that he indicated *all* Southern people were white trash, not just the ones who, for one reason or the other, were sorry and had a lot of naked babies running around.

White trash drank most all the moonshine. Not all moonshine producers were white trash, however. Some were businessmen who saw a demand and came up with the supply. Non-white-trash moonshiners used galvanized containers they bought at the hardware store in which to distill their moonshine. They also sold it in Mason jars, and when you bought a jar of moonshine from a non-white-trash producer, it normally didn't have any leaves, twigs, or dead bugs floating in it.

White-trash moonshiners used old automobile radiators in their process, and they sold it in old orange bellywasher bottles, empty mayonnaise jars, and discarded bottles that once held Wild Root Creme Oil hair cream for men. They would have sold moonshine in a paper sack if a paper sack would hold liquid long enough.

White-trash moonshiners also used a rather lax straining method. Buy moonshine from white trash, and you could pretty much expect there would be a lot of leaves, twigs, and dead bugs floating around it. Of course, saying that dead bugs were floating around in white-trash moonshine is redundant.

A roach that could check into a Roach Motel and stay there two weeks without even developing so much as a headache wouldn't last three seconds in a jar of white-trash moonshine. To take this even further, a lot of people who could drink a bottle of Wild Root Creme Oil hair cream for men if they couldn't get their hands on any moonshine, and show no ill effects, died from lead poisoning when they drank white-trash moonshine.

One also could spot a white-trash automobile quite easily. It always had mud all over the tires, a piece of cardboard substituting for one of the windows, was missing one or both fenders, had a 1951 tag in 1953 that was hanging on by one bolt, would crank only occasionally, and made a sound when it would crank like an outboard boat motor idling in a muddy lake. I'm not certain I can recreate that sound on the written page, but I will try:

"Blub, blub, blub, udden, udden, udden, dabloop, dabloop, dabloop . . ."

There were also some churches in the South of my youth—and some are still around—where people suddenly were slain in the spirit of the Lord in the midst of church services and would begin to speak in unknown tongues. They often sounded like a white-trash automobile, too.

"Blub, blub, blub, udden, udden, udden, dabloop,

dabloop, dabloop" in unknown tongues means "Go buy a Honda."

The Loot Starkins family in Moreland were a classic white-trash family. There were Loot and his wife, Clovis. Then there were the twelve little Starkinses. The boys were named Loot III, Coot, Toot, Boot, Goot, Root, and Poot, the youngest. Yes, Mr. and Mrs. Starkins named one of their children "Poot." In their defense, however, they did not realize "poot" was a term for flatulence. They were familiar only with "fart," as in Mr. Starkins saying to one of his children, "Is that dinner I smell cooking or did you fart?"

Little Poot obviously had it rough once he started school. His teacher, embarrassed to call his name out, asked Little Poot what his middle name was, but Poot didn't have one. Trying to think up twelve names for children was enough of a tax on the Starkinses' creative powers. Twenty-four would have been out of the question.

So what the teacher did was give Poot a middle name, "Marvin," and tried calling him that. But he would never respond.

The teacher would ask, "Marvin, can you tell us what two and two is?"

Poot wouldn't stir or speak.

Finally, one of the other students would say, "Hey, Fart Blossom, she's talking to you."

"Fart Blossom" was the nickname the other children came up with for Poot. They had a marvelous time with Poot's unfortunate name.

In the second grade, the teacher said, "It's going to be very cold tomorrow, everybody please wear their coats."

A youthful comedian spoke up and said to Poot, "Yeah, Fart Blossom, don't forget your windbreaker."

Poor Poot was in the sixth grade before he finally understood why the other children were always making fun of his name. Poot, on account of the fact he had to fight all his brothers for everything he got at home—food, a place in a bed, clothing— had become quite adept with his fists. So the first time anybody called him "Fart Blossom" after he had been clued in, he decked them with one blow and told everybody to refer to him as "Mr. Fart Blossom." Even a boy named Poot deserves respect.

So there were seven boys in the Starkins family. The five girls were Clovis Clovis, the oldest, followed by Clovis Mae and Clovis Sue, and then there were the young twins, Lootene and Lootette. All the girls were accomplished fighters as well, as they faced daily battles to fight off their brothers' advances every time they were sent to the creek to get a bucket of water. Clovis Clovis, as a matter of fact, is the only Starkins I was able to keep up with after I left home. She became a famous professional woman wrestler who went by the name of "the Masked Turnip" and once whipped a male wrestler, "Chopper Gaines," in an exhibition match in Baltimore. Clovis Clovis went for Chopper Gaines's eyes at the beginning of the match and rendered him temporarily blind with two quick finger pokes.

Naturally, Chopper complained to the referee regarding this tactic, but while he had his back to Clovis Clovis, she went into the audience and picked up a metal folding chair and brained him with it.

In professional wrestling circles, they still speak of how long it took to stop Chopper's bleeding and how Clovis Clovis also wound up whipping both the referee and the ring announcer before she finally was convinced to go to her dressing room.

It was a sight to behold to drive by the Starkins home while all the children were home. At least half of them were in the front yard naked most of the time, as I pointed out, a classic white-trash trait. One or two of the kids also would be wearing the filthy diapers and at least one of the boys, normally little Poot, would have on one of his sisters' dresses that Mrs. Starkins had made from a feed sack, because the other boys had on what few pairs of pants and shirts were available.

Besides Mr. and Mrs. Starkins and the twelve little Starkinses, Loot, Jr.'s mama and daddy, Loot, Sr., and Loblolly, lived in the one-room house. Loot, Sr., had worked as a sawmill hand until he got one of his hands cut off and had been forced to retire.

Also living with the Starkinses was Loot, Jr.'s youngest brother, Uncle Beede. The way it was told around Moreland, Beede went off to the service and was sent to Korea.

Upon hearing the first shot, however, he bolted and ran and was halfway back to Seoul before they caught him. Beede was examined by a psychiatrist and given the Rorschach inkblot test, which he failed miserably. He told the doctor one blot reminded him of his cousin, Clovis Clovis, with whom he admitted having sexual relations when he snuck up behind her down at the creek as she was dipping a bucket of water.

"Are other members of your family incestuous?" the doctor asked him.

"Naw," said Beede, "just 'bout every one of 'em gits bilious from time to time, though."

When Beede also admitted to the doctors he used to catch lightning bugs in a jar and then eat them, the doctor arranged for a discharge, and Beede was sent back to the United States where he spent six weeks in an army hospital being observed further.

Beede told doctors there he had once poured kerosene on a cat and lit it, was an accomplished pig thief, and was afraid of loud noises and haints (white trash for "ghosts"), so they discharged him and sent him back to Moreland to receive a monthly disability pension of $97.52.

Loot, Jr., occasionally would take a job as a Sheetrocker if all of Beede's pension was gone and it was more than ten days before Beede's next check was due. Otherwise, Loot, Jr., didn't see any sense working and figured Beede owed him something for allowing him to live in the house with Dildene, his wife.

That made eighteen under one roof, with more on its way. Dildene was pregnant with her first child back then, due to the fact Beede had a rather strong sexual appetite and usually didn't have the quarter to purchase a condom at Steve Smith's truck stop because Loot, Jr., had spent all his money.

It is normal for young couples, even white trash, to have sexual relations on a regular basis, but Beede and Dildene often would engage three times a day. The problem was, the family lived in one big room with five beds. So, whenever Beede and Dildene got the urge, the rest of the family had to go outside in order to give them some privacy. This wasn't much of a problem during the warm months, but when Beede and Dildene got into the mood on a cold January night, it wasn't pleasant at all for the rest of the family. But there was the matter of the monthly check for ninety-two dollars and change, so the arrangement continued.

It was rather difficult for Loot, Jr., to explain to

the younger children what they were doing standing outside in the cold while Uncle Beede and Aunt Dildene were in the house, warmed by the kerosene stove.

"What are they doing in there?" little Poot asked his father one night.

"Playin' a game," said Loot, Jr.

"What's it called?" Poot asked.

"Rooster and hen," answered his father.

"When they made us go outside this morning," said Poot, "I looked through a hole in the side of the house and saw 'em. It looked more like an old-fashioned fucking to me."

As I said earlier, Clovis Clovis was the only member of the Starkins family I managed to keep up with in the years after I left home. I do know Loot, Sr., died in '66 and that Beede and Dildene finally moved out of the house and rented a trailer at the Bide-A-Wee Trailer Park. This, I was told, was a terrible blow to Loot, Jr., who had to go to work full time as a Sheetrocker since he didn't have Beede's check coming anymore.

Normally, however, white trash married other white trash and had dozens of more children, and continued to drive cars with mud on the tires and fenders.

I don't know if there is any classic white trash still around in the South anymore. Regardless, they wouldn't refer to them as "white trash" anymore. Now, they would be "dumb rednecks," "goat ropers," or "Clampetts." Individuals from other parts of the country who avoid work at all costs, have children in double figures, and allow some of them to run around naked are called "underprivileged" or "poverty-stricken." There is an underclass in the country, and the rest of us need to help them. Free condoms and jobs cleaning up New York City and Washington, which are both terribly filthy, would be a great start.

But this isn't a book about curing social ills. It's about being a white Southern male who has ridiculous, insensitive ideas like the one I just expressed, which also is probably racist somehow and an affront to homosexuals who drive cars with muddy tires.

Stop me, before I offend again.

No, I didn't grow up as white trash. My mother was a college-educated schoolteacher. My father was an army officer before he lost his battle with an amber liquid. My parents had only one child, me, and I was never allowed to run around naked, and I doubt my mother ever allowed me to wear a dirty diaper, either.

My grandparents did, I admit, enjoy professional wrestling once we got a television when I was eight. As a matter of fact, my grandmother would live long enough to see a man walk on the moon. She believed that had been faked, however. But wrestling— "rasslin'"—was real.

We had more than one room in our house, and my mother bought a new 1955 green Chevrolet that never had a lot of mud on it and purred rather than sounded like an idling boat motor in a muddy lake.

We might have been poor by today's standards— Mother made a whopping $125 a month teaching in one of the county schools in 1953, but we had my grandfather's garden, and there were plenty of chickens to lose their heads and become Sunday dinner, and at least twice a month, my mother would cook pork chops.

We dressed up for church, and I was taught to say "Yes-sum" and "Nome" to my elders. There are no records of incestuous relationships in my family, and certainly no suspicions of it. We had a Naughahyde chair and sofa rather than discarded sofas and chairs with the stuffing coming out.

There was a report in a national publication not that long ago that some Southerners, even today, eat mud. Well, I must admit I did once eat some mud. I was four and it had rained, and I went out in my front yard and started playing in a puddle, which was very muddy. I picked up some of the mud, and it felt so good in my hand, I decided it probably tasted good, too. So I put some in my mouth, but I didn't swallow it. It tasted too gritty. I never tried to eat any mud again.

I loved growing up the way I did. I was raised by good and humble folk, who tried to teach me right from wrong.

Want a good example of how a straight Southern white male thinks? Okay:

When John Lennon was shot, it was like the president got it. There were network news specials and great sorrow and gnashing of teeth. It went on for days.

I was sorry John Lennon was shot. Such a waste. But John Lennon once posed naked on an album cover with his wife. Country singer Marty Robbins never did anything like that, and when he died, you barely could find his obituary in the newspaper, and he sang "El Paso" and "Devil Woman," both of which I think are better songs than anything the Beatles ever did.

See now what you are dealing with here?

··· 4 ···

Just 'Cause I'm Afraid of Copperheaded Water Rattlers Don't Mean I'm a Pissant

Most all straight Southern white males spend their entire lives trying to avoid being pissants. I'm not certain if "pissant" is the scientifically correct name for these insects, because I never took any classes in bugs, and even if I had, I probably wouldn't have paid attention.

I'm also not certain if there are pissants anywhere else besides the South. I think rats and alligators in the sewer systems are the big pests in the North, especially New York City. It is Southerners, by the way, who put the alligators in the sewer system in New York City to get even for Yankees retiring to the South, complaining about all the bugs, and driving slowly.

I once saw a bumper sticker in Florida that read, SAVE FLORIDA—BUY A YANKEE A BUS TICKET.

But back to the pissant. The pissant is larger than a regular ant. It has a big black body, and it will crawl on just about anything that is crawlable, like your arm or the mayonnaise-on-white-bread sandwich you have taken out into the yard to eat.

Pissants are nuisances. They, as far as I know, have no redeeming qualities, whatsoever, and with a name like pissant, they are disgusting.

Nearly all Southern coaches use the term "pissant" to cast aspersions upon their athletes. In Peter Bogdanovich's *The Last Picture Show*, the local high school coach in the small Texas town where the story takes place says to his basketball team as he is putting them through conditioning drills, "Run, you little pissants."

There is the story of the late University of Georgia football coach Wallace Butts, a stern disciplinarian, telling a big, slow tackle over and over, "You ain't nothin' but a worthless pissant."

In the midst of a game against Auburn, the big, slow tackle was missing block after block. Butts sent in a replacement for him and called the tackle to him on the sidelines.

Butts was going to tell his player just how lazy he was. So he said to him, "Do you know what you are?" figuring the player would have no answer, so he could then say, "You're lazy, that's what."

But when he asked, "Do you know what you are?" his player answered, "Yes, sir, Coach. I'm a big, dumb, worthless pissant," and smiled broadly at Butts, thinking he had pleased his coach by showing he had learned his station in life.

There are other things Southern coaches call their players. "Dingleberries," "maggots," and "piles of cow/mule/possum/horse/whale/dog/cat/and goat dung" all come to mind.

But "pissant" was the very worst. Some more examples:

—"You little pissants couldn't find your butts with both hands and a road map."

—"You may be the sorriest bunch of pissants we've ever had in this program."

—"If you little pissants think you're going to get my ass fired, you're pissing up the wrong rope."

—"I've seen some miserable little pissants in my day, but you dingleberries give new meaning to the term."

—"You pissants couldn't drive a boot up a mule's ass with directions written on the heel."

I had a coach in the early '60s who also referred to us as "faggots," "queers," and "homos." But when he really got mad, he'd go to "pissants," which gave me the idea that a pissant was worse than a faggot, queer, or homo, and those were really bad things to be in the early '60s.

Or maybe pissants, as well as being miserable and worthless, also had homosexual tendencies, which is why Southern coaches hated them so much and equated them with a sixteen-year-old boy who couldn't learn to hit the cutoff man on a throw from the outfield.

Yes, white Southern males who grew up when I did constantly were having their manhood challenged, and if you were a pissant, it probably almost meant you were homosexual, so you might as well be dead.

And we've all grown up to be homophobic? How could we have not? It was ingrained in us from our earliest years that a homosexual was a sissy, walked and talked funny, couldn't tackle or block his sister, had no business in the Boy Scouts, much less the military, and his mother allowed him to run around the house wearing one of her petticoats.

The closest I ever came to being called a faggot, queer, or homo was when my mother told one of her friends she was still having to tie my shoes and I was already nine. My mother's friend had a son in my class, and she told him.

At recess, her son said, in a voice you could have heard in Hogansville, which was seventeen miles away, "Lewis's mother still ties his shoes!"

The other children on the playground snickered and pointed at me. Frankie Garfield walked over and punched me in the arm, which made Marcus's nose bleed.

I tried to explain it was simply a matter of having little or no manual dexterity, but my classmates weren't listening, and I knew what they were thinking.

". . . Yeah, and he probably runs around wearing his mother's petticoat."

So, I had to prove my manhood. First, I thought of picking a fight with Frankie Garfield. Frankie would kill me, of course, but at least my legacy would be one of bravery, which might overcome the stupidity of picking a fight with Godzilla.

But I was never much of one for pain, which I certainly would feel. Frankie was a strong believer in slow death.

A boy in my class named Bobby Hosmer ate a live earthworm on the playground one day to impress the girls, and became the first Southerner ever to eat any bait, which would eventually be known as "sushi." Maybe I could eat a live earthworm. I also thought better of that, too. Throwing up, which I most certainly would do, was also a sign of weakness.

What I finally decided to do was to invite my friends over to the Atlanta and West Point Railroad tracks early one morning and prove my manhood by sticking my tongue onto one of the cold rails. It was rumored that a boy once stuck his tongue on a cold rail and then couldn't get it off. A few minutes later, the Crescent, westbound for Montgomery and New Orleans, came by and ran over his tongue and cut it slap off.

I had cringed every time I thought of that story, which everybody knew, but what better way could I show my manhood than by risking my tongue to a speeding passenger train?

I took a group of five over to the tracks one cold Saturday morning.

"I am going to stick my tongue to one of these rails," I announced, "because I am not afraid I won't be able to get it off and a train will come by and cut it slap off."

I must admit, however, I knew the westbound Crescent wouldn't be highballing through town—the train didn't stop in Moreland anymore—until much later in the day, and the worst thing that could happen to me was my friends would have to pull me and my tongue off the rail and all I might lose was a little skin off the bottom.

So I got down on my hands and knees and stuck my tongue to one of the cold rails. What I hadn't thought of, however, was that the *east*bound Crescent on its way to Atlanta was due a few seconds after I put my tongue to the rail.

As my friends stood and watched in complete awe, I heard the blare of the front-end diesel horn, as it rounded the curve a half-mile down the road.

What if my tongue really was stuck to the rail? The train was getting closer now. Fortunately, I was able to determine my tongue wasn't stuck, and I could, in fact, get it out of the way of the train. But shouldn't I wait until the train was almost upon me before I pulled away from the tracks? I would be a hero. I would be a legend.

"Lewis waited till that train was bearing right down on him and his tongue, and at just the last second, he pulled his tongue off the rail and dived out of the way!" It would be in the county weekly newspaper. They might even give me a parade. Grit might even want a first-person story.

"The train's comin'! It's gonna cut Lewis's tongue off!" the girls screamed, and one even started crying and invoking the name of Jesus.

"Jesus Christ!" said my friend Dudley Stamps. "This ought to be somethin'!"

I waited until the Crescent was approximately 100 yards away and closing. Then I pulled my tongue off the rail and flipped myself backward away from the tracks. The Crescent's horn was sounding a constant warning signal. It roared by, and the engineer shook his fist.

But I had proved my manhood. I was not a homo, and I had witnesses to prove it. There was much talk about my boldness at school, and my mother found out about it and gave me a whipping. I also had a bad taste in my mouth for about a week due to the fact railroad tracks normally are quite filthy and have such substances as kerosene on them.

But the experience had been well worth it. I'd be dead if I had picked a fight with Frankie Garfield, and I'd rather drink a quart of kerosene than swallow an earthworm anytime.

My father, who, as I mentioned earlier, is responsible for my being a straight Southern white male (Dad mentioned Mama did have a little to do with it, but he never went into details), is also responsible for the fact I wanted to be a ballplayer when I was a young man.

That sort of thing occurs all over, of course, but perhaps there are some differences with Southern fathers and sons. Do Northern fathers say to their sons when they toss a baseball in too limp-wristed a fashion, "I'll tell you one got-damn thing, ain't no son of mine gonna tho' no baseball like a got-damn girl."

Yes, the dreaded limp-wristed baseball toss. If you want to know what one really looks like, hand a girl a baseball and tell her to throw it. I realize that in the '90's, a lot of women are playing softball, and there was even a report I heard recently that women's running times are coming down at a faster clip than men's, which led some dolt on television to say, "There may be a day when the fastest woman can outrun the fastest man."

And there may be a day when a Volkswagen can outrun a Jaguar, too, but the good news is, I won't be around to see it. As long as most men can still outrun most women, which certainly is the case now and should continue until far past my lifetime, there's always hope for me. They can't bitch at what they can't catch. (Could that become a famous quote like, "He can run, but he can't hide," or "I don't like playing ball on nothin' a mule can't eat"? "They can't bitch at what they can't catch." I really like that.)

But despite women's increased participation in sports and despite the fact they're running faster, most women still can't throw a baseball like a man.

They never take their arms far enough back, for one thing. To throw a baseball, you turn your back to the target and heave it with your legs, butt, back, and arms all involved, sort of like when you try to make love to a woman who outweighs you by a hundred pounds.

Most women don't do anything close to that when they throw a baseball. They take their arm approximately back to ear level and then let it go like it was something dearly fragile. Most of their throw is wrist. The ball comes off the hand with absolutely no zip, and they couldn't get it from third to first in a week throwing that way.

With proper guiding and coaching, I suppose, women could be taught to make a better baseball throw, but most of them wouldn't want to go to the trouble. Today's modern woman would rather be down at the health club aerobicizing or pumping iron so she can look like Jane Fonda when she's fifty.

My father was a baseball player and basketball player in high school, college, and in the army. He later coached high school sports and was even once athletic director at Fort Benning.

My parents divorced when I was in the second grade, but I still had the benefit of my father's advice on such manly things as how to throw a baseball, and, before he died in 1970, I often accompanied him to ball games.

Once we attended a high school game together. He wasn't coaching in the game we were watching, but he did have a teaching position at the school, as well as a job as P.E. instructor.

My father, being an army veteran of two wars and having worn the jock himself, had no use for boys or men who he determined didn't have the slightest interest in athletics, much less wouldn't have the guts to storm a Nazi machine-gun nest.

He had a term for men and boys like that. I don't know where he got it, but he referred to them as "mully." Think of that word for a moment. It really

says it, doesn't it? "Mully." Would you want somebody who was "mully" to be responsible for giving
you a screen when you cut toward the baseline in a
basketball game? Would you want a "mully" individual to be the one you told, "Lay some cover, I'm
going after Heintz"?

"Mully." It stands for "weak" and "effeminate."
An Indian "mully" played by Kevin Costner probably would be named "Dances on Tippy-Toes."

Anyway, we were at this ball game, and my father
and I went out at halftime to get some refreshments.
In the concession area of the gymnasium stood two
boys, fifteen or sixteen, who weighed about a hundred pounds each, with their acne accounting for
about half of that. They were both puffing on cigarettes and holding them with their wrists cocked
when they weren't smoking them. (Women often
hold their cigarettes that way.) Both had what in
that day was considered extremely long hair (we are
talking late '50s here), and one had on a pair of
sandals with red socks. The other wore a pair of
shoes that looked like something Aladdin would
have worn if there had been Hush Puppies in those
days.

Both were terribly thin and fragile-looking, and
were very likely in the Science or Morning Devo-
tional or French clubs, perhaps even all three. Neither appeared to have had any Boy Scout training,
either, because their mothers probably wouldn't allow them to camp out. One's trousers, the one wearing the sandals, naturally—were too short, and the
other had on a silly-looking hat, the kind Matt Dil-
lon wore in *The Flamingo Kid* when he played a
greaser.

This was the kind of boy who would grow up later
to father children who would become punk rockers

and cut their hair with a weed-eater. They were "mully," is what they were.

My father, always dressed immaculately with close-cropped hair, couldn't resist. He walked over to the two boys and said, in a voice like the one the emcee will need on Judgment Day—brimming with power and certainty —"Boys, boys, boys!"

He looked them both over for several moments after addressing them, as an officer would inspect the sorriest of his ranks. His eyebrows were raised in utter disgust, and he rolled his eyes to express further disdain.

"I am Major Grizzard," he went on, "and I am an instructor and physical-education teacher at this institution, and never—*nevah, nevah, nevah*—have I ever—*evuh*—seen two more perfect examples of mulliness in my life.

"Look at your hair. Look at the rest of your persons. Where did you get those shoes, son?" he asked the one in the Aladdin Hush Puppies.

Before the boy could answer, my father asked further, "Are they your mother's shoes, son? Are they your sister's?"

He still wouldn't allow Mully No. 1 to answer. "How old are you, son?" he asked.

The boy managed to squeak out, "Fifteen."

"Fifteen, is it?" Daddy replied. "Why, you're practically a grown man, and you're going around in a pair of slippers like that? You should be ashamed. Son, you aren't homosexual, are you?" Daddy went on, as a crowd gathered. They were so in awe, even the other students, at his control and command, they simply watched.

"No, sir," the boy answered.

"Well, at least that's a relief," Daddy said.

Then he turned to the other boy and looked down

at his footwear, shaking his head, raising his eyebrows, and rolling his eyes again. By now, he knew the audience was with him, so he surged forth, even more appalled.

"Son," he said, "did you know Jesus wore sandals?"

Again, he didn't give Mully No. 2 time to answer.

"Yes, Jesus wore sandals, but I can assure you he didn't wear red socks with them as you have chosen to wear. Do you think you are better than Jesus and can wear red socks with your sandals?"

The boy tried to stammer out an answer, but he was too shocked and afraid to make a sound.

"Are you homosexual?" Daddy asked.

The boy shook his head, no.

"I served with a man like you in the bald hills of Korea once," Daddy went on. "He was a mully thing just like you. Do you know what happened to him?"

The boy shook in the negative again.

"The gooks killed him, Son. He hung around the high school gym just like you two are doing tonight. He smoked those old cigarettes like you two are doing. He was too sorry and lazy to take part in school athletics, and he wore sandals with nonstandard socks. He froze on the battlefield, son, too afraid to fight and too afraid to run. His mother still cries over his grave and wishes he had been a Boy Scout, but he'd have made a better Girl Scout.

"Now, here is what I want you two mullies to do. I want you to put out those two cigarettes you're smoking, and I never—nevuh, nevuh—want to see you using tobacco on school grounds again.

"Tomorrow is Saturday. I want you both to get a haircut. I want to see those ears. I then want you to go to a store somewhere—spend your little cigarette money—and purchase yourself some regulation gymnasium shoes, high tops. And I want you to wear them to school Monday and tell your P.E. teacher you have been asked to be switched to Major Grizzard's class.

"I'm going to make men out of you two mullies. Now, go back to your seats and cheer for those brave classmates on the floor out there who are representing your school. Go, go, go, go!"

They went.

Some months later, I asked Daddy if he'd been able to shape up the two mullies.

"Those two old dead cats?" he answered. "Couldn't do a thing with them. Sadly, Son," he went on, "once a mully, normally always a mully."

What we are basically talking about here are weaknesses. We were taught by these same coaches and fathers and other male role models (e.g., John Wayne, Roy Rogers, Humphrey Bogart, our scoutmaster, our shop teachers, and Argentina Rocca, the wrestler, who was so tough he always went into the ring barefoot and dared his opponent to stomp him on his feet, etc.) to avoid manifesting any signs of weakness of any sort so as to avoid any suspicions of pissantness or homosexuality.

I have discussed throwing a baseball like a girl and not learning to tie one's shoes by the time one has already learned to hit the cutoff man on any throw from the outfield.

But there were many, many other weaknesses. **Crying:** One of the all-time signs of weakness. What I had made up my mind to do if the Crescent had, indeed, come by and cut off my tongue was not cry.

"Lewis, you are really brave," one of the girls might have said to me. "The train cut off your tongue, but you didn't even cry. In the mid-'70s, when there will be the Pill and girls can become sexually promiscuous, will I have a few surprises for you."

"Goo, dunga, rapa, sim, sort," I would have replied, which is how "Boy, I am looking forward to that" sounds when it is pronounced by somebody with just a half a tongue left.

I sometimes cried in front of my mother, but I would always say to her, "You've already got me into enough trouble by telling about my inability to tie my own shoes, but if you want me to keep my tongue intact, please don't tell anybody I cried."

I normally cried in front of my mother either to get my way or to express my anger on, say, the occasion of being forced to eat liver, which I hated then and still hate today. I not only don't like liver myself, I don't even want to be in the same room with it.

The first time I was ever served liver, I refused to eat it.

My mother said, as all mothers say at some point, "How do you know you don't like it if you've never even tasted it?"

I was ready for that.

"I've never tasted brake fluid, but I know I wouldn't like it," I said.

"Well, young man," Mother went on, "you're going to sit here until we [she and my stepfather] finish eating ours."

I immediately launched into a fit of crying. I wrinkled up my face and bellowed out a few deep-throated sobs.

"Please don't make me stay at the table and watch the two of you suffer through eating liver," I said. "I can't bear it, I tell you. I can't! I can't!"

(I had heard an English actress say that once in a movie on TV. "I can't bear it, I tell you! I can't! I can't!" she said to her fiancé, Roland, when he told her he was leaving her for a lusty Spanish wench named Carlotta he had met while running the bulls in Pamplona.)

Mother was so moved by the fact I didn't want to see her and my stepfather suffer—as well as by the fact I was eight and could already do a magnificent English accent—she not only allowed me to leave the table, she later brought me a bowl of chicken-noodle soup and a glass of ginger ale in my room.

"I don't want you to go to bed hungry," she said.

"Oh, Muthah," I replied, doing my English accent again, "you are such a dear."

I was hit in the face once by a softball during school recess. I was playing third base, and I noticed Kathy Sue Loudermilk, the only female in history to be born with the breasts of a sixteen-year-old, hanging upside down on the monkey bars, a joyous sight to behold. As I gazed at her, the batter hit a line drive toward third. The ball caught me flush against my left cheek and my left nostril. At first, I thought God had hurled down a lightning bolt as punishment for what I was thinking as I gazed at Kathy Sue.

Then I remembered about Lot's wife and the pillar of salt. Had I been transformed in the same manner? Was I a pillar of salt, or worse, a pepper shaker, a syrup bucket or a jar of mayonnaise?

As I lay on the ground, motionless and in great pain, all these thoughts were running through my mind. Then I heard Dudley Stamps say to our teacher, who was supervising the softball game, "If Lewis is dead, can I have his dessert at lunch?"

I wasn't certain what I had been transformed into, but I was pretty sure I wasn't dead. My head was numb, but I still had the results of what I was thinking about as I gazed at Kathy Sue. I rolled over on my stomach on the dirt to avoid the embarrassment of anybody seeing that.

The teacher knelt down over me and asked, "Are you hurt?"

Am I hurt? The next thought that came into my mind was "What sort of education am I getting here?" How could anybody with a responsibility of molding young minds ask such a question?

I had just been hit in the head by a sphere going three hundred miles an hour. Of course I was hurt.

I was thankful to hear her call my name, however. Obviously, if my teacher still could recognize me, that meant I hadn't been transformed into anything.

At this point, I had to come to immediate grips with the fact that anytime you are in such an intense amount of pain, there is the tendency to cry.

But I didn't dare show such an overt sign of weakness. I had to fight hard against the tearful urge. Otherwise, when I finally arose sobbing, Dudley would talk baby talk to me, which is what you did when you saw another boy crying.

"Did it get its little head broke?" Dudley would mock me.

"Look at crybaby. It got its little head broke."

"Crybaby." It was right up there with "pissant."

"Walk it off, son," is what coaches said to you when you were hit in the head with a ball or caught one on your finger, which jammed your nail down next to the knuckle.

"Walk it off" meant, "Don't you be no crybaby, you little pissant."

So I arose from the dirt and attempted to walk off the pain. It didn't work. If walking had been good for pain, somebody like Dr. Crawford Long, who came up with ether, would have discovered it, not some ball coach. I mean, can you imagine calling your doctor and saying, "I just had my skull crushed, can you see me this afternoon?" to which he replies, "Go for two walks and call me in the morning."

I walked and just about everything north of my neck hurt, but I didn't cry. I sucked in my stomach, gritted my teeth, and curled in my toes to fight back the tears.

I had to do that the rest of the school day. When I finally got home, I ran to my mother screaming and crying like a person whose groin area had been attacked by killer bees.

My mother would never say, "Did it get its little head broke?"

Mother wiped away my tears, consoled me, and said, "Go ahead, darling. Cry all you want to."

Later, she brought me some more chicken-noodle soup and ginger ale to my room. My jaw was still hurting, but you can suck chicken broth and noodles, so I was able to avoid any painful chewing. As a matter of fact, all I could eat for a week after getting nailed with the softball was chicken soup, and a little applesauce. When my jaw finally healed and I was ready for a pork chop, a piece of Mama's fried chicken, or some of her marvelous country-fried steak, cooked in its own gravy, we had liver. I still refused to eat the liver or be with others eating it. I took a stick of butter and went to my room, and whimpered loud enough that Mama finally began to feel sorry for me and brought me a can of Vienna sausages and some saltine crackers, and she never mentioned to anybody else about my crying jag. One of the main reasons I haven't been able to stay married—and we will deal more with this in a later chapter—is my mother is the only person who ever delivered food to my room and didn't tell when I cried.

I cried once in front of my second wife when Green Bay fumbled on its own two and the Bears scored a touchdown and the Packers didn't cover, and she told everybody in her macramé class.

"Did it lose its wittle bet?" she had said.

We divorced a few months later. The judge said, "And Crybaby here will pay alimony in the sum of . . ."

Wearing Shorts in Rural Elementary School in the '50s: I attended first grade in Columbus, Georgia, a metropolis compared to Moreland, where I entered in the second grade after Daddy and Mama split and she took me to live with my grandparents. When it was warm, Mama sent me to the first grade wearing shorts, and nobody uttered a word about how sissy it was to wear shorts to school.

In second grade, however, Mama sent me to school wearing shorts on my first day, and they had to stand in line to take their turns at beating me up because I was wearing them.

Many of my male classmates in Moreland second grade wore overalls, like Loot and Beede Starkins. "Dee Cee" was the preferred brand of overall. Overalls had a little loop near the waist where you could carry your hammer around. Frankie Garfield came to school my first day at Moreland with, sure enough, a hammer hanging in his hammer loop. He was first in line to beat me up for wearing shorts, and he bopped me over the head with his hammer.

Honestly, I didn't know why shorts were so unpopular with the other boys in Moreland second grade. I finally asked Dudley Stamps the problem, and he said, "Don't you know anything? Sissies and crybabies wear short pants. Where are you from, anyway?"

"Columbus," I said.

"Where the hell is that?"

"I'm not sure," I said.

"Do they wear shorts to school in Columbus?"

"And nobody beats them up if they do."

"I never heard tell of that," Dudley said, "but if you wear those shorts tomorrow, you're not going to be able to see out of that other eye, either."

Mama took me to Judson Smith's discount clothing—used furniture—auto parts—recap tires—fresh produce—and chiropractic-clinic warehouse after school and purchased me a pair of "Dee Cee" overalls, saving my life. I carried the banana I would eat at recess in the hammer loop of my overalls and made it through the day without anybody laying a hand on me.

This experience has remained with me, however, and even until this day when I wear a pair of Bermuda shorts, say, to the golf course, I sometimes get a headache and have this urge to rush to the nearest Polo shop to see if they have a pair of Ralph Lauren overalls with a loop in them in which to carry your sand wedge.

Liking Girls: Any boy who showed anything but utter disdain for a girl until sometime during the fourth grade when Kathy Sue started wearing her first bra was considered weak. After that, anybody *not* liking girls was suspect. In fact, the only time after the fourth grade it was okay not to be messing around with girls was when your sport was in season. Messing around with girls during, say, basketball season, would cut your wind. As my coach used to tell us, "Now, you little pissants stay away from that cooter until the season's over. I don't want to get your wind cut."

I had a few problems with that. One, if we were

pissants, then we likely also were sissies and perhaps even had latent homosexual tendencies, so why would we mess with girls in the first place?

Second, you had to date a girl for a year in those days before she would allow you to engage in what was known in those days as "heavy petting," which always sounded to me like something that had to do with a dog. What it meant, however, was getting to the point you were swapping spit during long kisses. Spit-swapping was quite erotic, if hygienically incorrect, but I still didn't see how it would cut your wind. I could kiss and swap spit and hold my breath during nearly the first quarter of the movie *Pillow Talk*, starring Rock Hudson and Doris Day, at the drive-in in the county seat of Newnan. Had I known what would have happened to Rock, however, I'd have cut out the spit-swapping part, but in those days, we thought anybody named "Rock" was a man's man. Later, all of us found out he was gay, of course, and the term "man's man" took on an altogether new meaning.

It was a year after the kissing part before a girl would allow you to touch her breasts, and then only on the outside of her bra or her blouse. I never saw a bra that wasn't hanging on a clothesline until I was nearly eligible to vote. How could touching a girl's breast on the outside cut your wind? I often asked. In fact, I even asked my basketball coach one day as my girlfriend and I entered the first anniversary of when we started spit-swapping. Breast-touching, I was certain, loomed on the horizon.

"It just does, you little pissant," he explained.

Not Being Able to Complete All the Requirements to Get Lifesaving Merit Badge in the Boy Scouts: Actually, it was not being able to complete just one of the requirements to get Lifesaving merit badge in the Boy Scouts that was a sign of weakness.

That one requirement was to go to the public swimming pool in nearby Grantville—we didn't have one in Moreland—with your scoutmaster to do the old float-with-your-inflated-blue-jeans trick.

Here was the deal: You went into the deep end of the Grantville swimming pool, wearing a pair of blue jeans over your swim shorts. The idea was to take off your blue jeans while treading water and then to pull them over your head somehow and get air into them.

Once you did that, you had to hold on to your blue jeans and float for thirty minutes without drowning.

There were four of us who attempted to pass that requirement for Lifesaving merit badge together. Our scoutmaster, Charlie Bohannon, stood on the edge of the pool and watched us.

I didn't have any trouble getting my blue jeans off. But they became waterlogged and heavy, and I must have treaded water trying to inflate the damn things for forty-five minutes. The other three boys didn't have any trouble whatsoever and were out of the pool pointing and laughing at me, which just made it worse.

I even tried to hold the bottoms of my jeans closed and blow air down from the waist. That didn't work. Now, I was getting tired. I was overcome by frustration. It was at that point, I decided probably the best thing to do was to go ahead and drown. I would not have to face the ridicule of the other three boys telling everybody they knew, "Lewis couldn't get his blue jeans inflated."

Before I simply let go of my jeans and stopped treading water and allowed myself to sink to the bottom and drown, Scoutmaster Bohannon said, "If you'll promise never to use this merit badge on an application for a job as a lifeguard, I'll go ahead and give it to you for being one of the great water-treaders of all time."

By this time, I'd been in the pool during most of the first shift over at the Grantville cotton mill.

I promised, and he allowed me to get out of the pool. A few weeks later, I received my Lifesaving merit badge. I never displayed it on my Scout uniform, however, because I always felt it was tainted somehow. And that experience is one of the reasons I always laugh when I hear a flight attendant say, "Your seat cushion may be used for flotation."

Not mine. It would sink right to the bottom, and I'd have to tread water without it, waiting for the rescue team. This also is one of the reasons I've always been nervous about flying. My seat cushion wouldn't float, and I'm certain I couldn't get a pair of Duckhead khakis, which is what I wear now instead of blue jeans, inflated, and there is a limit to just how long I, one of the great water-treaders of all time, could keep myself from drowning if my plane went down between Atlanta and Chicago in a farm pond just outside Indianapolis.

But the shame of never successfully completing that requirement for Lifesaving merit badge hung with me for years, and I was convinced it was a sign of weakness.

Being Afraid of Snakes: The problem growing up was, there were a lot of boys who *weren't* afraid of snakes. This is because they were under the misguided impression there actually were different kinds of snakes, including varieties that wouldn't bite you.

I'd been walking through the woods and spotted a snake. As I recoiled in horror, these misinformed individuals would say, "You sissy. What are you afraid of? It's just a rat snake. They aren't poison-ous."

Bobby Hosmer, the boy who ate the earthworm, even brought a snake to school one day. When I saw it slithering down his arm in the school yard, I screamed "*Snake!*" ran into the third-grade room, and crouched under the teacher's desk.

The boys who weren't afraid of snakes thought this was a riot.

"It's just a garter snake," they said to me as I hovered under the desk. "Garter snakes aren't poi-sonous."

I knew what was coming next. Bobby Hosmer put the snake on the floor next to the teacher's desk. Suddenly, I was eye-to-eye with my first, and only, snake. I was halfway past Steve Smith's truck stop, running from that snake, when the principal drove up and told me the snake was gone and I could come back to class.

After that, I was always being teased about snakes. Dudley Stamps's brother, who was home on leave from the Navy, took Dudley to Atlanta to the Southeastern Fair, where he won a rubber snake. He won it picking up ducks, a carnival game that involved just what the name implies. There are some plastic ducks floating in water. You pay the guy a quarter and then pick up a duck. There is a number written on the bottom of the duck. You look on the shelf and find the prize with the same number, and the prize is yours. Of course, the prize you won had cost the carnival about four cents, but there re-mained the sense of pride that came with winning something. The first time I went to Vegas, I lost a quick thou at the craps table and tried to find a pick-up-the-duck game to salve my wounded pride. What I found was Keno, however, and I couldn't have afforded even a pick-up-the-duck game when I was through with that.

Anyway, Dudley picked up a duck and won a rubber snake as a prize. Dudley wasn't afraid of snakes. Dudley wasn't afraid of anything, not even bulls or yellow jackets or climbing water towers. He climbed the water tower in Moreland one day and wouldn't come down until his mother promised him she wouldn't make him go to college, something that she had casually mentioned to him. Dudley was in the second grade at the time and couldn't deal with the prospect of fourteen more years of school. And, sure enough, Dudley never went to college. He became a millionaire painting water towers.

Naturally, Dudley brought his rubber snake to school. He snuck into the classroom before I got there and put the snake in the bottom of my desk, the place where students kept their books. I reached into the bottom of my desk to pull out my Blue Springs arithmetic book and touched something cold and slimy.

My defense mechanism went off immediately.

"It's either a snake or a lawyer," I alerted myself.

When I pulled out the object and saw it was a snake, I bolted and ran again. This time I was almost to the city-limits sign when the principal stopped me and took me back to school.

He also confiscated Dudley's rubber snake and made him stay in for morning recess the next three days. I thought he should be sent away to reform school for what he did, but the principal said, "I don't want anything like that on Dudley's permanent record. It might hurt or impede his progress as the Earl Scheib of water towers."

What the other boys in school didn't know that I

know is that there is only one kind of snake, and that is the dreaded copperheaded water rattler. Copperheaded water rattlers are quite dangerous and even more cunning. They often go disguised as rats or garters. You remember when Moses turned his staff into a snake? It was a copperheaded water rattler. The pharaoh knew darn well what it was.

"A copperheaded water rattler!" he screamed. "Let this man's people go this instant!"

"You bet your ass, Your Highness," said a nearby aide, who also was afraid of snakes.

Copperheaded water rattlers grow to be very large, and they are very aggressive. Let's say you see one on your way home from school. It naturally will start chasing you. But you make it home just in time.

You'd think a snake would say to itself, "Well, that one just got away."

Not a CHWR. What they will do is hide in the bushes at your house and wait for you to come out the next morning and start chasing you again.

There was the story that went around about a man who was being chased by a CHWR. The man managed to get himself a room at a Holiday Inn in order to escape the snake.

That doesn't bother a copperheaded water rattler. The snake in question here checked into the room next to the guy, and bit him the next morning in the lobby as he was checking out.

There were all sorts of notions about snakes when I was growing up. I even heard it said, "Snakes won't bite you under water."

A copperheaded water rattler will. That's one of the reasons I couldn't get my blue jeans inflated in the Grantville pool. Just because there might be a cement bottom instead, it won't stop a CHWR from submarining you. I was so busy checking for an underwater snake assault, I couldn't concentrate on my jeans.

It's also the main reason I wouldn't go swimming in Lamb's Pond in Moreland anymore after somebody said he spotted a snake. At least in a swimming pool, you've got a chance to see the snake swimming toward you. Lamb's Pond was too muddy to see your hands a half-inch under the water. Fourteen CHWRs could swim right up to you and bite you in a crazed frenzy, and you wouldn't have had any chance to get out of the pond and attempt to outrun them back to your house or the nearest Holiday Inn.

You don't think something like that could happen? Did you see *Lonesome Dove* on television? There was that scene where they were crossing the herd through a river and the kid fell off his horse and about a million snakes bit him and killed him.

"What kind of snake would do a thing like that?" Augustus McCrae (Robert Duvall) asked Deets (Randy Glover).

"Most likely copperheaded water rattlers, Cap'n," answered Deets, who knew everything there was to know about horses, cows, and snakes.

Remember Marlin Perkins on Mutual of Omaha's *Wild Kingdom*? Marlin would always say, "My assistant, Bob, will put his head in the lion's mouth while I stand back here behind my Range Rover."

Marlin was big at finding animals and getting somebody to film them, but it was always his poor assistant, Bob, who actually had to go over and deal with the animal on a personal basis.

What finally happened was one day Marlin was doing a special on copperheaded water rattlers. He was at a pond, much like Lamb's Pond, just outside Sylacauga, Alabama.

Marlin said, "While my assistant, Bob, takes the camera down to get a closer look at the snakes, I'll just step into this snakeproof cage and watch."

The next week, Marlin was being assisted by a new assistant. They never even said what happened to poor Bob, but I knew. The snakes got him. I always hoped after that that something would get Marlin, too. If not a copperheaded water rattler, then at least a hippopotamus, which could make a mess of you if one happened to step on you.

I like to think I was then, and remain today, intelligent for being afraid of snakes. But, of course, that was another sign of weakness on my part.

To compensate for my snake fear, by the time I was eleven I had worked so much on not throwing a baseball like a girl that I had become a terrific pitcher.

I had a great deal of zip on my fastball and a wicked down-and-out curveball and could strike out most of the boys in school, which sort of made everybody forget about the snake thing.

Even Indiana Jones was afraid of snakes, but did you ever notice how many Arabs he could waste in one scene? If you show a sign of weakness in one area, you may escape any questioning of your manhood by being potent in another.

Not Having a Lot of Chores to Do: The Japanese should have been around to check out the work ethic in Moreland in the '50s. It was extremely powerful. I can remember my grandfather talking about the Ku Klux Klan. He wasn't a member, and he never suggested the Klan should do anything harmful to black people. What he often suggested, however, was that if a man wouldn't work and his family was suffering, "The Klan ought to tan his hide."

What I heard throughout my formative years was continuous derision of people who wouldn't work. They were termed "sorry," a word harkening back to the Starkins clan. A good example of this derision went like this: "That So-and-so is so sorry he wouldn't hit a lick at a snake."

That was, indeed, sorry in my mind. Somebody who wouldn't even hit a copperheaded water rattler with a nearby stick was, to me, the epitome of lazy and deserved to be bitten by the snake.

They didn't use the word "welfare" when I was growing up. It was "relief." So strong was the work ethic, any person who had to "go on relief" was not only sorry, this person was a skunk, a scoundrel, and probably didn't even trust in Jesus Christ as his personal Savior.

Charity was one thing. A family got down due to sickness, say, and the community would respond, whether it meant taking over food, helping rebuild a burned-down house or barn, or even planting a crop for those who couldn't do it themselves. Such a tradition has lived even until today in some parts of the South, Moreland being one of the examples.

My Aunt Una and her husband, John, moved back to Moreland after John retired from the army. Despite their advancing years, they still felt it necessary to plant several acres. They had corn, tomatoes, butter beans, peppers, squash, cucumbers, and onions.

But John came down with a bad heart, and his fields needed plowing. Aunt Una certainly couldn't do it. They were greatly perplexed.

Moreland has changed in a few ways, but it has remained a neighborly place in which to live. And there's been an influx of ex-urbanites. Moreland is just off Interstate 85 South. It is easier to get to the Atlanta's Hartsfield Airport from Moreland than it is from my house in the middle of Atlanta. If you're driving out of Moreland, you simply take I-85, and in twenty-five minutes you're at the airport, which is located south of downtown. From my house you've got city traffic, fourteen stoplights, and probably a truck carrying cantaloupes jackknifed just after where you pull onto the interstate.

As a result of its easy access to the airport, a number of pilots have bought farms in and around Moreland. One lives near Aunt Una and Uncle John. Aunt Una said it was the darndest thing.

"John and I were sitting here watching *Kojak*, and we heard a ruckus in the yard. I got up and looked out the window and saw this pilot friend of ours drive by on his tractor. He drove straight out into our fields without even stopping at the house to say anything, and started doing the plowing we needed.

"I offered to pay him, of course, but he wouldn't hear of it. Lord, I don't know what we'd have done if it hadn't been for him."

It's difficult for Southern men my age to understand welfare. It's because we come from a background that detested it so. We don't want people to starve, but we, indeed, become concerned over Ronald Reagan's welfare Cadillacs.

And today's homeless problem? A friend said recently, "Didn't we used to call the homeless 'bums'?"

I know times have changed. The end has come to the agricultural-based South. The influx to the cities has brought about an entire new set of problems.

But, oh, how that hatred for relief, the public dole, was pounded into us. And although I have worked steadily since I was fifteen, I can still feel some guilt for some of my own reluctance to do various sorts of work.

I've always been the sort of person who would work his butt off, night and day, day and night, as long as it was something I enjoyed doing. But give me a task that bored me or took too much physical effort, and I became a whiner, too.

My grandmother, my grandfather, my mother, my stepfather, my aunts, and my uncles had all worked in the fields as children. When I was back in Moreland in 1953, the family hadn't lost the sense of a collective work pool to tend to the acreage on which we lived. We still grew a lot of the family food.

To be perfectly honest, up to that point, I hadn't hit much of a lick at a snake, figuratively or otherwise. We'd lived on army posts up to that point. Not too many rows to hoe there.

But now, I'm in Moreland, and I'm getting a lot of stuff like, "Go out to the garden and help pick up potatoes."

I love potatoes. I love them prepared any way it is possible to prepare them, especially mashed and French-fried. I take the idea of mashed potatoes that come out of a box and frozen French fries as an affront to God, who created this wondrous vegetable.

But I learned quickly that eating potatoes was a lot better than picking them up. Here's how that worked.

Daddy Bun would harness his mule and plow through the potatoes, which had been growing underground. The idea was to walk behind him and his mule, pick up the potatoes, and put them in a large bucket you were carrying.

The problem was that you had to bend over for

long periods of time. Not only was that such an effort, a large amount of potatoes in a bucket can get rather heavy for a child. Especially a child like me.

As I picked up potatoes behind my grandfather and his mule, I even had the thought, I wonder if I told them I just wouldn't eat any more potatoes, would they let me out of this?

But give up potatoes? Really? Never.

So what I did was every time I would see my grandfather and his mule heading for the potato patch, I would go hide in the pump house. The problem was that besides the pump house, the only other place to hide was under my bed, and that's where I used to hide when my mother wanted to give me a dose of Milk of Magnesia. That was the first place she would look if she figured I was hiding from work.

There weren't any woods in which to hide, except half a mile away at Red Murphy's place, and every time I went to Red Murphy's, he'd always put me to work with his two sons, Mike and Danny, doing something like picking up pecans in his pecan orchard, which was something else I didn't like to do.

So after Mama looked for me under the bed, she would go straight to the pump house and find me there, and I'm back in the potato patch with my bucket.

Pulling corn was even a worse experience than picking up potatoes, because corn doesn't want to be pulled by an eight-year-old boy. Corn shucks are attached to cornstalks like a tongue to a cold rail. It takes a lot of strength to pull corn off a stalk. What's worse, you always perform tasks like this early in the morning, and you get wet from the dew. I would do anything to get out of pulling corn, including feigning a change in a wart or mole, threatening to hold my breath until I turned blue and passed out, and promising I wouldn't eat any more corn. Corn I could live without.

Nothing worked.

Besides pulling corn and picking up potatoes, there were things like hoeing weeds out of the butter-bean patch, gathering pole beans, picking a mess of turnip greens, gathering okra, which got okra fuzz all over you, and pulling the poots out of peanuts.

I wish I could be more specific about the last one, but I haven't pulled a poot out of a peanut since I was about eleven, which was the last time my grandfather said, "Come help me pull the poots out of the peanuts." I even tried to contact various peanut experts for an up-to-date explanation, but Booker T. Washington (or whoever it was) is dead, and Jimmy Carter is off trying to change the world somewhere.

Just so you know, that's what my grandfather called it. You sat down in a chair with all these peanuts that had been in the sun drying. You had to pull each peanut off the vegetation on which it had formed, and it took hours and hours. That was "pulling the poots off peanuts," but the next time you eat any peanut product, try not to think about it.

Since I figured out early in my life agriculture wasn't in my future, I did manage to get out of a lot of the chores set out for me.

I was spoiled. The problem was, the rumor got out that I didn't like work.

I had other friends who were comparative slaves. Mike and Danny Murphy's father always had them out in the fields somewhere. Mike was my age and was a dear friend. He was already plowing on his dad's tractor by the time he was ten. As a matter of fact, Mike sort of got into tractors by the time he was ten. His father had a John Deere tractor. Mike decided that since his father had a John Deere, John Deere must be the Cadillac of tractors, much preferred over the Studebakerish Allis-Chalmers.

I panicked when he asked me my opinion on tractors. Which did I prefer, he asked, John Deere or Allis-Chalmers? I knew the wrong answer would further deem me a weakling when it came to the manly art of plowing and such. But I had to answer. I couldn't say, "Frankly, I don't go around thinking that much about tractors. I'll take your word for which is best."

I had to have an answer. "Allis-Chalmers," for some reason, sounded like it might be a better tractor than the other one. So that's what I blurted out to Mike.

"Allis-Chalmers?" I answered. The fact I had posed a question back told Mike I was no card-carrying farm boy.

" 'Allis-Chalmers?' " he said back to me in a distinctive mocking tone.

"Well," I stammered, "not *all* Allis-Chalmers."

"Ain't no Allis-Chalmers of no kind better than a John Deere," Mike corrected me.

"You want some of this Three Musketeers bar?" I asked him. He not only took some of my candy bar, he berated me for fifteen minutes for being tractor stupid.

Then he asked me the question from hell.

"You aren't a Mama's boy, are you?"

If being a pissant was a thing to be avoided at all costs, being a Mama's boy was twice as bad as that. Not only was being a Mama's boy a sign of weakness, it also delved into one's courage, strength, and heterosexuality. "Mama's boy" in those days certainly carried with it definite hints of homosexuality. "Mama's boy" could, in fact, be used as a polite way of saying what we said in those days—i.e. "queer," "homo," "faggot," and a lot worse.

I already had one strike against me. Recall my mother did have to tie my shoes. The incident at the railroad tracks helped defuse some of that, but here I was still being asked if I was a Mama's boy.

There also was the undeniable fact my father wasn't around, which meant to an outsider I had a good chance of being attached more closely to my mother than a boy with a father to teach him about tractors. The outsider did not know of my strong relationship with my most important male model at the time, my grandfather, who couldn't afford a tractor and, the truth be known, was a bit of a traditionalist when it came to plowing and preferred a mule anyway.

Still, I had to wipe out any suspicions that might be in Mike's mind. So I said, "I may not know a lot about tractors, but I can plow a mule."

Actually, I'd never plowed a mule *by myself,* but Daddy Bun had allowed me to hold on to the plow handles once while he walked behind me with the mule reins. I also knew a mule joke my grandfather had told me. I repeated it to Mike.

"Did you know our mule talked?" I asked him, emphasizing the *our.*

"Mules can't talk," he replied.

"Ours can," I said. "When Daddy Bun goes to feed her at night, he says, 'How many oats do you want?'

"And the mule lifts its tail and says, 'Ah-fuuuuuuw.'"

Mike laughed at my joke. At that tender age, we were heavy into any joke that dealt with flatulence.

He also forgot about the Mama's boy thing, and the experience taught me a valuable lesson—if you think of a good joke when your back is to the wall, sometimes you can get yourself out of that situation. Later in life, I often tried that same tactic with wives, girlfriends, employers, and policemen.

One of my wives was berating me one morning about not squeezing the toothpaste tube from the bottom. I'm not certain why every woman I've ever had to deal with—including my mother—thinks it's some sort of biblical edict that you squeeze the toothpaste tube from the bottom. There's just so much toothpaste in a tube, and I'll eventually get it out of there one way or the other.

Anyway, as my ex-wife was giving me the business about the tube of toothpaste, I interrupted her with the joke about my grandfather's talking mule.

When I finished, she said, "I don't get it," and went back to berating me.

Sometimes the tactic works, sometimes it doesn't. But I learned another lesson in this instance. If you're a straight Southern white male with an agricultural background, never marry a former debutante, which is what this particular wife had been. They don't know anything about mule farting, which can create a large gap in the communication process.

After divorcing this particular wife, I was in a bar one evening and met another lady. I told her I was recently divorced.

"My wife just didn't understand mule farting," I said.

Lesson No. 3: That's really a bad pickup line.

So, growing up had taught me to be quite careful about showing any tendencies toward weakness, to avoid being known either as a "pissant" or a "Mama's boy," which could lead to being known as a lot worse.

I also learned not to hang around bus stations an inordinate length of time, which is my clever way of moving on to the next chapter and taking you with me.

··· 5 ···

This Chapter's Gonna Get Me in a Whole Bunch of Trouble

I FIRST HEARD THE PHRASE "BUS-STATION QUEER" WHEN I WAS about twelve. I was with a group of older, and sexually wiser, boys, and they were discussing a boy who was suspected of homosexuality. I shall call him "Ralph," certainly not his real name, and that doesn't mean I think Ralph is a homosexual name. It just came off my fingers as I was typing here.

One of the older boys asked another, "You think Ralph is really a homo?"

And the other replied, "Hail, yeah. That son of a bitch would go down on you faster than a bus-station queer."

That phrase intrigued me. *Bus-station queer.* Were bus stations gathering places for homosexuals? I'd ridden a Grey Dog a few times by then, going back and forth on visits to my father, but I hadn't seen any man I thought might be homosexual. I'd seen some winos, and I had changed buses in Columbia, South Carolina, once on the way to see my father, who was living in Cheraw at the time, and I'd witnessed a near cutting.

There were two men in a heated argument.

"You shut you got-damn mouth," one of them said to the other.

"You don't tell me to shut my got-damn mouth," said the other, at which time he reached into his pocket and pulled out a switchblade knife.

The other man recoiled.

"Put that got-damn thing away," he said. "I didn't really mean your wife was uglier than death backing out of a shithouse readin' *Mad* magazine."

No wonder the man pulled his knife. That wasn't ugly. That was double ugly. Maybe even quadruple ugly. Ugly like that could scare, as they used to say, a dog off a gut wagon.

The knife-wielder put his blade away, and the two were in the midst of shaking hands when I boarded the bus to Cheraw to see my Daddy.

I pondered on the "bus-station queer" reference as the older boys continued talking about Ralph. Finally, in my innocence, I asked aloud, "What's a bus-station queer?"

"It's somebody who hangs around the bus station, and when some little pissant is going to ride the bus and goes into the rest room, he goes in there with you and goes down on you."

" 'Goes down'?" I asked.

"Don't you know nothin'?" one of the older boys asked.

Apparently, I didn't. Later, I would learn what it meant, of course, one man performing oral sex on another. I also never went inside a bus station rest room again, no matter how much in need I was. I think I got permanent bladder damage once when I went all the way to Paducah, Kentucky, to see my father, where he moved after Cheraw.

Back to Ralph: Nobody had really seen him in any sort of compromising situation with another male, and nobody knew of any exact incident of him actually having sex with another male.

It was just that Ralph had what was considered a lot of funny ways about him. He had that terrible trait of throwing a baseball like a girl. Ralph didn't want to play baseball, but when he was in the seventh grade, his teacher had heard the talk and thought if she got him into a baseball game, he might be a natural and take up the game, thus removing all doubts about him. Nobody had ever heard of a homosexual ballplayer in those days. The term was considered oxymoronic.

She had to pull Ralph screaming and crying onto the diamond. She put him in left field. He never touched the first pop fly that came his way, and when he retrieved the ball, he got it halfway back to the shortstop, the cutoff man.

Poor Ralph. The boys knew. They just *knew*.

There was also the rumor that Ralph's mother had dressed him like a girl until he started school. She'd had three other sons by that time, and desperately wanted a girl. When Ralph came along, the story went, his mother was extremely disappointed and had been certain she was going to bear a daughter—she had prayed for it the entire nine months she was pregnant. She went to Judson Smith's warehouse and bought girl baby clothes months before Ralph was born. It was only when Ralph was about to start first grade that his father put his foot down and told his wife not to send the poor child to school dressed like Shirley Temple.

But Ralph had developed very noticeable effeminate habits, due, one supposed, to the fact his mother sent him to school as a boy, but had continued to refer to him as "my little Ralphine."

Ralph spoke effeminately. He walked effeminately. We called it "prissing" or "trying to walk carrying a corncob in his butt."

When Ralph put his hands on his hips, he did it with his fingers pointed backward, like an interior decorator looking over a room in a house, saying "Beige! Beige would be just perfect here."

As any straight white Southern male knows, when you put your hands on your hips, when, for instance, you're watching a bus-station cutting, you put your hands forward and kept your elbows in. You just do, is my only explanation for that.

Where Ralph made his fatal mistake, however, was trying to become the first boy to enroll in home ec in high school. Ralph's mother had taught him a lot about cooking, and he had plans to become a chef when he grew up.

But a boy wanting to be in home-ec class? The foundations of the high school building shook. Somebody suggested calling out the National Guard. The principal passed the issue over to the superintendent of schools, and he went to the school board with it. The local paper carried a harsh editorial against Ralph being in the previously all-girl home-ec classes and quoted the Bible. The local chapter of the Veterans of Foreign Wars, the Moose Lodge, the Masons, the Eastern Star, the Daughters of the Confederacy, nearly all the town's preachers, and the guy who ran the bus station all went anti-Ralph as well.

The school board finally compromised and said there was nothing wrong with a man cooking and mentioned Uncle Ben's rice, Duncan Hines, and Curley Wippert, the grill man at a local diner. They did say, however, it wouldn't be a good idea for Ralph to be in the same class with all those girls and agreed to have Curley come to the school once a week and give Ralph cooking lessons.

But Ralph's fate as an obvious homosexual was sealed. Nobody would shower next to him after P.E. class. He had no male friends, except Curley, who said, "Ralph might be queer, but he shore can fry a fine egg."

I went along with all this, but even though I'm a straight Southern white male, I certainly felt bad about my part in making Ralph's life miserable. Especially when I heard, ten years after I'd gotten out of high school, that Ralph had a successful restaurant somewhere out in Arkansas, was married to a former Miss Little Rock, and had had two children with her.

So I find myself today, nearly at the half-century mark, living in the '90s and being confronted with lifestyle changes and the New Sensitivity, trying to deal with my feelings about homosexuality.

Let me say, I have come this far at least: I have learned to say "gay," instead of all those other terms. There is one term I still say when I miss a two-foot putt on the golf course or Florida beats Georgia in football, but I am also trying to learn to deal with that.

Not too long ago, I was invited to play golf at a very exclusive club in Florida. I am a member of the Ansley Golf Club in Atlanta, founded in 1912. I love Ansley and my fellow members, and we've still got one of the last men-only grills, and that word—a three-syllable C- word—is often uttered in the grill card room when one is ginned upon with two naked kings or there's too much vermouth in one's martini.

The person who invited me to the exclusive club in Florida warned me not to say that word on the course or in the clubhouse.

"It's just not done here," he said.

"But what if I miss a two-foot putt and get ginned upon with two naked kings, and I just blurt it out without thinking?"

"What you must practice before we go there," he explained, "is learning to say 'rutabaga' instead of [the three-syllable C-word]."

So I practiced. I went out on the putting green at Ansley and purposely missed two-foot putts. Each time I did, I shouted, "Rutabaga!"

We had lunch in the Florida clubhouse. Not once did I make a mistake. I said, when the waiter brought my cheeseburger and it was nearly raw when I had ordered it well-done, "They didn't cook this rutabaga worth a doo-doo." (I had been warned about the S-word, as well.)

I shanked a seven iron on the second hole.

"Rutabaga!" I shouted.

I hit my tee shot out of bounds on Thirteen.

"Rutabaga!"

We were playing a ten-dollar Nassau. My partner and I were up two bets on the back when we got to Eighteen, and I had hit a three iron to four feet on the green in two on the challenging par four. A lot of money was at stake with my putt.

My partner pulled me aside and said to me before I putted, "Now, look. I want you to just relax, take your time, and don't feel any pressure. But whatever you do, don't miss that putt."

I never even touched the hole.

"Rutabaga!" I shouted when the ball rolled five feet past the cup.

"[The three-syllable C-word]!" shouted my partner. "You're the shittiest putter I've ever seen."

So if I slip occasionally and say that word, it really
has nothing to do with homosexuals. It is just a word
that has hung in my vocabulary from my youth.

Today, I say "gay." I really do. Several differences
with the Speech Police (aka, my editor, liberals,
leaders of minority groups, etc.), have taught me it
is not worth the hassle to refer to an individual or a
group in any manner besides the one they prefer.

So, if it's "gay" they want, it's "gay" they get from
me. And I don't know if I speak for all straight Southern white males, but I basically don't care what any
two (or more) adults want to do to one another's
person. I would suggest, however, always using a
condom. I once read about a homosexual group called
Queer Nation, which had set up a chapter on the
blessed campus of my alma mater, the University of
Georgia.

It was interesting to me that a gay group would
use the term "queer," since I had worked so long to
say "gay." But this was, by its own admission, a
radical group that espoused demonstrations (say, in
front of bus stations) where members kissed and fondled one another in public in order to shock
straights.

I wrote a newspaper column about this group, and
even mentioned trying to call the chapter's leader in
Athens. I wrote something like, "I decided not to
place the call, however. I had no condom handy, and
I was afraid to talk to somebody like that on the
telephone without one."

The column never saw print. The Speech Police
arrested it.

If members of the Queer Nation want to kiss one

another, it's okay by me. Honest. But I draw the line when they decide to do it in public, just for the shock value. I don't particularly want to see heterosexual couples engaging in a lot of touchee-feelee-kissee in public, either. Public displays of affection, I have always thought, were a bit tacky. Go get a motel room, for goodness' sake. What are you people, exhibitionists?

But wait a minute. There were all those rumors about gay quarterbacks in the National Football League, so just because a guy happened to be a ballplayer, does that mean there's no way he's homosexual? I suppose not. But I can say I know for certain Johnny Unitas isn't gay. He wore those high-top football shoes when he could have had the sexier low-cuts the other guys were wearing, and I've just got the feeling somehow that if he were gay, he'd have gone for the more flamboyant low-cuts.

Which brings me to flamboyancy, from whence the word "flaming" derives. We are told now there are many homosexual males who show no effeminate characteristics whatsoever. I found out about a man like that. He once worked in a restaurant where I ate. Big guy. Heavy beard. Then, one day, he wasn't at the restaurant. I asked one of the waitresses where he was.

She said, in a hushed tone, "There was this big gay party, and they brought out this huge cake, and all of a sudden |the guy's name| came out of the cake with no clothes on, and several of the men had their way with him. It was about that time the police came in. A lady across the street from the house where the party was going on heard a bunch of screaming and moaning and thought somebody might be getting hurt, so she called the cops. They got |the guy's name| and the others on all sorts of charges, like lewd behavior and disturbing the peace. It's hard to believe that kind of thing goes on." But you know, (the guy's name) didn't act like no (the Q-word). I'm trying to be as careful as I can here.

So I know there are macho-type gay men, I accept that, but let's face it, there are the "flamers," too—the ones with their fingers pointed backward when they put their hands on their hips. They are the ones who work in those spiffy restaurants that serve the green beans cold and the tomatoes hot, which is absolutely contrary to how they should be served, and come to your table and say, "Hi, I'm So-and-so, and I'll be your waiter this evening."

I always want to say, "I'm Lewis, and I'll be your customer. But that's as far as I'm going, Jack."

Flamers, I have noticed, don't touch the ground when they walk. They just sort of float across a room. I suppose that is where the phrase "I think that boy's a little light in his loafers" comes from. Other flaming characteristics:

—Wet, soft handshakes. Straight Southern white guys, especially, will attempt to break each other's hands when they shake, mostly to avoid any thoughts of light loaferness.

—Enjoyment of flute playing. Could Doug Flutie have been one of the . . . *nah!*

—The wearing of earrings. Look, I'm urbane and smart enough to know not every man who wears an earring is gay, but I grew up believing the only men who wore earrings were homosexuals and pirates, and there are darned few pirates anymore since the Coast Guard got all those fast boats.

—The wearing of ponytails. It was popular for men to wear ponytails back in the eighteenth century. I studied history. But that's because there were no barbershops back then, and if you were off fighting the Revolutionary War, for instance, your hair would grow long and unmanageable, and to avoid getting it hung in a tree or bush during a charge against Redcoats, it was a good idea to put your hair in a ponytail.

But the Revolutionary War's been over for two hundred years. And there are barbershops all over the place. Okay, so not every guy who wears a ponytail is gay, either. But those who tie it with a cute little piece of ribbon and stick a flower in it are. That's simply my story, and I'm sticking to it.

—Holding one hand in the air while prissing across the room to greet someone while saying, "Oh, my very favorite poopsie, it's sooo nice of you to come."

—Drawing out words like "soooo." Other examples are: "Youuuu just take my breath awaaaaay!"; "Ohhhhhh, Pierre, you are such a nauuuuuuughty boy"; "Daniel, you look absolutely diviiiine"; "Mr. Policeman, would you like to put your handcuffs on meeeeee?"

—Wearing pants that are too tight. "Ohhhhh, poooopsie, turn around and let me see you from the back."

—Watching football games just to see players pat their teammates on their behinds.

—Using a straw to drink anything unless you are in the hospital with two broken arms, which got a former pro-football-player-turned-CBS commentator fired once. He said of a player with two broken wrists—"Now, when he goes to the bathroom, he finds out just who his *real* friends are."

—Having an overzealous appetite for mushrooms. Straight Southern white guys don't eat a lot of mushrooms, and we'd cut anybody who tried to put one on our cheeseburgers. Robert E. Lee never

liked mushrooms, and Bear Bryant didn't, either.
—Draping one leg completely across the other
with arms folded and fingers sticking up. Try that
yourself. See what I mean. SSWMs cross their
legs, but they usually put the ankle of one leg on
their other leg, and they hold their hands with
their fingers pointed downward.
—Thinking Willie Nelson might be gay because
he wears an earring and a ponytail. I mentioned
earlier that not all men who wear earrings and
ponytails are gay, and Willie is one of those men.
I believe that to the very bottom of my heart, and
I'm considering writing a country song with the
title "Willie Ain't Gay, He Just Got a Little Behind on His Taxes."
—Favoring cocktails that are served with cherries.
—Ordering white wine when there's plenty of cold
beer available.
—Using a jockstrap for a change purse.
—Renting the movie *St. Elmo's Fire* just to get
another look at Rob Lowe.
—Even considering voting for Michael Dukakis
for president in 1988. If George Bush is a wimp,
Michael Dukakis drinks out of a straw and doesn't
understand the infield-fly rule.
—Joining in a gay march against the fact there
are no known homosexuals on the United States
Supreme Court.
  There are probably other flaming characteristics, but I'm tired of thinking about this, and I'm
sure you understand, even if you don't agree, what
I'm implying here—that the reason most straight
Southern white males are homophobic is that gays
have many pissant tendencies, and we've been
taught to detest anything pissantable.

My critics will say and write, "Your stereotyping of gay men is atrocious and just shows your ignorance. Why don't you go stick your head in a bucket of your beloved beer?"

I did that once. We had a "bobbing for beer" contest at my fraternity house at the University of Georgia, which was in 1965. I came in second to the brother who submerged his head under the beer in the bucket and drank it halfway down before coming up for air.

Look, I certainly understand about stereotyping. I really do. I get it all the time. You know the drill. All straight Southern white guys are:

—Beer-swillers.

—Public belchers.

—Just a couple of rungs up the food chain.

—Subscribe to *Neanderthal,* the magazine for guys who tell Magic Johnson jokes.

—Drive a truck with a gun rack and a bumper sticker that says, I'M THE MAN YOUR MAMA WARNED YOU ABOUT.

—Or drive a van with a bumper sticker that says, IF THIS VAN'S A ROCKIN', DON'T BOTHER KNOCKIN.'

—Eat spaghetti with their hands and spit out the bay leaves.

—Look and think just like Jethro Bodine, who, liberals say, had an incestual relationship with his cousin Ellie Mae. There's even a white Southern straight male incest joke:

A mountain boy from North Georgia gets married. He had his pappy build a shack for him and his new bride to live in. The married couple goes up to the shack for their honeymoon night.

The next morning, Jethro comes out of the shack alone. His pappy said, "Well, Son, how was yor' weddin' night?"

"I had to shoot my wife, Paw."

"What's 'at, Son?"

"She war a virgin."

"Well, I don't blame you, Son. If she waren't good enough for her own, she waren't good enough for us."

—Go fishing a lot, and if they don't catch any fish, eat the worms (the Bobby Hosmer Theory).

—Bathe only on special occasions, like to go to a hog-calling contest.

—Won't wear any fragrance other than Old Spice, because that's what their daddies wear, and if they were to put on something else, their daddies might think they were gay and have the Ku Klux Klan beat them up.

—Carry around pictures of Robert E. Lee in their wallets and have at least one bird dog named Stonewall.

—Wonder, "What was that girl doing up in Mike Tyson's hotel room in the first place? Mike ain't known for playin' Monopoly."

—Would laugh hysterically over a country song with the following chorus: "I'd rather go back to the beach with Willie, than over the bridge with Ted."

Another reason for my, as well as other SSWMs' homophobia, is we hear a lot of stories about some of the weird things gay men do to one another sexually. Because we all know at least one doctor who had to intern in an emergency room and see what can happen when gay guys start messing around with one another.

There's a lot of rectal-insertion stories that go around, and if this offends you, know that I am mentioning this here in the name of broadening knowledge and asking the proverbial question all straight

Southern white males ask when they are astounded by something: *"Do what?"*

We all know, of course, homosexual men are bad to engage in anal sex. I saw a T-shirt on a straight Southern white male once that was an advertisement of the way to stop AIDS. On the back, one silhouette, obviously male, was having anal sex with another male. There was a red circle around the two figures with a slash across them. Underneath the picture, it read, NO INDA BUTT.

But do you know about the gerbil thing? (I'm not certain I can get through this.) Yes, the gerbil thing. The story has been going around for years about a gay man inserting a tube in another gay man and then sending a gerbil up the tube. I don't know, it's something about the gerbil feeling quite trapped and running around to find an escape route. And that brings joy to the gerbilee, not to be confused with the "jubilee."

Now what do animal-rights activists think about that? They're out there spraying paint on people wearing fur coats and demanding rabbits and mice not be used in medical experiments, and poor gerbils are going through what I just described? At least bears and rabbits and foxes and minks are safe from that fate. They don't fit the size requirement. (Chihuahua dogs might take note, however.)

The doctor I know who interned in an emergency room told me, "You won't believe the things we have to remove from the anal areas of men, especially on a Saturday night."

He mentioned shot glasses, light bulbs, various fruits and green vegetables, golf balls, salt shakers, and Old Spice bottles.

"Ever have to remove a gerbil?" I asked him nervously.

"No," he replied, "but I had a friend who had to remove a rabbit's foot."

I had a lot of difficulty dealing with the infamous Robert Mapplethorpe photographic display that was funded by the government as a means of supporting the arts.

I never saw the exhibit, but I did read about it, at which time I learned there was a photograph on display that showed a naked man with a bullwhip in his rectum.

I began to think about this, and I wondered what was the conversation between the photographer, Mapplethorpe, and the man who agreed to pose in the photograph mentioned.

Mapplethorpe: Okay, you big hunk, I want you to take off all your clothes first.

Model: I will if you'll turn up the heat in here. I'm freezing already.

Mapplethorpe: No problem. Jerome, cut up the heat, please. Now, what is this I am holding in my hand?

Model: It appears to be a whip of some kind. Be still my heart! Beat me! Chain me! Make me write bad checks!

Mapplethorpe: No, we're not going to do anything like that, at least not now. What this is, is a bullwhip, and what I want you to do with it, is put it in your rectum, and I'm going to take a picture of you and get some government money so I can hang the picture on museum walls.

I mean, something like that had to happen, didn't it? You just don't hand a naked man a bullwhip, and he automatically inserts it into his rectum. *Do you?*

The controversy that arose out of the Mapplethorpe photographs was, "Is this art and deserving of tax dollars, or was it just a picture of a man with a bullwhip sticking out of his rectum?"

I formed my own opinion in a heartbeat, and that was, "I don't care if they had Lash Larue himself, standing there naked with his bullwhip stuck in his butt, that's not art, and I'd rather my tax dollars go to buy a new set of tires on a welfare Cadillac than for something as disgusting as that."

I'm also for carving wrestling tights on all those statues of naked men you see in Europe. I think this should be done for a number of reasons. One is, I saw one in Florence or Rome, and there were fourteen pigeons perched on that statue's genitalia. Women see that and wonder why five houseflies can't line up on the one they got at home.

I cannot end any discussion of male homosexuality without at least one comment about AIDS, which is a horrible thing and may get even worse. Let's fund research, let's find a cure, let's all use condoms.

We know, of course, heterosexuals can get AIDS, too. However, since the entire female population got together when I was about fourteen and made a pact to do everything in their power to keep me celibate, I'm not too worried about getting AIDS in that fashion.

You can also get AIDS by using dirty needles to stick dope in your arms. I missed out on dope. I was out of school and married when I first became conscious of the fact it was available. A neighbor of mine once put some marijuana in the dressing and invited me over for a Thanksgiving Day meal. That was the first and only time I've ever been high on corn bread. So the chance of my getting AIDS from a dirty drug experience is about the same chance I have to engage in sex with Kim Basinger, whom I began to lust after in my heart (and other places) when she and Richard Gere waded through the Louisiana bayou together in a movie. Put Kim Basinger in a wet dress soaked through with bayou water, and she is something to behold. But why would she want to have sex with me? I'd be afraid to wade through a bayou. That's where there are a lot of alligators, not to mention swarms of copperheaded water rattlers.

You can also contract AIDS through blood transfusions, and I've had my share of those, because I've had two heart surgeries to replace the faulty aortic valve I came with.

My last blood transfusion was in 1985, and my doctors have given me the HIV test over and over, and so far, I'm safe.

But let's say I did get AIDS that way. I'd die, and that's bad enough. But worse than that, I know my friends, all straight Southern white guys, all too well. An SSWM wouldn't think twice, despite all the evidence, about saying, "I knew that sumbitch was queer all the time."

And that brings up a headline I saw in a newspaper once that said, TRAVOLTA DENIES HOMOSEXUAL CHARGE.

The Travolta, of course, was the actor/dancer/greaser John, whom I've never cared for, but that's not my point here.

There are a lot of terrible headlines you could read about yourself, but in my opinion "[Your name] Denies Homosexual Charge" is perhaps the worst.

Here's what I worry about:

I write this book and make a lot of gay people mad, so they start a whispering campaign that I, too, prefer drinks with cherries in them.

Well, this would start to get around, and pretty soon I'd have to hold a press conference to straighten this matter out once and for all.

"I am not a homosexual," I would have to say, "and if I'm lying, I'm dying."

The problem is all that is too long to fit into a headline. So the headline would say, GRIZZARD DENIES HOMOSEXUAL CHARGE, and the problem with that is, all a lot of people read in the newspaper is the headlines, and sometimes they don't even take in the entire headline. They would glance at the headline about me and see only two words: "Grizzard" and "Homosexual," and nobody would sit next to me in the men's grill at my golf club anymore.

It would be like being called a Communist at the McCarthy hearings. The charge, even if it's not true, is enough to get you fired at the movie studio or drummed out of your Saturday foursome.

I will admit here, however, I did once see part of a movie about gay men. But please read this closely and realize that was not my intention; you just have to be a bit more careful in these times of alternative lifestyles and other weird stuff.

It had been a long day; I'd sat at my kitchen table for eight hours straight doing some work that called for a lot of typing and reading, which can be difficult on the neck, shoulders, and eyes. When I finished, a wagonload of chiropractors and a witch doctor couldn't have made me stop hurting.

First, I considered having a drink. But it was only three in the afternoon, and if I start drinking at three in the afternoon, I am asleep before Dan Rather.

It was too late to play golf. I don't have a pool, so a long, relaxing swim was out of the question. I do have a Jacuzzi in the bathtub in my bathroom, but I've never been in it. One, I don't take baths because I don't want to wash my face in water I've been sitting in; and, two, I heard about a guy who got into a

Jacuzzi and some wires got crossed, and he got electrocuted.

I decided the ideal thing to do would be to go to a movie. I could sit there in the dark, and get my mind off how poorly and tired I felt.

I turned to the movie ads (SSWMs always say "movie;" never "film"). The movies that most appealed to me had already begun, and it would be two hours before they were shown again. But I was determined to see a movie. So, my college education kicking in as it does occasionally, I deduced, "The heck with it. I'll just find a movie that begins a few minutes from now, regardless of what it is, as long as it isn't *Amadaeus, Grand Canyon,* or *Kiss of the Spider Woman,* which I consider to be the worst three movies ever made."

A small ad caught my eye. The name of the movie was *Longtime Companion.* There were no pictures in the ad. If there's a picture with an ad, you usually can tell at least what sort of movie it is—war, love, horror, romance, comedy, etc., or Hopalong Cassidy and California.

So I drove to the theater. There was a poster for *Longtime Companion,* but it was just a larger reproduction of the ad I'd seen in the paper. Still no pictures.

A young girl with a serious acne problem sold me the ticket. I could have asked her, "What's *Longtime Companion* about?" but I didn't. Besides the acne, she looked like she might not speak English either. She wore a headdress with what appeared to be bananas and other fruits on it, and appeared to be some sort of descendent of Carmen Miranda.

Maybe it's a Carmen Miranda movie, I thought. Lots of dancing and bongo drums.

I went inside the theater and bought a soft drink

and a bag of popcorn. The person behind the counter appeared to be quite young as well. He had zits on his teeth. He also wore an earring, and his hair was a color that might have been chartreuse. He looked like, in an earlier life, he might have been the seat covers on a 1953 DeSoto. Where do they find kids like those two to work in theaters?

It was late afternoon, and there were only eight or nine other people seated to watch *Longtime Companion*. I took a seat down front. In case there are nude scenes in movies, I want to give my aging eyes every possible chance.

The movie began. A man was jogging along a beach. A jogging movie, perhaps. There's never been one, as far as I knew.

The man, in his mid-twenties, it appeared, stopped jogging and took off his T-shirt. Then he took off his jogging shoes. Then he took off his jogging shorts, and ran bare-butted into the water and took a swim. Was this *Splash II?*

Then the screen went black. The next scene opened. It showed somebody who looked a lot like the nude swimmer asleep in a bed. I'm a quarter down through my popcorn at this point. Now, I see there is someone else in the bed with him. Daryl Hannah, perhaps?

Then I see the other person in the bed.

It's another guy.

Maybe they're just camping out after the VW bug broke down outside Ames, Iowa.

Nope. They're in a bed. A real bed. And the next thing is, they're sort of messing with one another, and the horrifying realization hits me:

It's a movie about gay guys!

I slumped down under the back of my seat. Then I sat back up. I didn't want the other members of the audience to think I was up to anything Pee-Wee here. The next scene is a bunch of men in a bed with each other, and somebody is reading a small item out of *The New York Times* about some strange new virus that is attacking homosexual men.

I had to make a decision. I've spent all these years trying not to be a pissant, trying not to manifest any overt signs of weakness, and here I am caught in a gay movie.

Do I get up now and leave, and risk those sitting behind me recognizing me and starting rumors? Or do I sit here and watch the entire movie, and then wait for the house to clear before I leave my seat? I decided the best idea would be to leave as quickly as possible and shout out to the audience, "My God, there are homosexuals in this movie!"

What I did, however, was pour the rest of my popcorn on the floor and put the bag over my head and spring out of the theater.

I did stop long enough, however, to say to Carmen Miranda, "My God, there are homosexuals in that movie!"

She said, "*Carumba Diego, buenas noches*," which I think is Spanish for "You buys your ticket, you takes your chances."

Not a day passes, I'm not shocked by things I read in the paper and hear on the news. And a lot of it has to do with homosexuality. Which brings up the rather interesting question, "If you were in a jail cell with Jeffrey Dahmer, would you rather he be horny or hungry?"

Out in the Bay Area there's even been a movement to get the Boy Scouts of America to lift its ban on homosexual Scouts and Scout leaders. The Boy Scouts have said, "Tie a knot in it, we're not budging." The Boy Scouts have said it is all about basic values and standards, and to allow homosexuals would be to compromise its beliefs.

I agree with that. Boy Scouting is all about being trustworthy and brave, which are basic values and standards. Homosexuality is an alternative lifestyle, which is neither basic nor standard. Besides, if I'm going to share a tent with another guy, I'd sort of like for him to be on the same sexual wavelength as me. Otherwise, there could be a serious misunderstanding, and sleeping-bag fur could fly.

As to homosexual Scout leaders, it doesn't necessarily fly that just because a Scout leader is homosexual, he's also a child molester. But what is a homosexual Scout leader going to do when his troop says, "Hey, let's all go over to the Girl Scout camp and see if we can get lucky?"

If he says, "That's a bad idea, guys," then his troop will think, "Oh, we get it. You would rather go watch the college men's volleyball team practice in these tight pants."

I mentioned earlier one of my own Scouting experiences, my attempt to float in my blue jeans in a swimming pool in order to get the Lifesaving merit badge.

We didn't have any homosexual Scouts that I'm aware of. We had suspicions about a new boy who moved into Moreland and joined the troop, because he spent what we considered too much time practicing the piano, when he could have been playing ball, damming up creeks, and putting kerosene on top of anthills and then igniting the kerosene. I admit torching ants probably isn't strictly adhering to the Boy Scout code and its basic values and standards, but we were trying to make the world safe for picnics.

One Scout meeting, however, the new boy brought

a magazine his older brother, who was in the Navy, had left him during a recent furlough. The magazine showed black-and-white photos of a man and women, all of whom had black bars across their eyes, doing things twelve and thirteen-year-old boys never dreamed could be done. Some even seemed physically impossible unless you were Plastic Man.

"I don't understand how they can see to do all that with those bars over their eyes," Arnold Bates, the teacher's pet who was also quite stupid, said.

The new boy said, "They don't really have black bars over their eyes. The magazine put 'em there so nobody would recognize anybody."

"Oh," said Arnold.

We knew the new boy was okay after he brought the magazine, which he sold hourly possession of at a quarter an hour. He eventually became rich. The new boy's name was Scout Bob Guccioni, who made a shoe box full of quarters, invested wisely, and later started his own magazine, *Penthouse*, which just shows you what a great country this is. You will notice now that *Penthouse* doesn't put any black bars across the eyes of the naked people it shows pictures of. That was originally my idea.

One Scout meeting, I said, "Bob, if you ever grow up and publish your own magazine like the one your brother gave you, you might consider taking the black bars off the naked peoples' faces. I think the photos will become more personal. You simply want to see the face that goes with those hooters, and heinies."

Bob said, "I'll take that up with my staff twenty-five years from now."

I don't have a problem with the idea of the Gay Boy Scouts of America, open just to gays. I mean, aren't there gay rodeos, gay raft races, gay bobbing-for-apples at gay carnivals, and likely even gay duck-picking-up? So why not Gay Boy Scouts?

The flamers might want a few new merit badges that are available to them, like Hiking Without Touching the Ground, Husbandry, Kinky Cosmetics, Studying the Anals of History, and Gerbil Raising for Fun.

"The Scout motto is 'Be Prepared'. Don't forget to bring those condoms to next week's meeting."

What else happened in the Bay Area with this Scouting issue is that the United Way, which funds various Scout councils in the vicinity, said it would withhold its contributions if the homosexual ban wasn't lifted.

Buford Hill, western regional director of the BSA, was asked to comment on the United Way's stand. Before I tell you what he said, I don't know if Buford Hill is a straight Southern white guy or not, but anybody named "Buford" stands a good chance of being one. What Buford told the United Way also sounds a lot like what most SSWMs would have said if they had been in his place.

Buford Hill said the Scouts would go looking for funds in other areas.

Buford Hill said, "Our values are not for sale."

By God.

Of course, there also have been controversies regarding gay policemen and gays in the military. I don't necessarily think *all* gays should be kept off the police forces and out of the service, but let's be reasonable—if not politically correct—here, and say maybe the line should be drawn with flamers. Tough to get much respect out of criminals when you are involved in a drug bust and draw your weapon on a group of thugs and say, "You boys have been soooo bad. Now get those hands up; somebody handcuff me. No, that was last night. I'll handcuff you this time."

Think of what would happen if they allowed flaming homosexuals into the army. Advance to the rear would take on an altogether new meaning.

I realize this discussion has not once mentioned homosexual women. Okay, a joke involving homosexual women:

A guy is sitting at the bar. He looks down the end, and there sits the most beautiful and sexy woman he has ever seen.

He tells the bartender to send her a drink, and then he goes down and sits next to her.

"I appreciate the drink," she tells him, "but I'm a lesbian."

"That's okay," he said. "Your place or mine?"

"I don't think you heard me," the woman went on. "I'm a lesbian."

"I'll get some champagne, we'll build a fire . . ." the man continued.

"Look, fellow," the woman said. "Do you see that beautiful woman at the other end of the bar?"

"I see her."

"I'd like to take her home and make love to her all night long."

The man suddenly began to quiver and sweat.

"What's the matter with you?" the woman asked him.

"My God," he replied, "I think I'm a lesbian, too."

I realize it is a double standard to think of male homosexual sex as something sick and female homosexual sex as kinky, but frankly, I don't understand females having sex with males, because I sure wouldn't do it. Men are too hairy for one thing, and they look like they were put together by spare parts from Eve, not the other way around. If you're a man, ever take a real close look at your body?

I did that once, which is why I no longer shower at my golf club. I'm gnarly, for one thing, and as somebody said to me once, "You look like you traded legs with a stork and lost some ass in the deal."

I have the skinniest legs on earth, except for one other person, my friend Mole Fleming of Albany, Georgia. Mole and I each weigh about 160 each. We were playing golf one day. We both were wearing Bermuda shorts. We began to talk about our skinniness.

"I believe your legs are even skinnier than mine," I said to him.

"You're right," said Mole, "but I believe I got you in butt."

He was right, too. I have absolutely no butt. I don't know what happened to it. In high school, they used to look at the back of my trousers, which always appeared like it must have been vacated by the Chinese Army on bivouac and say, "My God, Lewis! They've stolen your butt!"

That really didn't bother me until the onset of feminism, when it was revealed women enjoy sex, too, and one of the arousable parts of the male body, women said, was his hindparts, and there I was, No Butt Grizzard. I managed to overcome this physical setback by doing things like telling women a lot of funny stories and giving them lots of money and being a pretty good dancer ("Shag Champion," State Key Club Convention, DeSoto Hotel, Savannah, Georgia, 1962, with partner, Louise Beavers, my all-time favorite redheaded cheerleader and erstwhile mixed-doubles tennis partner).

When Mole and I finished our rounds of golf, we

thought perhaps we'd better get a second opinion on who had the edge in legs and butts.

We were playing at the lovely Lake Nona Golf Club in Orlando, and we asked one of the servers, the ever lovelier Jerianne, to judge legs and butts.

We were correct in our original thinking. Jerianne said I had the biggest legs, but Mole had the biggest butt. She also said she wouldn't go out with me, just because I had bigger legs than a man who could floss his teeth with *his* legs.

But back to female homosexuality. I can fully understand desiring the female body. The only chance I'd ever have had of being a homosexual is if I'd been born a girl. As a matter of fact, I'm almost positive I'd've been a lesbian, but I'd have been a picky one. Kim Basinger, yes. Martina Navratilova, absolutely not.

I knew a woman once who was an admitted bisexual. Whoever would buy her things—like a car or jewelry—could be sexual with her.

She said, "I look at a woman's body as a work of art. Women's bodies are beautiful, and I can't help being attracted to them."

I feel the same way. So sue me.

My problem with all homosexuals, however, is that they have become a real group of whiners, too. They also have decided it's cute to flaunt their homosexuality, and they're getting downright pushy.

They break into network newscasts and disrupt them, they show up at political rallies and start screaming at the candidate. I don't mind screaming at a political candidate—God knows, we should do more of it—but at least I'm willing to wait my turn and not begin blithering like an idiot when he or she is trying to make a speech.

They go around demanding too much, also. I get

tired of people who go around demanding all the time. "We demand to be allowed to march in the parade." Hey, go form your own parade. Don't mess up somebody else's.

They demand not being discriminated against in the workplace.

If somebody owns a grocery store and doesn't want gay people working there for whatever reasons, it's that person's grocery store, it's that person who took the risk borrowing money to open it, and it's that person's right to say who works there and who doesn't.

If a black man opens a grocery store and doesn't want whites working there, that's his business. Where does it say the world is supposed to be fair all the time? If the world were a fair place, then fat Lonnie Smith would have scored from second base on Terry Pendleton's double in the 1991 World Series, and the Atlanta Braves would have won it. If the world were fair, I wouldn't have been born with a faulty aortic valve in my heart, none of the dogs I've owned would have been run over, and I'd have gotten to keep the stereo when my first wife and I divorced.

If a group of gay musicians want to name themselves the Gerbils and not include any straight people, I can understand that, too.

I got turned down for a job on a newspaper once because I said to the guy who was interviewing me, "Newspapers are dull as hell. Why don't we run some color occasionally?"

He said to me, "You're crazy as hell, and I'd hire a homosexual who enjoyed a gerbil in his butt before I'd hire you."

Little did he know about *USA Today* and the gerbil fetish that would one day be among us.

I don't like the fact there seems to be a tendency of gay people flaunting their homosexuality. I mentioned Queer Nation. Listen, I've mentioned my lust for Kim Basinger, but I'm not going to stand on a street corner and scream, "I'd like to give Kim Basinger the big one." (An actress thanked her husband for the big one on one of those television awards shows. I thought that was pretty tacky, too.)

I like to have sex with beautiful, well-shaped women, and a lot of other guys do, too. But, hell, we aren't going to parade down the street and put our hands on our women's hindparts! That's a homosexual symbol I've seen pictured before. Two guys walking down a busy street, and one of them has his hand on the other guy's butt. It that really necessary? If you want to play with each other's butts, why do you insist on doing it in public? It's trashy. It's tacky. It's irresponsible. It's flaunting for flaunting's sake.

Go back to your apartment. Or to a motel room. Register as Mr. and Mr. Smith. Fondle each other, dress up like chickens, I honestly don't care. But damn if I want to have to see you do it.

Decency. Remember that word? Decency basically means that if you're going to do something that not everybody wants to see, you go somewhere where you can be alone. At least Pee-Wee Herman picked a dark theater, even if he wasn't alone.

It all comes down to this: I don't care if you have sex with a goat, if the goat is in agreement, but, for Godsakes and in the name of decency, don't you and the goat run down on the field at halftime of a football game and get into it there.

And if somebody finds out you're a goat-screwer, don't be surprised if that person doesn't want to hire you, doesn't want to be around you, doesn't think you have the right to engage in your particular sexual choice around people who think what you're doing is sick, against the teachings of certain religious dogmas, and wouldn't hire you as a marketing consultant because you might bring your goat to the conference with the prospective clients next week. You're the one who decided you wanted to screw goats, which is certainly against the flow, and you have to live with the consequences.

To be perfectly honest, I never saw any of this coming. That's because I went my first three decades or so figuring there might be ten homosexuals in the entire world, and none of them would ever kiss one another on the mouth on the campus of my alma mater in order to shock people.

I said to a friend once, "Damn, where did all the queers come from suddenly?"

He replied, "I guess they were all in that closet." He thought for a few more moments and added, "I'll bet it was one helluva mess in that closet before they started coming out of there."

Before I leave this subject and go on to offend somebody else, I should mention something about the word "gay" itself. I read a letter to an editor on the editorial page of a newspaper recently that was complaining about homosexuals adopting their word.

" 'Gay' used to have such a wonderful meaning," the writer said. "I admit I'm a senior citizen, but 'gay' used to mean somebody who was happy or it described a happy, carefree situation. Parties were known as 'gay affairs' when I was young. People with pleasant personalities who always seemed to be happy were called 'gay', and it had nothing to do with their sexual preferences.

"Why did the homosexuals pick on that particular

word? I miss that word, and I resent them changing its meaning."

Okay, as I said earlier, I've even learned to say "gay" myself, but the writer had a point. We've really lost a pretty good word in "gay." People even used to name girl children that word before the homosexuals stole it. There was a town near Moreland named Gay, Georgia. It's still there. The problem is, somebody is always stealing its city-limit signs to put in gay bars.

Maybe I should start a movement to get the word "gay" back. We take "gay" back, and homosexuals come up with something else to call themselves. I'm a fair man. I'll even attempt to think of things homosexuals could call themselves other than "gay."

I think it ought to be a brand-new word, not one that has a perfectly good meaning already. Every year, new words slip into our vocabulary.

Why couldn't we come up with a new one for homosexuals? Just off the top of my head, I thought of these:

Gooblers
Dinky-Dos
Dinky-Don'ts
Funts
Yags ("Gays" backward)
Sliberg ("Gerbils" backward)
Holecorners (You figure that one out yourself)
Pootwooler
Pootootlers
Stoolienayias (Russian homosexuals)
Wiggywangers
Norts
Rumplers
Skcors (Plural of "Rock" spelled backward)

Hineygleamers
Wienerwanters (German homosexuals)
Or, Wantawieners (I'm not particular)
Poopydoopies
Suckiwukies (Japanese homosexuals)
Gingdingers
Abdulfokkers (Arab homosexuals)
Kareem Abdulfokkers (Black basketball-player homosexuals)

Pootwooler Pride Week. It does have a ring to it, doesn't it?

I've also been racking my brain here (that's not anything homosexuals do to one another, is it?) trying to figure out how homosexuals became to be known as "gays" in the first place. What's the connection? Heterosexuals are probably just as gay as homosexuals when they score.

The only thing I can think of is perhaps the two first two homosexuals ever, a couple of cavemen, (and I'm not going to say anything like their names were "Bruce" and "Keith") finished their business, and one felt sort of bad about the whole thing, being he was part of the first homosexual experience.

But his companion (okay, his name was "Oobie," as in "oobie do-be-do," caveman for "That boy walks a little funny, don't he?") said, "For goodness' sake, you're sooooo silly. Be like me. Be happy! Be proud! Be gay! Be my date at the Valentines Day Ball over at the Big Club Bar next week!"

So when the two arrived at the bar, hand in hand, the bouncer, Googa, said, "What the hell do you two wiggywangers think you're doing? This ain't no fruit inspection, it's a dance."

And Oobie replied, "Listen, you big brute, we're here and we're gay and you'd better get used to us."

And "gay" sort of stuck after that, and Oobie later

filed a suit against the Big Club Bar when it refused him service when he came in and ordered a Singapore Sling with extra cherries, wearing nothing but a sloth fur thong, and asked the waiter, Slurg, if he wanted to dance the Lambada.

He won the suit, incidentally, after it went all the way to the Cro-Magnon Supreme Court that had been appointed by President Nork, a liberal who wanted to reduce the amount of clubs in the military and give the money to the caveless.

Anything is possible, although there's no way you could ever convince me Fred and Barney were anything more than just pals.

••• 6 •••

So I Never Ate a Pig's Knuckle—I'm Still Proud to Be a Good Ol' Boy

W HEN THE 1992 PRESIDENTIAL PRIMARIES MOVED SOUTH, the media was full of references to "the Bubba vote."

Yet, when the primaries were in the East, nobody referred to the "Loud-talking Yankee vote." When they went to the Midwest, there was no mention of the "Frozen fools vote." When it was time for the California primary, there was nothing said about "the nut and fruit vote."

Just the South.

And I'm always a "Southern columnist," or "Southern humorist," or "that redneck from Atlanta."

Ever heard of Mike Royko being referred to as a "midwestern columnist"? Or Dave Barry, of *The Miami Herald*, a "Cuban columnist"?

If you're Southern, it's always going to be mentioned.

"Why don't you people forget the Civil War?" I've heard so often from Northerners.

Well, why don't y'all leave us the hell alone and stop thinking of the South as an odd appendage? How about stopping with the stereotyping already.

The "Bubba vote," indeed.

Allow me to explain "Bubba" once and for all:

"Bubba" normally comes from the fact little sisters have trouble saying "Brother." They have trouble with "Daddy" and "Mama," as well as "chrysanthemum," but that's another story. So "Daddy" comes out "Da-da" and "Mama" can come out "Mah-mah." But they don't normally stick.

But when "Brother" comes out something like "Bubba," it has a way of hanging on. "Bubba" is sort of cute coming out of a little sister's mouth, and pretty soon, the entire family is referring to the boychild that way.

I'm not so sure it's an all-Southern, all-white thing. In fact, I'm certain it's not. Remember Bubba Smith, the football player who went to the pros and was last seen in one of these *Police Academy* movies? Bubba Smith attended Michigan State, and he's black. I have no idea how he got stuck with "Bubba," but they used to wear buttons at Michigan State football games that said, KILL, BUBBA, KILL.

Wasn't that racist? Didn't that portray a black man as nothing more than a violent machine that had no feelings and reacted to the smell of blood? If Bubba Smith had played at Ole Miss or at Georgia, you can bet some smarty-pants from *The New York Times* would have taken "Kill, Bubba, Kill" and had a grand time with it, offering it as further proof of the backwardness and the racial insensitivity of the South.

I had a man write me a letter years ago with what he considered to be quite a dilemma. He had been called "Bubba" by his family and friends for thirty-

five years. He came from a small Georgia town and
had gone to work with a large national firm in Atlanta. His boss, he explained in the letter to me, had
been transplanted from New York City.

"My boss called me into his office," the letter said,
"and told me now that I held a high-level position
with the firm, I could no longer use the name
'Bubba.'

"He said it sounded too 'Southern and ignorant.'

"But that's the way everybody knows me. I don't
see a thing wrong with being called 'Bubba'."

"Nor I," I wrote in a column regarding this situation.

And I was incensed the son of a bitch from New
York City would say "too Southern and ignorant."

What if the man had been named "Booker T."?
Would that have been too "black and ignorant"? How
about "Lech" (as in Walesa), would that have been
too "Polish and stupid"?

What if he had been named "Dances with Fat
Girls"? "Too Indian and insensitive to persons of
size"? How about "Bertrand"? Too "Jewish and
cheap"?

What else I said, and felt, was that, quite frankly,
I'd like to do business with a man named "Bubba."
It's a name, I think, that says the person carrying it
is honest, down-to-earth, and you could roll up your
sleeves with him and dismiss with all pretensions
and get whatever task was at hand done in a lot
shorter time than if you were dealing with some guy
named "Vinny," which sounds "too New Yorky and
the kind of guy who'd order a hit on you if you didn't
like the sort of deal he was offering."

So I told the Bubba who wrote the letter to tell the
jerk who wanted him to drop his name to kiss his ass
and see if he could find a job with a firm that wasn't

being run by a lot of Yankees who looked down on Southerners and had their heads in their asses (*cranial rectitus*).

I never heard from this particular "Bubba" again, but I did hear from a lot of other transplanted Yankees with *cranial rectitus* who delivered long diatribes concerning what was wrong with the South.

One wrote, "I was transferred to Atlanta from New York six years ago. Every time I return to Atlanta on an airplane, I expect the stewardesses to say, 'Welcome to Atlanta. Set your watch back two decades.'"

A woman wrote, "You Bubbas are all alike. All you can think about is football, beer swilling, and hillbilly music. I've been in Atlanta six years. I'm single and I'm college-educated, but I haven't met a single Southern male who reads without moving his lips."

My response to the first writer was, "Oh, yeah? Every time I fly into New York, I expect the stewardess to say, 'Welcome to New York. Get off the plane at your own risk.'"

To the other, I responded, "Read this: Delta is ready when you are."

"Too Southern and ignorant . . ."

That makes my blood boil.

Allow me to get even here by doing a little stereotyping of my own. The Bubba vote? Okay, how about:

The Honker Vote: Honkers are loudmouthed Yankees who never shut up, and they get that way because in the North, especially New York, everybody tries to talk at once (throwing their hands around), and the only way you can be heard is to be able to scream louder than everybody else taking part in the conversation.

Honkers sound like about eight zillion waterfowl,

like ducks and geese, quacking and honking at once.

They pronounce "Bob" as "Baaa-b." And they always get cute with other people's names. Frankly, I don't like it when some honker tries to get familiar with me by calling me "Lew."

"It's 'Lewis,' " I want to say.

And "Nancy" can become "Nance," and "Vinny" can become "Vin," and "Mike" is "Mikey" and "Paul" becomes, inevitably, "Paulie."

Back off, you loudmouth Yankee son of a bitch. After we've known each other for a while and I've determined you have at least some sense, and you learn not to honk but to speak softly and not mock Southerners by using "you-all" in the singular sense, which is completely wrong because Southerners don't do that, I might allow you to become close enough to me, that if you mistakenly refer to me as "Lew," I might allow you to get away with it and say, "Please, it's 'Lewis,' " instead of, "It's Lewis, goddamnit."

But not before.

And, please, keep it down a few decibels, no matter what you are saying.

A friend of mine was describing what happened once when he was a spectator at the Masters golf tournament at the Augusta National Golf Club, where gentility has reigned for over fifty years.

This is a quiet place, a place of great beauty. There are azaleas and dogwoods. There is tradition and history. A sportscaster once referred to the Masters "gallery" as a "mob." He was never allowed by Masters officials (a committee of one, Cliff Roberts, who ran the tournament with an iron fist) to broadcast the tournament again.

Masters galleries for years have been referred to as "the most polite and knowledgeable" in golf.

My friend was sitting in front of the small pond that runs to the left of the par 3 sixteenth hole. It has been a favorite spot of galleries for years. Not only is it breathtakingly beautiful with the green of the turf, the green of the water, and the pinks and whites of the azaleas and dogwoods, it often has been the turning point of many Masters tournaments.

So my friend said, "I was sitting there with my wife, and these 'honkers' were sitting next to me. Not only were they loud, they used every golf cliché in the book and thought they were quite amusing.

"Nicklaus had an impossible putt from forty feet on a green that was like putting on the hood of a car. But he almost made it, leaving the ball just short on the lip. It was an incredible putt, but one of the honkers said, as aloud as he could, 'Never up, never in, Jackie!' and his buddies thought he was a riot. Everybody around him reacted to him as if he had just loudly broken wind.

"I had to get away from them for a while, and I decided to go to a concession tent for a beer. I'm standing there, and here come these idiots right behind me.

" 'Well,' one said when he reached the front of the line, 'what are we going to have to eat, fellows?'

"One of his buddies replied, after looking at the concession-stand list, 'Hey, that Masters sandwich sounds just delish—what about it, fellows?'

" 'Sounds terrif to me,' said the other honker, who then proceeded to ask the young black girl serving, 'Say, could you tell us what's in a Masters sandwich?'

"The girl said, 'There's some ham and some turkey and some roast beef, and some mayonnaise and some mustard, and some coleslaw and some pickles and some bread.'

" 'Sounds good to me,' said the first honker. 'Give us three Masters sandwiches.'

" 'We ain't got no mo',' said the black girl.

"I nearly fell on the ground laughing."

Most honkers are from New Jersey, incidentally.

The Whiny, Bitchy Vote: Usually, these are Northern women, who talk through their noses a lot. The woman who couldn't find a Southern man who read without his lips moving was, in fact, a whiny-bitchette, I'm almost positive.

Whiny-bitchettes don't shave their legs or under their arms. They were all ugly in high school and could never get a date. When they do go out with guys, after they are older and learn to wash their hair occasionally, they usually go out with wimps and weenies from New York City named Bernie.

They also wear running shoes to work, wear glasses, and whine and bitch until they get off at five, and they all live with cats, which are whiny, bitchy animals.

They have names like Mona, and they have clammy-looking white skin and small breasts. "I wouldn't have intercourse with her with your male sexual organ" is what a Southern guy might say to his friend if he saw a whiny-bitchette.

The Wimp and Weenie Vote: These are Northern men who like Wally Cox. The "Mr. Peepers" vote. Bernies. Marvins. They marry whiny-bitchettes and produce more whiny-bitchettes, as well as wimps and weenies, who all wear thick glasses, go prematurely bald, and never take part in sports. They are too busy with their science projects and are too frail, anyway. They become editors of newspapers and college professors who are pissed at how much the head football coach is making, experts with computers whose eyes bug out of their heads eventually, liberal

columnists, liberal lawyers, and politicians, and they take their ugly little whiny-bitchette wives to the beach once a year, and they wear Bermuda shorts and sandals and long black socks and can become terribly sunburned after three minutes' exposure to the sun. They're pissants, is what they are.
The Rocky Vote: These are men who talk like Rocky Balboa and rarely make discernible, humanlike sounds. They say "duh" and "dis" and "dese" and "yo" a lot. They say, "Yo, Paulie, would yuh look at dis." Actually, they don't talk at all. They grunt. They wear black leather jackets, stupid-looking hats, and they all have greasy black hair.

They also usually have at least one tattoo, work in the shipping department, slobber a lot, do nothing more interesting on their off-time than stand around on street corners, making obscene remarks to female passersby. They are uneducated, uncouth, and they are greaseballs. A lot of them live in Philadelphia. More live in Newark, and New York City is full of them. If they aren't named "Rocky," then there are "Tony," "Sal," or "Dominick." A lot of them wind up in the Mafia.
The Hang 10 Vote: Idiots with blond hair who start every sentence with "I'm like," and for "she says," they say, "she goes" and they all live in southern California. You want stereotyping, I'll give you stereotyping. The male hang-tenners are all named "Shawn" or "Kevin," and they've got sand for brains. The female hang-tenners all have names that end in "i," like "Debbi" and "Vicki" and "Poopi," and they are where all the blonde jokes come from. Hear about the blonde who had a pet zebra named Spot?

I could go on and on here. *Newsweek* can get away with using "the Bubba vote." But what if it offered a few of the ones I've mentioned before? It wouldn't, of course, because everybody who works for *Newsweek* is a creep or creepette who went to some school that has bad football teams and is either a wimp, a weenie, or a whiny-bitchette.

The poor Bubba/redneck/good ol' boy. Call us ignorant, racist, sexist, slovenly Neanderthals. We're the last group that hasn't risen up, formed some sort of coalition, and said, "You can't talk about us that way," because one of us would probably say, "One more word out of you, you little Yankee wimp faggot, and I'm gonna cut you," and that would be playing right into the hands of our detractors.

So what do we do? We take it, for the most part. Occasionally, one of us rises up, like me, but we are normally brushed aside as individuals still living in a sordid past of lynchings, queer-rollings, and Klan-rallyings, and who want to keep all women down—in addition to barefoot and pregnant—and make up the part of the nation H. L. Mencken once referred to as a "cultural Gobi," meaning we'd rather go to a rat-killing than a cultural performance.

A few words about that. H. L. Mencken was from Baltimore, and nobody from Baltimore has any right to cast aspersions on any other part of the country. Also, it was later discovered H. L. Mencken was guilty of at least some degree of anti-Semitism, the lousy hypocrite. And to think I actually wasted my time studying some of his writing in journalism school.

Also, I did go to my share of rat-killings in my youth. What you do is you go down to where the corn is stored at night and take positions with .22 rifles. Then somebody switches on a light, and the rats, which are eating the corn, are temporarily blinded, and you shoot as many of them as you can, thus helping save the corn.

But I also have seen Pavarotti live—once in New York and once in London. I have been to the Louvre, museums in such places as Vienna, and have eaten caviar at Maxim's in Paris. I enjoyed both ends of that spectrum, to be perfectly honest, and I'm probably located on the cultural pole somewhere in the midst of those two ends.

I enjoyed my rat-killing days, but I can sing along with Pavarotti when he sings, *"La donnaè mobile."* But I'm most at home now at a University of Georgia football game, a Willie Nelson concert, or a performance of *Miss Saigon* at the Drury Lane Theater in London.

I do like caviar, but I like pork barbecue better. I attended an opera, *The Marriage of Figaro,* in Vienna and was quick to figure out that the whole thing was about how every guy in the cast had the hots for the rather plump ladies' maid. I do admit leaving after the first act, but that was because it was too hot in the hall, and I thought I might faint.

I have two pairs of Gucci shoes in my closet, I wear Geoffrey Beane cologne, and I have a red Chevy Blazer that is six years old. I do not have a gun in a gun rack behind the front seat. I have a gun rack, but that's a four-iron, not a gun, that is resting in it.

And I will not, under any circumstances, turn my back on my heritage. I am proud of it, as a matter of fact, and I wouldn't have had it any other way, and allow me to tell you why you are wrong to use the word "redneck," if you do, indeed, do such a thing and show your own narrow-mindedness and dearth of intelligence.

Here is how the word "redneck" came to be and took its modern-day definition by people who don't know any better and are terribly biased (and ignorant) as well.

You are a Southern farmer. You're not a rich planter. You are a Southern dirt farmer. You don't own any slaves. Nobody in your family ever owned any slaves. It's simply what you do to make a living, a humble, honest, hardworking living.

You go to church, and you believe in God. You're patriotic, you care for your children, you care for your neighbors. You're the salt of the earth. Perhaps you haven't had a great deal of formal education. There wasn't time. Your father worked in the fields, and his father before him, and you have fallen into line.

You are in the fields before dawn because you know the amount of work that is to be done in order that your family be fed. You often stay in the fields after dark.

You live in the South where it's hot. The sun beats down upon you. You work in a pair of overalls, and you plow and you plant and you reap, and that sun just keeps pounding down upon you.

There is a town not far from you. It is perhaps the county seat. It is where you go on the weekends to buy supplies, to buy equipment, to take your wife shopping for what family needs you don't produce yourself.

And they can spot you in that town, and they can tell immediately you aren't a banker, a doctor, a businessman, or even a barber, a car salesman, or a mechanic.

More than likely, you have worn your pair of clean overalls to town. You have those work shoes on. And then they look at your neck.

It's red. It's red because of the hell-hot Southern sun that beats down on the Carolinas, the Georgias, the Alabamas et al. It's red because it's your plot in life to work the soil. You feed yourselves. You feed the whole damn world.

But you're not polished. You're not assertive. You're neither politically correct nor incorrect. You might think about politics some but in your position, you know nobody wants to hear your views.

More often than not, you're gentle and kind to children, and dogs love you. You hunt and fish when there is time for recreation. Your language is filled with colloquialisms, and instead of "his," you say "his'n," because that's the way you learned to say it.

You listen to the "Grand Ol' Opry" on the radio, because it's music to which you can relate, music from the farms and the railroad shanties, Ernest Tubb sings, "Keep them cards and letters comin' in, baby. Keep them cards and letters comin' in. It's a long way from Nashville to Berlin, honey. . . ."

Little Jimmie Dickens sings about sleeping at the foot of the bed, and Hank Williams sings those mournful blues.

You never complain. Your needs and your desires are simple. You are a good man to know if your barn burned down and needs rebuilding. You're a good man to know if you're poor and black and need some work, because you know he'll do what he can for you. He'd share his last biscuit with somebody he thought was needy and worthy.

You took a little boy who was six. His daddy had left him. And you raised him and taught him and gave him a memory he will never forget.

Yeah, you were a redneck. And we put you back in that red clay of Georgia when your heart gave out on you in the fields one April day.

You're Charles Bunyon Word of Heard County, Georgia. A foot-washin', shoutin' Baptist.

You're Daddy Bun, my grandfather.

You're a redneck. And you got that way honestly, and you were the kindest, gentlest, most loving man I've ever known, and when they put you in the ground, it broke my heart. I can still see you, hear you, smell you. You took me fishing. You watched ball games and westerns on television with me.

You were my world for seven years before you died.

And you are a redneck, Daddy Bun. Your neck was parched by the sun for the seventy years you followed a mule and kept your family fed.

Yeah, the redneck. The rube. The bumpkin. The hayseed. The hillbilly. They were looked down upon even by some Southern townsfolk. They never belonged to country clubs or sat and had brandy and cigars and discussed Herbert Hoover and the stock market.

But there were some mighty good Americans who were rednecks, and I'm sorry to have seen that word suddenly stand for not only ignorance, but for racism, insensitivity, and cultural lacking.

"Redneck," like "Dixie," simply got tangled up in hate. Not that there haven't been or don't still remain, Southerners with a bad case of the "sorries," but to call them "rednecks" is, in my mind, completely wrong. The original "redneck" was a man or a woman who, lacking in education or the ways of the urbane, raised families, refused "relief" at any cost, worshiped his or her God, and fought and died for his or her country.

I want to take the word "gay" back, and I want to take away the connotation "redneck" has come to possess today. A man or woman is filled with hate, is slovenly, is ignorant, not because of a lack of opportunity, but a lack of effort; is hurtful, is willing to deprive others for reasons of prejudice, farts, and belches at the wrong time—such a person is not a "redneck" in the purest and original sense of the word. We need a better word. I have a few thoughts there, as well. How about:

Turd-Tappers: The only time I ever heard that phrase is when Atlanta mayor Andrew Young called fellow civil-rights activist Hosea Williams one. But it sounds to me like a "turd-tapper" might be one who is ignorant as a dog turd. It also has no regional bearing, which I like. There are turd-tappers throughout the fifty, I'm sure.

Booger-Eater: I really like that one. Says a lot about a person, as in, "Get away from me with all that bullshit about the false Holocaust, you booger-eater."

Riffraff: Good phrase, too. "You take the rest of that riffraff you've got along with you and get out of my restaurant. You're loud, you're obnoxious, you're not wearing any shoes, and you have no manners. I don't know what the hell is going wrong in New York City, but if we don't do something soon, the riffraff is going to take over."

Jacklegs: A group of Jacklegs attacked a black resident of the city last evening and beat him severely. It is the most recent outbreak of racial incidences in New York/Boston/Atlanta/Miami/Detroit, you name it.

Call the scum of the earth—regardless of their color, or origin—what they really are—"the scum of the earth," not "redneck."

I would really appreciate it, because I don't want anybody talking bad about my grandfather. Otherwise, I might jump out of my Chevy Blazer when you least expect it and bonk you over the head with my four-iron, which I think I could do because your head is a lot bigger than a golf ball.

We need to make some progress in this area. Automatically assuming anybody from the South, in general, and any straight Southern white male has a sheet hanging in his closet, is just as prejudiced as thinking all black people will steal whatever isn't nailed down.

And as long as we're on the subject, I've got some problems with the term "good ol' boy," as well.

I'll tell you where G.O.B. originally came from. That term was once used in the South to indicate that a male might have a few weaknesses, but he basically was a nice person who would come over and help you plant corn if you really needed him.

That went something like this: "Harvey, he's bad to drink, but he's a good ol' boy."

Or, "Bubba's bad to get chicken manure between his toes, but he's a good ol' boy."

"Good ol' boy" is Southern for the most universal "ol' boy," as in the "ol' boy network in Washington," which is what women with hyphenated last names curse when they get turned down for a federal post.

"Ol' boy" refers to a white male, who has ascended to some position of power, like president or senator, or secretary of defense.

"Good ol' boy," however, again connotes ignorance, pickup trucks, beer-drinking, football-watching, gay- and race-baiting, ad nauseum.

Frankly, I don't know how that happened. "Good ol' boy" originally connoted an individual with bad points and good points both. Sort of like all of us.

I've even heard, "good ol' girl," as in "Nadine is uglier than a speckled-heart butter bean, but she's a good ol' girl."

As I mentioned, I've often been referred to as a

"redneck"; some of these references were in jest, others were not. And how many times am I described as a "good ol' boy"?

No problem, if it's the original meaning, such as, "Lewis is bad to play golf all day and play gin at the men's grill until midnight, but he's a good ol' boy."

But if it means I want to hurt other people, and all those other things, I damn sure don't care for it.

What I hope I am is a person of diverse interests who certainly has his faults, but just because he often writes about his native South, it doesn't necessarily mean he wants for the white race to take the country back and throw out every vestige of multi-culturalism. Hell, if anybody ought to take the country back, it's the Indians. But if they want to be called something besides Indians, I don't think Native American is the ticket.

"America" was named after an Italian. I sort of like, "the people who were here first," as in the Atlanta People Who Were Here First's Most Courageous topped the Cleveland Just Plain People Who Were Here First in the first game of the World Series.

(Who am I kidding? The Cleveland Just Plain People Who Were Here First have as much a chance getting into the World Series as I do of getting asked to deliver the keynote address at the National Organization of Women Who Are Just Plain Mean and Ornery annual convention.)

Bubbas and rednecks and good ol' boys have accomplished a lot. We're not perfect, of course, but neither is anyone else. But we are damn tired of being the villains.

If Cracker Barrel won't hire you because you're gay, it's probably because they are afraid it might hurt their business. Whoever first put up the money to build the first Cracker Barrel and has built it into a large chain of restaurants that specialize in Southern foods is the one who took all the initial risk and is the one who stands to lose the most if there is a problem in the business. I'm not saying hiring gays would necessarily hurt business, but it might, and a capitalist who used his own funds, or those he borrowed from a bank and must pay back, should be entitled to do whatever this person thinks needs to be done, or not done, to make his investments secure.

If you're gay and you want a job waiting tables in a Cracker Barrel, why don't you get a job instead in one of the many restaurants that specialize in gay waiters—and they are legion in Atlanta—save your money and perhaps make a deal at the bank and open your own restaurant. If you don't want to hire heterosexuals, that's your business.

This doesn't mean I don't think just because a person is gay/black/yellow/orange/purple/a communist/a bedwetting liberal/anything, he or she should be turned away from a restaurant, a hotel, or a public conveyance. I simply think private property is that, and what was once a damn fine Civil Rights Act has been so used, abused, misinterpreted, and taken to limits that are downright silly, we are now into a period of backlash that is growing as divisive as the Jim Crow laws of an earlier time.

It's the old whining thing, and anyone who dares wonder, "Jesus Christ, isn't this still the best place to live on this earth, and if ever one society has bent over backward to repair the wrongs it did to another people, it's this one, so why don't they get off their butts and go out there and hump it like the rest of us," immediately we'll be covered from head to toe with labels.

I took another little hit from *The New York Times* over some things I wrote regarding the Shoal Creek controversy in Birmingham. One might have thought Bull Connor was back, and he had the German shepherds and the fire hoses out again.

Here is what happened: Shoal Creek is a private golf club in Birmingham that was designed by Jack Nicklaus. It has hosted two championships of the Professional Golfers of America, one of four major golf championships.

The first PGA tournament at Shoal Creek went off smoothly: Lee Trevino, Hispanic in origin, won it. He got a lot of money.

The PGA returned to Shoal Creek in 1990. A great stir came about when a newspaper reported there were no black members of Shoal Creek. Nobody asked if a black had ever applied for a membership at Shoal Creek and had been turned down.

A black guy with $35,000 to spend on being a member of a private golf club because he wants to play golf, and not get a lot of publicity and perhaps a few city, state, and federal grants and contracts because of that publicity, is one thing.

But that had never happened. No black had ever applied. The man who founded the club said, "It's just not done in Birmingham," which wasn't the smart thing to say to a member of the Speech Police.

What came as a result was about 14 zillion newspaper stories, columns, and editorials. Major sponsors pulled out of the tournament, every contestant in the tournament was asked a zillion questions about the controversy, and I thought the whole thing was a lot of overkill.

What I wrote was, "Aren't there more pressing issues than what black millionaire is a member of what golf course?"

A *New York Times* columnist said I meant the Shoal Creek thing was "integration run amok."

No, I didn't. What I thought it was, was stupid. And the result of it all was stupid.

The founder of Shoal Creek got on the horn, found a wealthy black man in Birmingham, gave him a membership, and said, "Satisfied now?"

And the story went away, and now there's even a wealthy black man who is a member of Augusta National.

All that ink and that tape. Wealthy black people can do quite well, thank you. What really needs to happen in this country is for wealthy black leaders not to jump and scream and attempt to keep racism and divisiveness alive, so they can continue riding in private airplanes and appearing on *Nightline*.

Most black people and white people get along. And most black people don't want to go to the Grand Ole Opry with whites; and most whites don't want to go to a Black History Week Music Festival with blacks. Nothing wrong with that. If we truly are multicultural, then *vive la différence*. I don't particularly like fajitas, but it doesn't mean I hate Hispanics.

So the question obviously must arise—Lewis, you redneck, are you a member of an all-white golf club?

Three of them. Ansley Golf Club in Atlanta, Atlanta National Golf Club (guess where that is located), and Lake Nona Golf Club in Orlando. I'm also member of a fourth club, Melrose, on Daufuskie Island, South Carolina, just off Hilton Head. We had a black member, but the last time I talked to him, he said he was thinking of dropping out because he didn't like the greens. We were having a drink together at the time.

I checked with all three of the all-white clubs to

which I belonged to ask if any had a policy that said no blacks would be allowed to join.

No.

I asked if any black members had ever applied. I got the same answer.

So I asked the next logical question; if a black person applied for membership and had the means to pay the initiation fee (an average of $30,000 at the three clubs), would this person be turned down?

The answer was that if a black person did, indeed, have the money for the initiation fee, this person would then go through the same process as any other person attempting to join the club. This mainly involves getting two or three members to write and recommend a prospective member.

Now, I'm not stupid enough to think there might not be members of any of these clubs who would object to a black member. There *might* be.

But I'm also not stupid enough to think that in 1992, any of these clubs would want to get into a Shoal Creek kind of thing and have to take on the wrath of the Speech Police, by turning down a black person qualified to join, simply because this person was black.

And, for the record, there are also no rules against women members at any of the four clubs to which I belong, nor are there any rules against Jewish members, Hispanic members, Asian members, Native American members, or any other kind of members. There might even be homosexual members, but, as far as I know, none have come out of their lockers.

I will admit, though, there are some separate facilities for men and women in my clubs. At Melrose, the men's and women's locker rooms are separate. That's also the case with the locker rooms at my three other clubs.

At Lake Nona, there also is what is known as the "Gentlemen's Smoking Room," but women certainly are allowed inside it. I think the reason this room is called what it is is that an Englishman founded the club, and the whiny-bitchettes aren't nearly as vocal in England as they are in this country.

At Atlanta National, there is a men's grill, but we have female waitpersons who serve, and an ex-girlfriend of mine was even invited in one time.

At Ansley, there's a little different setup. There is, in fact, a men's grill and women are *not* allowed in it. Here's the main reason:

In order to get to the men's grill, one must walk through the men's locker room where the showers and sauna are located. Men often walk back and forth to the showers and the sauna naked. I walk to the shower naked, as a matter of fact, and I stand in front of a mirror naked and shave.

Thankfully, we have not reached the point where the whiny-bitchettes have demanded they be able to walk around in men's locker rooms to see them naked because men can go into strip bars and see women naked.

It's the old thing about the female sportswriter and the locker rooms. Damn, if you can't have some privacy where you shower and go to the bathroom, where can you have it? And if I were covering, say, Wimbledon, I don't think they would allow me in the women's locker room so I might get a chance to see Gabriela Sabatini naked. I'd like to see her naked, but I'm not going to take it to federal court.

To me, the men's grill at Ansley is a place of great comfort. I can eat there. I can drink there. I can play gin rummy there. I can curse there. I can break wind there. I can belch, I can espouse radical political and social beliefs, I can watch ball games on TV without hearing a whiny-bitchette say, "How much longer is this going to last?"

I can be myself there. I can do some male bonding there, as in calling my gin opponent who threw a queen of one suit and I followed with a queen of another suit and he picked it up to put on the end of a run a "baiting prick."

I can be as loud and as obnoxious as I want to be, and I can talk ugly about whiny-bitchettes, and I can scratch whatever it is that happens to be itching at the time.

And, please note, there are locker room facilities for women, and they have their own lounge, and if they need to do a business deal over lunch, there certainly is a place they can do that.

I firmly believe there is such a thing as the right of privacy. I firmly believe if three boys build a tree house and don't want any girls in it, they can say, "Hey, go build your own tree house." (Note: I was involved in the building of a tree house once. We welcomed girls, but none would ever get near it.)

I believe in the right to gather, the right to choose your friends and companions, the right to say, "Sorry, members only."

I would dearly like to be a member of the Augusta National Golf Club. What golfer wouldn't? It is Valhalla. I'd also like to be a member of the Royal and Ancient Golf Club in St. Andrews, Scotland. I'd like to be a member of the Harvard Club, for that matter, as a place to hang out when I'm in New York.

But I'm not going to get into Augusta National nor any of those other places. Do I think, then, Augusta National is discriminating against me? Hell, no. Augusta National can admit who it wants when it wants, and it's no business of mine.

What am I supposed to do? Go over there to the

gate and demand I become a member? Privacy. Nothing wrong with it.

But am I saying the same thing about public accommodations like hotels and restaurants? No. There are limits and boundaries for everything. To exclude individuals from a hotel or a restaurant because of color is to deny these individuals a place to sleep and eat, necessities of life, and would be downright cruel. And facilities funded by governments should be open to all.

On the other hand, if I owned a restaurant and I wanted to exclude people who aren't wearing shoes or shirts, that's my business, too. (I still like the sign I saw in a Longhorn Steak House in Atlanta—NO SHOES, NO SHIRT, NO SERVICE. PANTIES OPTIONAL.) If I allowed turd-tappers or booger-eaters into my restaurant who weren't wearing shoes or shirts, then my other customers might not come back, and I'm out of business and have lost my tail.

I don't wear ties. When I attempt to enter a restaurant, and I am told, "Gentlemen are required to wear ties," I don't scream about my rights. I do one of two things, depending on my mood or how much I want to eat in this particular restaurant. I either say, "Thank you, I'll go someplace else," or I say, "Do you have a tie I can wear?"

I've never been in any tie-demanding restaurants that weren't happy to provide me one. I was in New York staying at The Donald's Plaza. I was having a business lunch, and when I approached the maître d's stand at the restaurant, the gentleman standing there told me I could not get in without a tie. I was wearing a golf shirt and blue blazer.

To be honest, I didn't like the maître d's snippy little way of saying I needed a tie. I also didn't like his looks. He appeared Ichabod Cranish and peered down his lengthy snout at me when he informed me of the tie rule.

But I figured Ichabod didn't make the rules, so I asked, "Do you have a tie I can wear?"

"But of course," he replied, and brought me three from which to choose. All three were fashion nightmares, but I took one.

I did one further statement but just for the record:

"What's really silly about this," I said to Booger Well, "is I'm about to put on an incredibly ugly and outdated tie on a golf shirt. I simply want to point that out, to say just because a man is wearing a tie, it doesn't always improve his appearance."

Then another problem arose. It had been so long since I had worn a tie, I couldn't remember how to tie the damn thing. I finally gave up and tied it in a hard knot—and went in to lunch. People stared at me, and one of the people who stared at me was The Donald, who was having lunch at the very same restaurant I was.

After lunch, the maître d' had to go fetch a pair of scissors and cut the tie off me, since there is no way to loosen a bowline half-hitch turnaround without an acetylene torch.

But I don't own the Plaza, and I had to abide by its rules. It's like I told Marla Maples later over drinks in the Oak Room: "Look, if The Donald wants you to put on a chicken outfit and run around the room flapping your wings and cackling, that's just what makes the man's grapefruit squirt, and he's paying the bills."

"I guess you're right," said Marla. "But I am going to draw the line at pretending like I'm laying eggs."

We must get back to this redneck, good ol' boy thing, though, and take on the stereotypes that are always put upon us, that of being beer-swilling, hillbilly-music-listening, football-watching, truck-driving, big-bellied, drawling cavemen, who likely would carve such things on their cave walls as "How 'bout them Dawgs"; "War Eagle!"; and "Anybody who don't like Hank Williams can kiss my ass."

I'll just start with beer.

There's nothing wrong with drinking beer. In fact, there are a lot of things right about drinking beer. In the first place, you have to drink a lot more beers than you have to drink Beefeater very dry martinis suddenly to run outside and howl at the moon, pull down your pants in a public place, fall on the floor, and go under a table and make boorish remarks to a Supreme Court justice, pass out in your soup, or eat your host's or hostess's cat.

A lot of men prefer beer. I understand Paul Newman is one. But you throw the word "swilling" with beer, and here comes that image again of Billy Carter throwing 'em down, and his belly getting bigger and bigger and his neck getting redder and redder with every swallow.

I don't swill beer. To me, swilling is turning up a bottle or can and not taking it down from one's mouth until the bottle or can of beer is emptied. Swilling also implies some of the beer running out the sides of one's mouth, and then dripping down the chin and onto one's T-shirt that says, IF I'D KNOWN IT WAS GOING TO BE THIS MUCH TROUBLE, I'D HAVE PICKED MY OWN COTTON.

As far as I know, most beer-swillers are college boys, and they swill just as often, I'm almost certain, in the Big Ten as they do in the Southeastern Conference. College boys still have many, many oats to feel and chug-a-lugging (swilling) is one way that is manifested. Throwing up after thirty-seven swills (aka "calling Ralph") is another.

But get this: During the Carter presidency, I sat in Billy Carter's service station in Plains and drank a few beers of my own. When Billy came in, however, he didn't drink a single beer. He was drinking some sort of clear liquid out of a plastic cup. My best guess would have been Seven-up and vodka.

One of the reasons a lot of us drink beer is because it's a lot less trouble than trying to drink liquor in some locations.

At the beach. I've tried to drink screwdrivers at a beach, but the ice melts too fast, and what you wind up drinking is a mixture of barely chilly water, orange juice, and vodka.

Also, you have to take along a lot of cups, and because cups have large mouths, more sand can get in your drink than can get into a can of beer.

And drinking liquor on a hot beach can cause one to go to sleep (aka, pass out) and get a horrible sunburn and/or miss college girls walking by in thongs.

With beer, you just fill up the ice chest. You don't have to worry about mixers, stirrers, your ice melting, cups, or getting sand in your drink. Getting sand in your bathing suit is bad enough.

At baseball games. Think what would happen if they served liquor by the drink at ball games?

People would get even drunker than they do on beer, and if it happened to be Bat Night and everybody who came into the game got a miniature bat, there would be even more bat fights in the stands than there already are if they aren't serving anything but beer.

At company picnics. You know damn well if liquor was served, office grudges would come out a lot sooner, and a knife fight might even break out. You could also get cross-eyed and invite yourself to whip your boss's butt, or ask his wife if the slob is any better in bed than he is managing people. Also, if there happened to be horseshoe tossing at the company picnic and everybody was liquored up, concussions could result.

At bars where there are also pool tables. There are, in fact, bars where there are pool tables, and liquor is also served. These places rarely last very long, however. That is because patrons do things like kill one another over an argument regarding a particular game of pool, whether or not a Ford can outrun a Chevrolet, or somebody makes a remark about somebody else's girlfriend, like "Your old lady needs a douche that will keep her fresher, longer."

After about ten or so killings, the place gets a reputation as being "tough," and then only the bikers will show up, but they'll eventually move on to where there's been twice the killings, and you're out of business.

Patrons also tend to wreck such places at least twice a week and even burn them down if the fancy occurs to them if they think they've been overcharged or were made to check their bazookas at the door.

I went into one of those places once near Valdosta, Georgia. There were pool tables in one corner, a dance floor in the middle, and a bandstand.

Somebody brought over the owner and introduced him to me. The owner apparently wasn't too interested in journalism, and, because it was very noisy in the place (the band was playing "Jeremiah Was a Bullfrog," I seem to recall), he apparently misunderstood and thought I was some sort of law-enforcement official or a politician in charge of liquor licenses.

He said to me, "We don't never have no trouble in here. I promise you that."

While he was saying that, a fight broke out behind him. Two men were taking turns beating one another over the head with pool sticks.

The owner just kept going: "I don't allow no rough stuff here, no sirree."

One combatee finally rendered the other unconscious and went back to the pool table. The owner had never noticed them. I said to my companions, "Let's get out of here before the band starts playing 'Feelings' and there's a shoot-out over somebody trying to cut in on a slow dance."

If there's just beer being served, there still can be violence in a pool hall, but usually all that is required is a few stitches, not the coroner. To be completely on the safe side, these places often serve beer only in cans made of soft aluminum. Beer bottles certainly can become lethal weapons. It is difficult, however, to harm anybody with a soft aluminum beer can—unless one person forces another to eat a soft aluminum beer can.

Beer simply is a man's drink, a male-bonding drink, if you will. Guys who go fishing and camping together reach into the ice chest, open an Old Milwaukee, and say, "It doesn't get any better than this."

Why they do and say that is they hope the Swedish bikini team does, indeed, suddenly appear, and things get a lot better. But if you opened a bottle of vodka and said, "It doesn't get any better than this," the Russian Women's Olympic Tractor-Pulling team might suddenly appear, drink all the vodka, and smash the bottles into the fire, scaring away all the fish.

Southern men probably do drink more beer than other men, but there are reasons for that, too. One, it gets hotter in the South, and beer certainly can be a pleasant thirst-quencher. Two, there are still a lot of counties in the South that don't allow liquor sales but are perfectly happy with beer, so a lot of beer joints get opened. A "beer joint" is known as a "tavern" in other places.

Southern beer joints are a favorite of mine. To qualify as a true "beer joint," a place must meet the following requirements:

—It must have an all-country jukebox. Even a jukebox with Elvis on it is suspect. If it has "In the Garden" by the Statler Brothers, "Six Days on the Road" by Dave Dudley, "Hello Darling" by Conway Twitty, "Waltz Across Texas" by Ernest Tubb, you're in a top-of-the-line Southern beer joint.

—Somewhere on the wall, there should be one of those Miller beer signs, where colored lines go from one side of the sign to the other. Your woman has left you or your dog has died, or you have wrecked your truck, you can drink beer and stare at one of those signs and get things back into perspective.

—There should be at least one of the following things to eat: pickled eggs, pickled sausages, Slim Jims, and even pickled pig knuckles. To be honest, I've never eaten a pickled pig knuckle, but I did once eat four dozen raw oysters in an oyster bar in Destin, Florida, so I'm okay.

—It wouldn't hurt if there were those little wooden signs for sale that picture a pregnant girl saying, "I should have danced all night."

—In Billy Carter's service station, a bona fide beer joint, there was a poster that said, "In case of nuclear attack, put your head between your legs and kiss your ass good-bye." That's just as good as the pregnant girl.

—Handwritten signs with at least one misspelled word are necessary, as well. My favorite was a sign I saw in a Georgia beer joint that had a pool table. The sign said, NO GAMBLING. ANYBODY CAUGHT GAMBLING WILL BE "PROSUTED."

—The bartender should be a male named Rooster or Harld (beer joint for Harold), but that doesn't always have to be the case. The first beer I ever drank in a beer joint was in Grantville, Georgia, and was owned and operated by Lucille Drake. It was a great beer joint because Lucille didn't care how old you were. If you could reach high enough to put thirty-five cents on the bar, she would, in fact, serve you a cold Pabst Blue Ribbon.

—There should be some sort of animal that hangs around. The best would be a dog. A sort of mangy ol' dog is even better. One named Cooter or Biscuit, the kind of ol' dog that would go get under a truck and go to sleep in the shade and get oil drippings on its back. Nobody would remember where the dog came from. Rooster, the bartender, would explain, "He jes' showed up here one day. I reckin somebody gave him part of a pickled pig's knuckle, and he decided to stay around."

I'm not sure if a cat would qualify as a good beer-joint animal. I think of cats and I think of whiny-bitchettes, who certainly wouldn't be allowed in a beer joint. Ol' girls named Roxanne, or Darlene, or Mae would, however, and they would be in charge of taking your money over to the jukebox and playing "Statue of a Fool," the original by Jack Green, not the recent remake by Ricky Van Shelton.

I did, however, once have a Best Beer Joint in the State of Georgia contest. There were the aforementioned requirements, and patrons of such places were supposed to write to me and explain why they thought theirs was unique.

First prize was I came to the winning beer joint and drank beer with the winner all afternoon and picked up the tab.

My selection was a beer joint in the far South Georgia town of Willacoochee, population, a few. The beer joint was the "No Name" beer joint, because it didn't have a name. What I'm saying is, there was no sign on the front that said, NO NAME BEER JOINT. There was no sign whatsoever, just a little cement-block building with two booths and a bar with maybe six stools.

The No Name met all the requirements, but what put it over the top was the coon.

"Every night," the winner wrote me, "we got this coon that comes in. He scratches on the screen door until somebody opens it for him. Then, he gets on top of the bar and people put beer in ash trays and he drinks it. 'Bout half drunk, by the way, that's one mean coon."

Something else would happen at the No Name that always would endear it to me. Even naming the No Name the Best Beer Joint in Georgia couldn't keep it open but a couple of years. The owner just closed it down one day. Somebody said he found the Lord, but that was never verified.

A few months later, however, somebody else re-opened the No Name, and I was invited down for opening night. There was a man singing country songs live inside the No Name, and outside they were having a fish fry. What they had was a big black pot filled with grease sitting on an open fire. Somebody had caught a lot of bream and had cleaned them. The men doing the cooking would drop a bream in the grease and then put it on your paper plate when it was done.

On a table near the pot were several loaves of white bread. That was it. Bream and bread.

I was standing outside eating a fish off my paper plate, when a man wearing large rubber boots walked up. Without a word, he took two pieces of white bread off the table and grunted at the cook he wanted a bream.

The cook forked it out and placed it between the man's two pieces of white bread. The man then proceeded to take a large bite. He got meat, skin, fins, bones and all. No mayonnaise. No tartar sauce. Just a bream sandwich in its purest state.

When the man walked inside the No Name, the cook said to me, "He's a hog farmer. I never did meet a hog farmer that had any sense."

Just look at it this way: Just because a man is Southern and he happens to drink beer, it doesn't necessarily follow he would be a swiller and void of redeeming qualities. I still like beer joints because they remind me of Steve Smith's truck stop in Moreland. That was about the only place to hang out in Moreland, and I still remember sitting on the hood of a car on a weekend night in Steve's parking lot, listening to the music that was piped outside from the jukebox, talking about how far we got with the dates we had just taken home, which usually was fraught with exaggeration.

So, it's a nostalgia thing with me.

As for Lucille Drake, she died, and her beer joint closed down, too. Several years later, the interstate came through, just a few yards from her old place. The last time I drove by, it was a convenience store.

Pity.

As for nonalcoholic beer, I refuse to discuss it. Wimps and weenies drink nonalcoholic beer, not to mention bottled water.

So get off beer and Southern men who drink it. I might still be able to locate Willachoochee's favorite coon.

If you are still using the term "hillbilly music," you are extremely outdated and, to be quite honest, a bit ignorant yourself. One might still use the term when one is speaking of bluegrass music, which certainly can be nasal in tone. It was a couple of bluegrassers, Lester Flatt and Earl Scruggs, who did the theme song for *The Beverly Hillbillies*. The term "hillbilly" itself is close to "redneck" in origin.

People from the Southern hills didn't get to town very much, either, and when they did, they often stood out like rednecks. Some didn't wear shoes, for instance, and others, like the Clampetts, called swimming pools "cement ponds."

But most of them were good and true folk, even the moonshiners, who basically didn't think it was any of the federal government's business what they happened to do with their corn crop, and I heartily agree. The government has about as much business saying who can distill what and who can drink it as it does running a railroad, which is why Amtrak is rarely on time, the help can be snarly, and the air conditioner never works in my roomette.

The proper term for what somebody might erroneously call "hillbilly" music today is, of course, "country music." I don't even think "country western" is correct, because most of it is recorded in Nashville, which is the South, but clearly is not in the country. Granted, a lot of country songs are about such things as cowboys, rodeos, and desperadoes. And a lot of country artists do wear cowboy boots and cowboy hats, but if rock singers did songs about the aforementioned and wore cowboy boots and hats, it would still be "rock," not "rock western."

I think "country" is a perfect term for country music, though, because it implies a certain earthiness. If there's anything country is, it's earthy.

Conway Twitty sang, "Even with your hair up in curlers, I'd still like to lay you down," and that's about a good three feet into the ground there.

I think country music is also "real life" music, as in all the real-life television that is offered on the networks today. Country talks about bad women, good whiskey, Mama's old brown hymnal, and Daddy's hands. Country is about all the family a man has left since his woman has gone; country is Brother Jukebox, Sister Wine, Mother Freedom, and Father Time.

I've helped write a few country tunes of my own with a man I mentioned earlier, Dick Feller of Nashville fame. Dick is on board with Sony-Tree Publishing in Nashville, as I am.

We've written songs about such things as getting drunk and making calls in the middle of the night; the last time I saw my mother and father dance together; a game called pig polo for ordinary folk; my grandmother's yard; and not telling old friends you love them when you occasionally run into them after long absences.

Willie Nelson has sung of Bloody Mary mornings. Alabama has sung about Sunday being the only day "Daddy wouldn't work." Garth Brooks has sung of infidelity and wife-beaters, Johnny Cash on prisons, Merle Haggard on the blues of a working man, and Tom T. Hall of "Old Dogs, Children and Watermelon Wine," one of my all-time favorite country songs.

But don't dare look down on me or my kind from being countryphiles. Read this:

Country music is now the most popular music in the United States. It has even touched some of the country's youth.

"There's a reason for that," Dick Feller has said. "Rock sucks."

Indeed. And it not only sucks, it is void of melody, it's too loud, the people who sing it are mullies, and why wasn't Michael Jackson arrested when he got on top of that car and fondled himself in his latest video? Didn't we lock up Pee-Wee Herman for basically the same thing? At least Pee-Wee had the decency to go inside a dark adult movie theater.

I mentioned earlier, I was a fan of early '50's and '60's rock and roll. I liked Elvis, the Everly Brothers, the Platters, Jackie Wilson, the early works of Marvin Gaye ("Stubborn Kind of Fellow"), Maurice Williams and the Zodiacs, the Drifters, Bobby Vee, Bobby Vinton, Gene Pitney, the Corsairs, the Showmen, and, hallowed be their names, the Temptations and the Four Tops.

I was at the University of Georgia from 1964 until 1968, a time of great musical appreciation on my part. I was a member of Sigma Pi Fraternity. We had a jukebox in the dance room that may have been one of the great '50s and '60s rock-and-roll jukeboxes of all time. And you didn't have to put any money in it.

The jukebox rocked around the clock for the entire four years I was connected with the fraternity. It's probably a dead heat what song got played the most—Marvin Gaye's "Stubborn Kind of Fellow" or the Temptations' "My Girl."

We did a dance called the "shag" back then, a slow form of the jitterbug, which was particularly popu-

lar in the Myrtle Beach area. High school and college kids flocked there in the summer to dance to
mostly all-black bands. From that, "beach music"
got its start, and it has made a comeback in recent
years with forty- and fifty-year-olds, dancing to the
music of our college days. I'm country, but I still
enjoy beach music. Let me also say, I was, in fact,
named the dance champion at the 1962 Georgia Key
Club State Convention at the DeSoto Hilton Hotel in
Savannah, dancing with Louise Beavers, my favorite redheaded cheerleader of all times, to Maurice
Williams and the Zodiac's immortal "Stay."

When the Beatles came, I was a senior in high
school in 1964. I didn't like the Beatles, I didn't like
their music, I didn't like their accents, and I didn't
like their hair.

And I still don't.

As a matter of fact, I blame the Beatles for having
a large part in creating the havoc in my otherwise-
comfortable world of the first sixteen or seventeen
years of my life.

Here is what all I blame the Beatles for:

—The Rolling Stones, the Dave Clark Five, and
all those other silly-looking English groups that
suddenly came forth into America. What we
fought the Revolutionary War about was putting
those bloody kidney-pie-eating, wrong-side-of-the-
road-driving blokes in their place, and here they
were ruining the American music scene.

—Hippies. The Beatles introduced long, unkempt
hair in this country. You know what happened
after that. Drugs, Woodstock, campus unrest, a
less than full commitment in Vietnam. Sure, I
blame the Beatles for that.

If they hadn't come along with all that hair and
there hadn't been hippies, then the government

might have listened to General Curtis (Bombs Away) LeMay, who said we ought to nuke the North. That would have saved a lot of American lives, because about a millisecond after the first nuke hit Hanoi, the Vietnam War would have been over, as was the case in World War II when we *Enola-Gay*ed the Japs.

—Hard rock, heavy metal, punk rock, rap, MTV, Boy George, Madonna, Michael Jackson fondling himself on television. Sure, the Beatles caused all that. If it hadn't been for the Beatles, none of those similarly nerdy longhairs would have thought they could have made it in music, and they all would be delivering Domino's pizzas today, instead of banging on musical instruments and wearing hair that looks like a birth defect.

What's happened to music is exactly what's happened to a lot of other things in this country—it's gone crazy. It's gone worse than that. It's become sick, demented, nasty. It's become dangerous.

Call me whatever you want to call me, but rap is getting people killed and raped. One of those goofballs "sings" about putting a bullet in the head of any Korean who gets in a black's way. In case you missed it, the blacks and the Koreans aren't getting along in New York City.

The Koreans open grocery stores and make decent livings, which pisses off the blacks in the neighborhoods. And why shouldn't it, the racist little gooks? How dare they open grocery stores near black neighborhoods in order to feed themselves and their families? What they should do, of course, is give away their grocery stores to the angry blacks. Rev. Al Sharpton could show up and make a speech, get himself on television, and probably get himself a nice little percentage of the grocery-store business, for as long as it lasted without the Asian work ethic.

Rap is violent, it uses every possible bad word it can get out of its filthy mouth, and that's just great for inner-city kids to listen to.

"Yo, let's listen to some rap and then go out and do a drive-by shooting."

I wrote my own rap song. I'm Lewis Iced T.

Muthafuka, Muthafuka,
Kill, rape, kill,
Muthafuka. Muthafuka,
It ain't no big deal.
Shoot 'em in the head
Shoot 'em in the mouth.
Shoot them little babies
Sleepin' in the house.
Muthafuka, Muthafuka,
Don't say no to me
I'm black, I'm mean
And I'll break your knee.
Muthafuka, Muthafuka,
Yo man, yo yo
You'll be a dead Muthafuka
Bleedin' on the flo'.

Apparently you can get thrown out of college these days for using language that might hurt or upset somebody or cause a riot. Then what's this rap crap? And why is it allowed? If you're a parent, go upstairs right now and search your child's room for violent, sexually demented, sick, and filthy rap music. Take it downstairs and burn it, and then go back upstairs with a large stick and beat your kid until he or she promises never to spend your hard-earned money on such filth and bring it under your roof again.

That's better than censorship. As long as there are sick, demented kids with money to buy sick, demented music, they will. So cut the little suckers off. Feed 'em and house 'em, but don't give them a single dime unless they promise to spend it on something that doesn't suggest killing and raping or maiming somebody else.

That will also put the rappers out of business, and maybe drive-by shooting will end, or at least slow down a bit, unless, of course, Los Angeles gangs get their hands on nuclear weapons. Which could happen. Really.

Let's say a gang or a group of dope dealers make about 15 septillion dollars selling cocaine. But they need a lot of heavy armor to protect themselves from the police and other drug dealers. Uzis are fine, but what if they had a nuclear warhead?

> Muthafuka, Muthafuka,
> Yo, man, yo yo
> We gonna nuke you
> Till you glow.

Where would they get a nuclear warhead? Hey, they've got enough money from selling cocaine to buy a lot of food for the former Soviet Union. They make a little deal with Boris Yeltsin. They buy everybody in Russia something to eat, and Boris lets them have a few warheads. He doesn't have any use for them anymore.

See where this rap crap could lead?

Okay, enough about rap. Then how about Madonna? May she get terminal zits. Why is this woman dancing around in her underwear onstage with a riveted bra? Why is she having oral sex with a bottle of water? Why does she have a video where she's in bed with three guys, two women, and a polar bear? She isn't a musical act. She's a porno act. Dress her in what Janie Fricke wears during her country act, and make her just sing for a living, and she'd starve to death. At least she and that creep Sean Penn didn't have any children together. Maybe her breed will simply die away one day.

Punk rock. I was reading my *own* newspaper, the *Atlanta Journal-Constitution,* one day, and came upon a review of a punk-rock concert in Atlanta.

I'm not sure why I read it. Other times when I have attempted to read articles by rock-music critics, I haven't gotten past the first paragraph, because rock-music critics do not write sentences or paragraphs that make any sense whatsoever to anybody without pink hair and a spear-gun arrow stuck through its nose, and "its" certainly is proper here.

Here's what a rock-music critic might write:

". . . Then, the big dep dingo strains buffoed dingelberriedly upon the stackline foosilbenders of the lead bingondaanterists and fired the audience into a frenetical maelstrom reminiscent of Third Public Hemlock's gritch-grassiness of the mid-'80s."

Rock-music critics are as sick as the people they cover, but newspapers pay them anyway, which always astounds me, because how many punk-rock fans read the newspaper? These people don't read. After the concerts, they all go off and strakeline each other's foosilbenders.

At any rate, I was reading this review, which was making no sense whatsoever to me, and I came upon the name of one of the groups that performed.

Ready for this name? The group was called the Butthole Surfers.

A couple of things came to mind. Maybe more than

that. I'm just not certain I can stay on this subject much longer without having a stroke.

First, how did this group come up with such a name as the Butthole Surfers?

"Okay, we've got our first gig tomorrow night at the Vomit and Green Pus Club. What are we going to call ourselves?"

"How about the Sexual Deviate Mother Killers?"

"Nah, somebody already used that."

"Okay, how about the Twin Engine-Fart Company?"

"Sounds too sixties."

"I've got it! How about the Butthole Surfers?"

"Great!"

Second, I was incensed the word "Butthole" had appeared in the *Atlanta Journal-Constitution*, the South's Standard Newspaper, the newspaper of Ralph McGill. I had an editor cut "jock itch" out of a column once because he said it was too harsh. Too harsh? What's the Butthole Surfers, if jock itch is "too harsh"?

I did get away with writing a column the next day on "butthole" appearing in the *Atlanta Journal-Constitution*. I asked, "Where is decency these days?"

Then I answered myself, "Probably in somebody's butthole."

I realize the adults raised all hell when I was coming along about our timid rock and roll and Elvis. But, God knows, what is "Rock Around the Clock" by Bill Haley and the Comets compared to "Come Sit On My Face While I Have Unnatural Sex with a Rogue Elephant" by the Butthole Surfers? What was Elvis compared to rockers who pull their Johnsons out in midconcert and wave them at an adoring crowd of fourteen-year-olds?

And country is "hillbilly"? Country is *sane*. It's

moral. It's sweet and it's tender. It speaks, God forbid in the '90s, of values.

I think a phrase of a country song applies here, and perhaps applies to every other thing I've been writing in this book. The phrase is "Anybody who don't like Hank Williams can kiss my ass."

I can sit right here, without making any phone calls, and give you a list of people who don't like Hank Williams and can etc. etc.

—Ted Kennedy doesn't like Hank Williams.

—Guns N' Roses and other groups that get concerts canceled because violence usually breaks out don't like Hank Williams.

—Jane Fonda doesn't, and even if Ted Turner did, after they married, Jane probably said, "Turn off that hillbilly and come over here and hold my legs down while I do twenty-five thousand situps and figure out what kind of stink I can raise next."

—Rev. Al and Rev. Jesse don't like Hank Williams. They're too busy standing around in expensive suits talking about the poor people.

—Hammer Rammer Jammer, or whatever his name is, doesn't like Hank Williams, and neither does Spike Lee, who doesn't like anybody who's white.

Spike blames white people for everything. He blames them because he hasn't gotten an Oscar, and he said white people were afraid to go to the theater to see *Do the Right Thing* because they were afraid there would be blacks in the audience who might get violent.

Now why would anybody white think that? Just because black gangs tend to rumble occasionally in movie theaters and start shooting real bullets? No, it's a racist thing.

Take me. I thought about going to see *Do the Right*

Thing in a movie theater, but then I thought, "What if the Cruds or the Bloods are there, too, and when the black people go berserk and burn down the guy's pizza restaurant in the movie, they start looking around for honkies to shoot?"

What I did was wait for the movie to come out in video, and I watched it, behind locked doors, of course, on the VCR in my living room.

I gave it one star. And after the movie was over, I asked, "Now, wait a minute? Basically, they burn this man out because he's Italian, and he has Italian heroes hanging on his walls in his pizza joint, which he opened with *his* money. And some smart-aleck black kid wants Dr. Martin Luther King, Jr., and Malcolm X up on the wall because he spends his money there?"

That's like me calling the White House and demanding they put a picture of me on the wall since I'm a taxpayer and help pay the light bill.

If I'd been the pizza guy in *Do the Right Thing*, I'd have compromised. I would have said, "Hey, you want some pictures of black heroes on the wall? Go get some, have them framed, and stick them on the wall over your favorite booth."

But even if he hadn't done that, I still don't think he deserved to be put out of business. It's the Korean-grocery thing all over again. If the black kid wanted a black pizza joint in his neighborhood, there must have been some sort of federal-smederal minority something or other that would have put him in business. And probably sent over the anchovies as well.

Still one more thought: Did anybody think while they were burning down the man's store, "Hey, if we do this, where are we gonna get pizza tomorrow?"

Nah, Spike Lee doesn't like Hank Williams, and I hope he gets ripped off at the next Cannes Film Festival by the same beach boy who, the first and last time I was ever in Cannes, charged me about a hundred American dollars for two beach chairs, an umbrella, a Coke, and a copy of *The International Herald-Tribune.*

What does any of this have to do with country music: Well, if it's good enough for Charley Pride, I don't understand why Spike Lee thinks he's too African-Americanized to like Hank Williams, who inspired Charley Pride, I've heard tell, to go into country music.

By the way, if you've never heard of Charley Pride, he's had about a dozen or so huge country hits, and the man is black. Spike Lee breaking into movie making as a black producer is one thing. Charley Pride making it in Nashville more than twenty years ago is something else altogether.

To heck with Spike Lee. Somebody ought to give Charley Pride the Color-Barrier-Breaker of All Time Award.

I'm also pretty certain Michael Dukakis, Jerry Brown, all other liberal Democrats, and Gloria Steinem don't like Hank Williams. I'd guess Bill Clinton probably does, but his wife doesn't. Tough to keep a mixed marriage going smoothly all the time.

I've accomplished a few things during my lifetime of which I have been quite proud. I've had a hole-in-one on the golf course. I managed to get my VCR to tape a television program (I only accomplished that once, but I felt it was still quite an endeavor for someone so mechanically impaired as I am). And once I appeared on the television show *Designing Women.*

They never invited me back, but I still think just being on the program once was a great accomplishment, since my only previous acting experience was my role as a nonspeaking tree in a third-grade play.

But something happened in the early spring of 1992 I marked down as truly a remarkable feat on my part.

Radio Station WSM in Nashville is *the* country-music station. It has broadcast the Grand Ole Opry and sent it out on its nightly clear channel to a great portion of the country-music audience since about the same time Miss Minnie Pearl bought that hat and forgot to take the price tag off.

It was the very first voice of country music. Now, there are about six jillion country stations with fancy FM names like Big Country 94 and Kicks 105, but WSM was shooting out country music to the masses long before you had to plug the instruments into anything.

I always enjoyed the commercials on the WSM's Grand Ole Opry, which I could pick up on my Sears radio in Moreland on Friday nights.

There was the Goo-Goo candy bar and its song, "Gotta get a Goo-Goo, right now!" I still enjoy an occasional Goo-Goo, and figured out "Goo-Goo" yet? It's "Grand Ole Opry."

There was also something called Cardui Tablets, which I think was a pioneer pill for PMS, although I'm not certain. They could have been for yeast infections, too, although nobody talked about such a thing back then. Now, they're on television with it.

And Black Draught, which I'm almost positive was a laxative, although the phrase "Constipation can be a problem" didn't come along until TV carried it years later, either.

I seem to recall the announcer discussing very little details regarding what Black Draught was for, but there were two pronunciations that were accepted. "Black Draught, some say Black 'Draft,' " the announcer would begin.

At any rate, WSM was the station of country music's birthing, and I still cherish my memories of it.

I mentioned earlier I've been writing a country tune or two with Dick Feller in Nashville. We wrote a song called "Grandma Willie's Yard." The idea came from a column I'd written recalling the many days I'd played everything in my grandmother's yard—from Cowboys and Indians to kick the can, dig up the worms, and *I Led Three Lives* with Richard Carlson.

So we put the song on a comedy album we recorded live in Shreveport, Louisiana. I sing it. Dick Feller plays guitar, and Timmy Tappan, the other third of the Lewis Grizzard Trio, plays piano, and they do some humming and harmonizing in the background, which helps me cover the rough notes.

I claim not to be Garth Brooks. Nor Lonzo nor Oscar, either. But I can carry a tune a few feet. The song has a lot of talking in it, too, and I always could talk.

"Grandma Willie's Yard" by Dick Feller and me:

We put Grandma to rest
By that little Baptist Church
Where she sang for the Lord
All her days.

I wiped the tears from my face
And drove back to Grandma's place
For one last walk
Through grandma's yard
And the thought came to me,
As I parked my car . . .

(CHORUS)

I have seen the world
In Grandma Willie's yard
The Spanish Main
The desert plain
And the changing of the guard.
I've chased a thousand outlaws there
And whipped 'em long and hard
When as a child I saw the world
In Grandma Willie's yard.

(RECITE)

Summer days have magic ways
With the dreams in a young boy's head
Why I've seen pirates by that low stone wall
And Martians in the flower bed
There was Robin Hood by the tire swing
And kings and queens by the fence
When evergreen trees hid foreign thieves
And magnolias were circus tents.
Oh, life's never been as simple since.

(Repeat first part of chorus, then more recitation)

And if there is a heaven,
And I must believe there is,
And if we all should go there,
I believe we go as kids.
And our grandmas wait
By the pearly gate
For us with outstretched arms,
'Cause heaven's just another place
Like Grandma Willie's yard.

Then, there's a big finish with the chorus again, and I've done the song live thirty times, and nobody has thrown anything at me yet. One lady at the Majestic Theatre in Dallas told me it made her cry, which is what a good country ballad is supposed to do.

So I was in Nashville in early spring 1992 to perform at the Annual Disc Jockey Convention and Seminar. As a part of it all, I was on WSM one morning, and they played the tape of me singing "Grandma Willie's Yard," and the disc jockey said he liked it.

Imagine that. Me singing on WSM. I had been where Tubb and Snow and Williams and Acuff had trod. I never expected to do anything like that. And, to be quite honest, I'm not certain if WSM will ever play my singing again since I'm a forty-six-year-old country-music rookie, but I was there once, by God. It made my decade.

I saw a picture of Wynonna Judd on the cover of *Calendar,* the Sunday entertainment section of the *Los Angeles Times.* Country has its own network show now, *Hot Country Nights.* Its own cable channel. There's a country station in New York City, and country's even big in Europe and Asia, as well as parts of New Jersey, speaking of foreign locales.

I'm proud of it. Another of my favorite lines from country is, "I was country when country wasn't cool."

Me, too.

Now, *we are* No. 1.

So, now I've managed to say everything I have to say about beer-swilling and country music. Let's take college-football-watching from the strict Southern male viewpoint.

A former colleague of mine, Ed Hinton, was a

sportswriter for the *Atlanta Journal* when Georgia and Herschel Walker won the national championship by beating Notre Dame in the Sugar Bowl at the end of the 1980 season. He had flown to New Orleans on New Year's Eve from Atlanta, on a flight loaded with Georgia revelers. Hinton did a piece later on their obnoxiousness. Seems they gave a Notre Dame kid a lot of grief. Somebody probably barked at him, but I don't remember exactly.

Hinton's piece ran the day after Georgia had won its first national title, and the state was in a frenzy of celebration. As the result of his negativeness, he became, for a time, the least popular man in the largest state east of the Mississippi.

One Georgia fan said to him, "I remember growing up in my little Georgia hometown. About once every two or three years, we would get a little snow. All we kids would run out and play in it. But there was always one bigger kid who thought it was funny to piss on our snow. That's what you've done, pissed on our newly fallen white snow."

Hinton later told me what his mind-set had been when he wrote the piece.

"I'm from Mississippi," he said, "and we've been the target of more abuse than any other state in the country. I guess I was just jealous. Here was Georgia, which I never thought was any better than Mississippi, going to the Sugar Bowl with a chance to be Number One, and I just got mad."

But Hinton and I continued the conversation, and he was most insightful, I thought, on just why Southern men can take a life-or-death stance on a college football game.

"You think about it," he said, "except for Vietnam, which was like getting tied by Wake Forest, the Southern white male is the only American male ever to lose a war. That shame has been passed down from generation to generation. That, and the idea that the North looks down on us and thinks we're all Jed Clampetts.

"I think the white Southern male of today is just as combative, just as proud of his heritage, as they were in Civil War times. But there's no war. But what there is, is college football. It's something to attach oneself to. It's a cause, it has to do with pride, and it gets all tangled up into politics, lifestyles, and bitter rivalry."

I've often thought about Hinton's deduction. I think he's on target.

I was in the Louisiana Superdome for the Georgia–Notre Dame game on New Year's Day, 1981. I was so nervous before the game, I couldn't spit. During the game, which was very close, my language became so abusive, my wife left and went back to the hotel room.

"I just don't see why you're this emotional about a football game," she said.

Later, I thought about that question again, and then I answered it.

I'm pretty emotional about all Georgia football games, since it's my alma mater; the head coach, Ray Goff, is a friend of mine; and God never made a lovelier place than Sanford Stadium in Athens, Georgia, on an October afternoon, and I've been to the Greek Isles, which was nice, but nothing like Athens, Ga.

But Georgia–Notre Dame was something else. I could get into something like that because it brought out all the Southernness that is in me. This was Notre Dame we were playing, the Notre Dame of all those movies, and the Notre Dame that is the home office of college football. The Notre Dame that always seems to get its way because it's Notre Dame.

Notre Dame. Yankee Dame. They-Think-That-They're-Better-Than-Us Dame. This wasn't a football game in my mind. It was to prove our way of life was better than theirs. This was Gettysburg again. This was for the way they mock the way we talk, the way they think we're all ignorant redneck scum. This was to prove Jesus is on our side, too.

Georgia won the game 17–10. I don't want my beloved Dawgs ever to play the Irish again. That way, we'll always be 1–0 against them.

Bear Bryant at Alabama was never able to beat Notre Dame, but what he accomplished at Tuscaloosa probably churned up more pride in a Southern state than had ever been done previously.

Alabama, like Mississippi, has always been suspect in the rest of the country. There was all that George Wallace stand-in-the-schoolhouse-door thing, and Bull Connor and the dogs and hoses in Birmingham. And Alabama was usually right at the bottom when poverty levels and education levels for the country were listed.

But the Bear gave Alabama something it could strut about. He won national championships at Alabama college football for a long time.

And Bryant accomplished what might at one time have been the unthinkable at the University of Alabama. He integrated his football team, and not a hose was turned on.

I'm not saying Bryant was out there on the cutting edge of the civil-rights movement, but he *was* the first Southern coach to realize he needed black players to compete nationally.

I covered the game that convinced him in the early '70's. Alabama met Southern Cal in Birmingham. Southern Cal had a black back named Sam Cunningham who ran over Alabama's all-white defense that day, and the Bear wasted little time after that in recruiting black athletes.

Soon, the rest of the South followed, in order to keep up with the Bear, and now most Southeastern Conference teams are dominated by black players.

What really makes me laugh is all this recent garbage about the "exploitation of the black athlete" and the "plantation mentality" of major football programs. The criticism is normally aimed mostly at Southern programs.

After years and years of segregation, black athletes were given the same opportunity as white athletes to compete. But then came all the nonsense that some schools simply were using black kids to further their athletic programs and make the head coach and athletic director rich with no concern for how the athletes were doing in the classroom.

We found a new statistic, "graduation rate," and newspapers went to great lengths to obtain that statistic as a means of pointing out the "hypocrisy" in college football.

Here is how a black athlete is exploited at most schools today.

He (or she) gets a paid-in-full college education. He, or she, lives in an athletic dorm, gets steak for dinner, the latest in equipment, the latest in training methods.

He, or she, gets to travel all over the United States on airplanes and some even get to go to Tokyo to show the Japs what football is all about. What the athlete must do in return for all that is practice his or her butt off and keep his or her butt academically eligible to play under rules that are getting stricter each year.

What that basically means is athletes, black and white, have to go to class. If there's something they're having trouble with, tutors are called in to help free of charge.

How is that "exploiting"? So this athlete or that athlete got out of Jock Strap A&M and reads on a third-grade level? All he had to say was, "Hey, I'd like to read a little better. What time will the tutor be in my room?"

The dean of the journalism school at Georgia didn't make sure I was in class every day, didn't lead me by the hand to the library to study, didn't provide me with tutors.

I worked twelve hours a day, six days a week and was married in college. I didn't sleep for four years. Big deal, a lot of people had it tough in college, but a lot of people also hung in there and got their degrees. If they didn't, it was nobody's fault but their own.

In a perfect world, every student on every campus would have made a perfect score on his or her SAT. But it isn't a perfect world, and that means not every student who enters college is going to graduate.

A woman professor, Dr. Jan Kemp, raised a stink at Georgia over what she saw as preferential treatment of athletes. She was fired and then sued the school and won a cash settlement. The roof caved in over low SAT scores for athletes and a low graduate rate. That came out of testimony.

The attorney for Georgia at the opening of the trial said something he was greatly criticized for. His statement, some said, doomed Georgia's case from the start.

I'll paraphrase his statement:

He said, not every athlete who comes to Georgia graduates, but it is the school's hope those who don't can get enough exposure to the academic atmosphere of a university, can at least see the importance of some education, that they can go back to their homes after one or two years and at least become civil servants, such as postmen.

The sparrows chirped, "What does this mean? That the University of Georgia is some sort of trade school? That the failure to graduate is acceptable somehow?"

I interpreted the statement a little differently.

The kid is poor and black. His father isn't in his household. His mother is working and trying to raise six children on a meager salary.

But the kid can play ball.

So he signs a scholarship. For whatever reason, a couple of years later, he is dismissed from school for academic reasons. He goes back home with two years of college.

He has been in an academic atmosphere. He has met people with different viewpoints. He has traveled. He would have learned *something*, wouldn't he? Wouldn't he, in most cases, be better off for the experience, even if it lasted only two years?

So he goes home and becomes a postman. What if he'd not been allowed to enter school for any length of time? He might have become a cocaine dealer, or a mill worker, instead. The experience has improved his life.

I have at least two brilliant suggestions of how to handle college athletics from now on:

Brilliant Suggestion No. 1: Pay the players. Playing college sports is a job. Give them some money for doing it. Some athletes arrive at school with two T-shirts and a pair of jeans to their name. Alumni can't give them clothes or money. Alumni can't give them anything.

So they're walking around campus seeing other students in Corvettes. The reason they can't enjoy

the full campus experience like other students is
they can't afford it. Make it worthwhile financially
for them to stay in school.

Brilliant Suggestion No. 2: Offer a major in football. (And other sports, too, but let's keep it simple.)
The student learns to play football and perhaps can
become a professional player.

Or the student learns how to coach football, or
how to make a football, or sell a football. Nothing
wrong with any of those jobs. What's the difference
between a football major learning to work in a
sporting-goods store and a music major who learns
to play guitar and then goes out and sings in Holiday Inn lounges for money? What's the difference
between that student coaching football after college
and a journalism major covering ball games for a
living?

None.

What I basically think is happening with college
sports today is that administration and faculties,
who have had a bad case of the reds for years because coaches have their own TV shows, and they
don't, want to get even. They simply can't deal with
Bear Bryant's line: "Eighty thousand people never
showed up to see a chemistry test."

What I can't figure out is what fault anybody could
find with eighty thousand people having a great time
on an autumn Saturday? These are the alumni who
use athletics as a means to stay connected with their
schools.

Georgia Tech won a co-national championship in
1990 after years of having a drug problem, according
to a friend of mine, Bugar Seeley, of Albany, Georgia, a fellow Bulldog.

"They were drug up and down the field every time
they went out to play," said Bugar.

But Tech loosened its academics and suddenly was able to get the burner wide receiver with the 700 SAT.

Alumni contributions went up dramatically after the National Championship. So did the number of students trying to enroll.

That's bad? No, that's good. When will the reformers realize that big-time sports isn't hurting anybody? It's helping a lot of us to enjoy life, and it's helping the schools as well.

I have formed lifetime friendships over Georgia football. Both male and female friendships, by the way. I know many women who bleed red and black. God bless them. And they also fry chicken and make deviled eggs for tailgate picnics. They dress in red, wear bulldog earrings, and "Woof!" with the rest of us.

Unfortunately, they're all married.

All this criticism about college sports and the constant calls for reforms, I believe, is rooted—and I firmly believe this—in the fact that all those former nerds, geeks, and lizards in high school and college are trying to get even. Yes, the Revenge of the Nerds.

Remember them? They didn't play sports, they didn't drive fast cars, they didn't date, they wore funny-looking clothes, and they tended to join things like the Science or French clubs. The girls had premature facial hair, didn't wear makeup to hide their zits, were either fat or terribly skinny, and always knew the answers in ancient-history class. Some of them played trumpet in the band, and some of the fat ones played tuba. Some of the fat ones *looked* like tubas.

After school, you didn't see any of them anymore, and you probably didn't think about them anymore.

Well, you know what happened to them? They

went right on being geeks, but they were also very smart, as you recall now, and they've wound up in certain positions of power, like presidents of colleges, editors of newspapers and magazines, officials of the National Organization of Women. Some of the ones you thought were a little light in the loafers in school, in fact, were, and now they're chairpersons of some Gay Alliance of Something or Other.

You might have given some of those people some grief back in school. Or, worse, you probably ignored them—and now they're back! And they have some power! And they remember you! And they remember how much they hated you, hated sports, hated cheerleaders, hated the Homecoming Queen, hated fraternities and sororities. Yes, revenge is what they want. They want to shut down most of the things you really like, and they come up with terms for you, just like you had terms for them.

You are a Neanderthal, a bimbo, a redneck, a good ol' boy, a blonde, or a jock who never grew up. I see them in many facets of American life. They're Phil Donahue, rock singers, and lawyers for the ACLU. They're liberal op-ed newspaper columnists, politicians, research scientists who come up with all the things that aren't good for you anymore, like smoking, drinking, eating, having sex, breathing, walking, driving, and going to college football games.

There are not as many of them as there are of us, but since they have so few outside interests, like going to sporting events and barking at other fans, they have a lot of time to plot that revenge.

They are trying their best to ruin everything for the rest of us like college sports and fried-chicken eating. Fortunately, as I mentioned earlier, there are more of us than there are of them, which is why the Democrats can't get a weenie like Michael Dukakis elected president.

And I finally believe we will never surrender and will win out in the end. The infidels will finally try to go too far, and the masses will revolt. Let Georgia go with a string of lousy seasons in a row, and the reformers' heads will roll.

There is nothing wrong with college football now, and it doesn't need repairing. It needs nurturing, it needs protection from the nonbelievers.

Does this sound like a holy war? It is to me. It is to a lot of straight Southern white guys. A man I knew surveyed Sanford Stadium in Athens one evening before a Georgia–Clemson nationally televised game.

The stadium was filled to capacity. People were happy. Georgia football, and college football in general, has so much more over pro football. There's the tradition, the pageantry, and nobody goes on strike. It was an enchanted night.

He said, "When I was in Vietnam, I really used to wonder what I was fighting for. I believe it was for this."

Hand me a piece of fried chicken, another deviled egg, and a cold beer. Kickoff is nigh, Bubba.

What remains in this discussion of stereotypes of Bubbas, is to take a look at those who could be called truck-drivin', tobacco-chewin' and/or big-bellied.

I have a truck. Well, a sort-of-truck. It's a 1984 Chevrolet Blazer, a red one. Why I bought it has to do with my dog, Catfish, the black Lab. When I got Catfish, I also owned a black Mercedes two-seater convertible. I was very proud of that Mercedes, because I was the first member of my family to own one.

My Uncle Johnny, a doctor, became the first mem-

ber of our family to own a foreign car. He bought a
VW bug during the '60's. I was rather upset with him
for doing that, because I had always held it wasn't
right for Americans to buy cars from countries with
whom we've been to war.

But upon returning to Atlanta after three years in
Chicago in 1977, I had no car whatsoever. I didn't
need a car in Chicago. Actually, I could have had a
car, but there wouldn't have been a place to park it,
and I don't think I could have gotten a VW bug or
any other car through the front door of my second-
floor near-north apartment in order to have some
place to put it at night.

So I just took cabs, all of which were being driven
by people who didn't speak English and who often
had trouble locating the Loop, where I worked.

But upon returning to Atlanta, I rented an apartment with a large parking lot, so I could have a car
again.

Unfortunately, I couldn't afford a new car at the
time, so I borrowed one from my stepfather, H.B., a
brown 1974 Pontiac.

One day, I drove it to a friend of mine's house. My
friend had a tennis court in his yard, and I was a
tennis player at the time. I later had to quit playing
tennis because my right arm fell off, but that's another story.

My friend's wife, a native Californian, happened
to own a red two-seater Mercedes convertible.

"You shouldn't own a car produced by a country
with whom we've been to war," I told her.

"You good ol' boy rednecks never know when a
war is over," she replied.

After tennis, my stepfather's car wouldn't crank.
But my friend had some jumper cables.

"You put the jumper cables on the battery," I said to him, "and I'll crank the car."

The reason I didn't want to attach the jumper cables to the battery is, I never can remember what cable goes where, and I'm convinced if you put jumper cables on a battery wrong, the battery will explode in your face.

We got the Pontiac cranked. But when I tried to close the hood, it wouldn't close anymore. As a matter of fact, it wouldn't stay down at all. It kept going to an erect position, blocking my view out of the front window.

What we had to do was wire the hood down with a couple of straightened-out clothes hangers. To be quite honest about it, the entire situation was rather embarrassing, and it got even worse when my friend's wife said, in typical California fashion, "All this makes you wonder who *really* won the war, doesn't it?"

It was at that point I decided owning a German-made car wasn't all that bad a thing to do.

It took a good six years to become financially well off enough to buy the black Mercedes two-seater convertible.

When I drove it home to Moreland to show it to my family, my stepfather said, "What is it, a Rolls-Royce?"

I said, "Heavens, no. I'm not on television, I just work for a newspaper. It's a Mercedes."

"That's German, isn't it?" my stepfather, a veteran of World War II, asked.

I said, "Hey, the war's been over for forty years."

He just grunted.

Anyway, I was proud of my Mercedes, and it was the only vehicle I needed until I got my dog, Catfish, a gift from the head football coach, Vince Dooley, of the University of Georgia.

The Dooleys were giving a dinner party in their backyard. A number of chairs and tables had been set up, and guests were having cocktails before the meal was to be served.

Barbara Dooley said she heard a lot of chairs falling and looked over at the dinner area. To her amazement, not to mention embarrassment, their two dogs, Herschel and Miss Georgia, were quite involved in, well, a form of what might be called puppy love.

From this union came nine little Herschels and Miss Georgias. The Dooleys gave me one of them, and I named him Catfish. I'm still not certain why, but I sort of liked it as a dog's name. It certainly was better than Blackie, or Bingo, or even "Lil" Herschel.

But I owned dogs before, and I knew of what sort of things they could get on their feet. Mud is one of the better things. You don't want to put a dog with mud on its paws in a new black two-seater Mercedes convertible.

So I decided to buy the Chevy Blazer to carry Catfish around on the occasions I needed, or wanted, him to join me on a drive.

My Chevy Blazer is, indeed, a truck, and I do, indeed, drive it. But it's not a real truck, not in its purest form. For one, I don't have a bumper sticker on the back that says, I'LL GIVE UP MY GUN WHEN THEY PRY MY COLD, DEAD FINGERS OFF THE TRIGGER. I was driving on the interstate in Atlanta and got behind a truck that had that exact bumper sticker. I pulled off at the next exit and waited fifteen minutes before I got back on the interstate. I figure a guy with a bumper sticker on his truck like that *wants* to shoot somebody.

My truck doesn't have an open back to it, either, which makes it impossible for me to say those immortal words, "Get in the back of the truck and shut the hell up." I've got to say, "Get in the backseat and shut the hell up," which doesn't carry the same connotation of being completely fed up as does the former.

If one is banished simply to the backseat, then one is not really isolated. One is still under the same roof of the vehicle and one can continue bitching and nagging about something, and the driver can still hear.

But if one is banished to the back of the truck, it means one is completely isolated from the one who banished one there. One can beat on the back window, but one will eventually tire of being ignored and one will sit in the back of the truck and shut the hell up.

White Southern males who actually own trucks are liable to banish any number of individuals to the back of the truck, but here are the ones most likely to be treated in this manner:

His Wife: "I'm sick and tired of riding up here with this stinking dog sitting between us." *Reply:* "Then get in the back of the truck and shut the hell up."

His Brother-In-Law: "Damnit, Harvey, I really need ten dollars. I'm taking Doreen to the rasslin' matches." *Reply:* "I ain't loanin' you no more money, Grover. Now, just get in the back of the truck and shut the hell up."

His Business Associate: "Why don't I ever get to push the wheelbarrow?" *Reply:* " 'Cause you don't know a got-damn thing about machinery. Get in the back of the truck and shut the hell up."

His Cousin, Earl: "Hey, Harvey, I defended you the other day. Fellow said you ate horse manure and ran

rabbits. I said, 'Hell, Harvey can't run that fast.'"
Reply: "Earl, you're about as funny as a train wreck.
Get in the back of the truck and shut the hell up."
His Fiancée: "But you promised we'd get married
sometime this summer. I'm tired of Mama always
saying all you want from me is one thing." *Reply:*
"Well, you tell your Mama it ain't none of her business, and you can just get in the back of the truck
and shut the hell up."

"You can't talk that way about my mother."

Second reply: "You want to walk to the motel?"

Not only is there "Get in the back of the truck and
shut the hell up," there is also "You wait in the
truck."

Telling someone to wait in the truck means one of
several things. It means this person often can be an
embarrassment, and it would be better for all concerned if this person just sat in the truck until the
business at hand was completed.

Basically, however, "you wait in the truck" is an
excellent way of putting down somebody and keeping him in his place. I was at a country-music concert years ago. Roy Clark was onstage. Roy Clark
sings a song called, "I Never Picked Cotton."

Throughout his performance, a man in the audience kept screaming, "Hey, Roy! You ever picked
cotton?"

After a half hour of this, Roy finally replied to the
man, "Didn't I tell you to wait in the truck?"

The man never made another sound. I covered
the 1980 Democratic National Convention in New
York City. It was like covering a zoo, but that's
even a longer story than the one about my arm
falling off.

I can recall walking around in the press headquarters and coming up on the CBS area. The back

door leading to it was closed. There was a sign on the door that said, ESSENTIAL PERSONNEL ONLY.

That sign intrigued me. If you work for CBS and were about to enter that door, how long would it take you to figure out whether or not you were essential? And if you decided you weren't, then what were you doing there in the first place?

It can be the same with "Wait in the truck."

I think Jimmy Carter would have been a lot better off as president if, when he moved to Washington, he'd told brother Billy to wait in the truck. That's only symbolic, but you should get the idea. If Billy had waited in the truck while Jimmy went to be president, Billy couldn't have kept getting his big brother into all that trouble for doing and saying stupid things.

Telling someone to wait in the truck, on the other hand, might become necessary when you realize that if a certain person accompanies you, you could look bad in comparison. Bill Clinton, a white Southerner like President Carter, should have told his wife, Hillary, to wait in the truck while he ran for president when it was becoming more and more obvious she was the one who should have been running.

It also means, "I can manage this on my own, thank you very much."

It's what MacArthur was saying to Truman when he went ahead and crossed the 38th parallel into North Korea. It was what Ronald Reagan meant in his famous line about the microphone during a New Hampshire primary debate. It's what Custer said to his sergeant when the sergeant looked across the field at Little Bighorn and said, "Uh, General, I think we made a wrong turn. Look at all them Indians."

Know also there are two kinds of Southern white

males who drive trucks. One kind drives a truck because his occupation calls for one. These include well-diggers, housepainters, Sheetrockers, carpenters, plumbers, farmers, goat-ropers, bug-killers, snake-handlers and/or ministers of churches where they take up the serpent to show their faith, professional hog-callers, septic-tank-cleaners, and driveway-pavers, both honest and the other kind, who will charge you $150 to pave your driveway then, three weeks later, it will crack and split, and you didn't get a good description of their truck.

Basically, if your job calls for you to haul a lot of stuff around, you need a pickup truck.

The next category of straight Southern white men who drive trucks are those who do it strictly for recreation. A fisherman needs a truck. What if the worms, lizards, or crickets got loose in the backseat of your Eldorado?

A man who hunts a lot needs a truck in case he kills something big, like a moose. A dead moose, for instance, will not fit in any sort of Japanese car. That's because the Japanese don't hunt moose. If they did, though, they would probably eat the sucker raw. You know darn well if you took a Jap fishing with you, he might get hungry on the way home and ask to get into the back of the truck so he could have some of those delicious raw catfish.

Then there are men who are just *into* trucks. (It's okay to mix in a little hippie-dippie California-chic talk isn't it? People in the '70s were *into* drugs, jazz, and art deco. Sometimes dogs are *into* sucking eggs and chasing cars. So can straight Southern white guys be *into* trucks? On second thought, maybe it's just better to say, "It's a trucking thing. You wouldn't understand.")

What I'm basically talking about here are those

guys who ride around in trucks three or four stories high. You need an elevator to get in and out of these trucks.

C-5A's don't have tires as big as the ones for this sort of truck. I've been seeing them for years, especially in areas where they don't play a lot of golf and would rather see Wild Bill Elliott outrun Davey Allison at the Darlington Motor Speedway than see Nicklaus win another Masters.

I'm just guessing here, but I think the way you wind up in a truck that could mash an elephant flat if one happened to be crossing the road is, first, you go out and buy a regular pickup truck. Then you go to the air force and ask if you can buy a few tires off whatever the largest aircraft they happen to have handy. Then you have your tires loaded on flatbed cars and have them delivered to a place where they put giant tires on pickup trucks. After your tires are on, you now have a pickup truck where the cab sits higher than one on a 727. What you do next is put some giant headlights on top of the cab of the truck and then give your truck a name. Normally, men don't name this sort of truck after women, like, "Have you met my truck, 'Nadine'?" They name them more macho-sounding names. Like Big Red. Or the Green Monster. Or Bus Eater. Or Elephant-Flattener.

I expect some of the men with these trucks just sort of drive around in them, wearing baseball caps that say, I'M THE MAN YOUR MAMA WARNED YOU ABOUT. They drive around and intimidate motorists in smaller vehicles, like semis, hauling hogs.

Others go pro and engage in driving over the tops of other cars, trucks, buses, and Roto-Rooter vans. Surely, you've seen this on television. Two giant trucks line up together, and then they take off and drive over the tops of a long line of such vehicles as were previously mentioned. They smash such vehicles, and the truck to finish smashing first is the winner.

That is what is known as *organized* Monster Trucking.

Unorganized Monster Trucking is where a couple of guys begin arguing who has the best Monster Truck. Then, to settle the issue, they go out and attach a chain to a couple of fast-food restaurants. The one who can pull his restaurant across town first is the winner.

I think trucks are to some Southern men what a good horse was to a cowboy. The truck, as was the horse, is an extension of its driver. The drivers, in this instance, enjoyed stomping ants and spiders when they were little boys, and all they've done is graduated to flattening out other means of mechanized transportation. Many of these men have fathers who drove tanks in World War II.

Anyway, I don't think you can throw me into the stereotype of good ol' boy truck-drivin'. Not with a Chevy Blazer. Too many suburban housewives drive would-be trucks like that and take their children to school, to ballet lessons, and to the country club for swim team. These women usually are also in the Junior League, and nobody has ever said, "Wait in the truck while I go to my Junior League meeting," or, "I have to go to a Junior League meeting tonight, Devroe. Are you using Bus Eater?"

My dog Catfish did ride in the Mercedes two-seater convertible a couple of times, incidentally. He did track some mud onto the seat, but on the other hand he never complained because I had a country-music station playing on the radio and he wanted to listen to a rock station, like a lot of women who rode in it did. I never had to say to him, "You want to walk to the motel?"

That leaves big-bellied and tobacco-chewin', of which I am neither. I am quite skinny, as a matter of fact, and I don't chew tobacco. I did *try* chewing tobacco once. It was right after the airlines said you couldn't smoke anymore. It was a long flight to the West Coast, and I figured I'd just put in a little pinch between my teeth and gums and enjoy that satisfying pleasure for four-and-a-half hours. Then I discovered there was no place to spit. I asked for a paper cup and put a napkin in it like I'd seen my grandfather do when he was dipping snuff and watching television.

When I dropped my first big dollop into my cup, the lady next to me began screaming.

"Tobacco!" she cried.

A flight attendant kneed me in the belly, and I swallowed the chewing tobacco. When I arrived on the West Coast, they had an ambulance waiting for me. At the emergency room, they pumped my stomach. Later I was questioned by the Federal Aviation Authority, BAN (Big-Know-It-Alls Against Nicotine), the Los Angeles Lifestyle Police, the Surgeon General's Office, the American Lung Association, the American Cancer Association, several pro-life groups, and a Harvard student doing a thesis on chewing tobacco and its relation to cowboy hats.

I don't have anything against anybody else chewing tobacco, but it's just not my cup of spit.

As for big-bellied, I do know a number of big-bellied straight Southern white guys.

I was with one, as a matter of fact, in a singles bar in Atlanta several years ago. He spotted a young woman with whom he wanted to become acquainted and walked to her table to buy her a drink.

She declined.

"What did she say?" I asked my friend when he returned to the bar.

"She said she didn't drink with anybody who had the Dick Do syndrome."

I asked what on earth was that?

My friend answered, "She told me my belly stuck out a lot further than my dick do."

Having a big belly doesn't necessarily make you a bad person, even if you are a Southern deputy sheriff.

There was one in my county named Sonny Bubba (Junebug) Johnson. He pulled over a couple of Yankee tourists from Ohio one day who were driving to Panama City, Florida.

He saw the Ohio license plates, noticed they were doing exactly fifty-five, and figured, "They got to be up to something."

Sonny Bubba (that was his real name, his Mama called him "Junebug") got out of his car, pulled his pants up over his own ample girth, and sauntered toward the car.

He asked the man driving for his "driiben lycunces." The man had no clue what he was talking about. In Ohio, they are called "driver's licenses."

When the man didn't respond quickly enough for Sonny Bubba, he said, "Whar' y'all from, anyway?"

The Ohioan said, "Columbus."

Sonny Bubba said, "Don't lie to me. I seen them Ohio license plates."

There have been a lot of great Americans—from all over the country—with big bellies. Presidents Theodore Roosevelt and William Howard Taft had big bellies. Tommy Lasorda, manager of the Dodgers, had a big belly until he started sucking down Slim Fast milk shakes. Babe Ruth had one of the big bellies of all time. General Schwarzkopf has some rotundity about him, as well.

Atlanta mayor Maynard Jackson, whose city won the 1996 Olympic Games site, is a person of size. I'm not saying he's fat, or anything like that, but I will say when he steps on a cigarette, that sucker is out.

It once was reported that it cost the city of Atlanta nearly a half-million dollars to protect Mayor Jackson. A lot of people thought that was excessive.

I noted, "Not if you compute it by the pound."

Fatty Arbuckle had a big belly. So did W.C. Fields. God may have a big belly, for all we know. Perhaps that is why He has let Oprah be all that successful carrying around more weight than a Greek fighter.

I rest my case.

"L" Is for "Leap into a Garbage Disposal"

I SUPPOSE THE ONE THING I'VE SPENT THE MOST TIME TRYING to figure out since 1962 is, with the exception of my mother, grandmother, and aunts, why I can't get along with women for more than, say, eleven minutes straight. I bring up 1962 specifically because that's the year I got my driver's license, which afforded me the opportunity to spend even more time with women than I had previous to that.

Previous to that, I occasionally walked with women, or rode bicycles with them.

I don't think women—or girlpersons—really take a man—or boyperson—seriously until he has his driver's license and can drive them to places in a car.

Walking with a girl before a boy is thirteen normally is out of the question. That's because his friends are playing ball or damming creeks or in a tree house somewhere smoking rabbit tobacco, or regular tobacco, if they can get their hands on it, all of which is more fun than walking with a girl at that point in a boy's development.

Plus, what do you have to say to a girl when you're under thirteen? What do they have to say to you?

Neither one of you know to say such things while you're walking together as "There's something wrong with our relationship," or "I simply need some space," or "I've got this little problem I need to talk to you about."

The "little problem" men and women talk about when they go on walks later in life can be any number of things, but I'll just mention the worst of them:

—AIDS
—Herpes
—Bankruptcy
—Pregnancy
—Being fired by her father
—Affairs
—Bad things that happen due to affairs: Herpes and AIDS are just two of them. There are other sorts of diseases and conditions that can occur due to an affair, as well, including one you need to buy some blue ointment for, but that's as far as I'm going.
—The press found out about (fill in the name), and I'm afraid we won't be living in the White House this time next year after all.
—A mishap with his Mercedes or her Jaguar.
—Pregnancy (It's worth mentioning again.)
—Palimony suits
—*Two* palimony suits
—I have never at any time been in a Miss Black America contest, so don't ask me another time if there's anything between me and Mike Tyson.
—We're moving into a mobile home.

Riding a bicycle with a girl is sort of the same kind of thing. You don't pedal alongside a girl on a bicycle and say, "I knew you slept with someone when you went to Milwaukee, but did it have to be Jeffrey Dahmer?"

In fact, until a boy is sixteen and able to get his driver's license, it's almost impossible to have any sort of real involvement with a girl. That's because girls fourteen or fifteen are all out at the drive-in or cruising the Dairy Queen with boys who are sixteen and over and have their driver's licenses. If you aren't old enough to drive yet, you spend a lot of time developing your curveball and counting the days until you're sixteen so you can go to the drive-in and cruise the Dairy Queen with girls fourteen or fifteen who will think you are sooo *mature*, especially when you pull out on the highway after leaving the drive-in and peel rubber. A lot of people might think peeling rubber is just the opposite of mature, and is in fact quite childish. Not to a fourteen- or fifteen- or sixteen-year-old girl out with a boy who already has his driver's license and is teaching her how to French kiss and is telling her her breasts need an occasional fondling in order to grow properly.

When I was growing up, "peeling rubber" was referred to as "getting a wheel." For a boy-man driver of an automobile, it was another sign of weakness if he didn't "get a wheel" at every opportunity to do so.

Leaving school was a very important time to get a wheel. Only pissants, science-club members, and other social misfits didn't get a wheel when they left school. Most of them also usually were picked up by their mothers and driven home for their piano lessons.

Not so the cool, mature guys. When school was out

at Newnan High (class of '64 here), it sounded like the Indy 500 time trials in the student parking lot. I'm convinced the cool, mature types single-handedly kept the Goodyear Tire Company in business between the years of 1960 and 1964, when I was in high school.

Getting a wheel involved putting your car in low gear, holding down the clutch, and revving on the engine for a good two or three minutes to build up momentum. Then you released the clutch and were doing sixty-five in a heartbeat. But that was only on your speedometer. Your tires were doing sixty-five, in one place. The result was that about half the tread on the tires your father bought you if you promised never to get a wheel was flying through the air. The resulting "errrrrrrrrk" sound they made on the concrete turned every head.

Once a car did lurch into forward motion, if you could get a wheel when you changed gears a second and third time, it meant you likely would end up on the cover of *Time* magazine as Man of the Year.

I received my driver's license at the LaGrange, Georgia, State Patrol headquarters on Saturday, October 20, 1962, my sixteenth birthday. The Newnan Georgia State Patrol office was a lot closer to Moreland, six miles, but that post didn't issue driver's licenses on the weekends.

Wait until Monday to get my driver's license when I'd been counting the days until this moment since they took the training wheels off my bike? No damn way.

My relationship with females began to go downhill the very first night I had my driver's license. I had a date with the woman who would later become my first wife, the lovely Paula. Naturally, our date

was to go to the drive-in and do some major fogging
up of the windows.

Our relationship, which ended in divorce in 1970,
began to deteriorate when I decided that before we
went to the drive-in, I'd cruise by the Dairy Queen,
now that I finally had come of age to do such a wondrous thing.

The cruising part went well. Friends saw me behind the wheel of a car, which gave me status and
acceptability. But when I started to pull out onto the
highway for the drive-in, the trouble began.

A couple of my friends, who were sitting atop the
hoods of their cars at the Dairy Queen because every
mother in the country wouldn't allow their daughters to date them on account of their reputations as
reckless drivers, screamed at me, "Hey, Lewis, get a
wheel!"

As much as I had wanted to get my driver's license, I didn't do a lot of studying or thinking about
automobiles beforehand. I didn't know one thing
about carburetors, glass packs, Earl Scheib, painting flames on the side of your car, hanging foam-
rubber dice over your rearview mirror, or putting
your name on the driver's door and your girlfriend's
name on the passenger door, which a lot of guys did,
as in "Ducky" and "Sylvia."

And there was another problem. The automobile
that I was driving had no clutch. It had an automatic
transmission. It was a 1958 blue-and-white Pontiac.
I actually preferred an automatic transmission, pissant as that might be, because a straight stick involved three foot pedals, instead of two, and a lot
more mechanical knowledge and ability than I had
at the time. (I'm still suffering from being mechanically impaired, as a matter of fact, manifested by
the fact I usually have to have an attendant come

out to show me how to operate the pump when I pull into a self-serve filling station.)

So there I was, my moment to shine. To join that great fraternity of wheel-getters. To follow in the steps of some of the great wheel-getters and reckless drivers like Dudley Stamps and Raiford Smith, famed tire-tread destroyers, both.

I stopped before pulling out onto the highway, but I felt deep panic. I'd never gotten a wheel before. I knew it had something to do with stomping on the accelerator as hard as you could from an idling position.

But was I supposed to put the gear in "L" first or would "D" suffice?

I knew "D" was for drive. But what was this "L" thing?

I decided, in my panic, "L" probably stood for "Leap." So, I pulled it down to "L," stomped the accelerator, and shot across the street into a large trash receptacle in front of West's Body Shop, which was located across the street from Dairy Queen.

My first thought was not, were my girlfriend and I dead, or had I totaled the family '58 Pontiac. It was, did I get a wheel?

I was fairly certain I hadn't. One, I hadn't heard an "errrrrrrk." I had heard only a "huuuuuuuume!" the sound a 1958 Pontiac makes when it is in low gear and somebody presses the accelerator all the way to the floor and it lurches out from a Dairy Queen and barely misses a collision with a produce truck loaded with turnip greens and sweet potatoes and crashes into a trash receptacle at West's Body Shop.

I then looked into the rearview mirror to see what the reaction had been to my first attempt to get a wheel. They were doubled up with laughter. Some

lay across car hoods on their stomachs and beat on
the hoods with their fists, howling and bellowing.

I didn't get out of the car to check any damage. I
had to leave that place as quickly as possible. So I
put my car in "R," backed into the street, nearly
colliding with the Greyhound bus from Carrollton,
turned it toward the drive-in and put the gear in
"L" again, and lead-footed the accelerator one more
time. The Pontiac's rear end went toward the pavement, and the front shot upward. But still no sound
or smell of burning rubber. To make matters
worse, when we finally got to the drive-in, the
movie was Robert Mitchum in *Thunder Road,*
where Robert Mitchum played a guy who drove
cars loaded with moonshine across mountain roads.
The movie lasted about an hour and a half. At
least three quarters of that were taken up by Robert Mitchum getting wheels throughout the entire
state of Tennessee.

I could tell Paula was terribly upset.

My first clue had been, as we "huuuuuuuumed"
toward the drive-in from the Dairy Queen, she said,
"This is the most embarrassing moment of my life."
I've always been perceptive that way.

At the drive-in, embarrassment turned into disgust, and disgust turned into anger, and anger
turned into, "I don't know if I'll ever be able to show
my face at Newnan High School again."

I tried to explain to Paula that I'd been real busy
playing ball and getting the Lifesaving merit badge
the years previous to getting my driver's license,
and I simply hadn't paid that much attention to cars.
"If you really loved me, you would have," she replied, which was the first time—but certainly not
the last—a woman would say something to me that
made absolutely no sense whatever, but if you asked

for further explanation, it simply would become even more confusing.

I replied, "What's not knowing about cars have anything to do with not loving you?"

"Why don't you just pick me up on your bicycle next time?" is how she replied to that.

"But what has any of this got to do with whether or not I love you?" I pressed on, inexperienced as I was.

"Just take me home," she explained.

I became frustrated and even more confused. I should have kept quiet at that point, which I would learn to do later in life. But I didn't.

I said, "Just because my car has an automatic transmission and doesn't make sounds like a carrier landing has nothing to do with the way I feel about you."

At which point she began to cry, and I had to suffer a setback even greater than the one at the Dairy Queen. We stayed through the entire performance of *Thunder Road*. And watched every second of it. My window remained completely unfogged.

Luckily, there was only a small dent in the front bumper of the Pontiac as a result of the collision with the dumpster in the parking lot of West's Body Shop. I told my mother somebody had backed into me as I was parked at the Dairy Queen, which she believed, which is one of the reasons I got along with my mother. She usually believed, or pretended to believe, most anything I told her, and most of the time, I told her the truth. This was different, because had I told my mother the truth, she would have gotten the wrong idea about me as a driver.

The truth was, I didn't want to drive foolishly and recklessly. I didn't like speed. I used to beg Dudley to slow down when he decided to see if he could drive his Thunderbird, with me in it, the six miles from Newnan to Moreland in less than three minutes, which he nearly accomplished at times.

The Moreland Straight was our Bonneville Salt Flats. It was a mile stretch of straight Highway 29 that extended from the airport curve (adjacent to Coweta County Airport, or as I always referred to it, Moreland International) to the city-limits sign of Moreland.

I'm not certain why nobody was ever killed on the Moreland Straight, especially me. Whenever Dudley announced, upon entering the straight, "Let's see what this son of a bitch will do"—the words still give me chills—I would beg him and plead with him to keep it under 120. He'd laugh that sinister laugh of his and say, "Hell, I can hit a hunnerd and twenty in third gear," and I'm sure he could. Dudley had a nuclear power plant under the hood of his 1960 convertible that his parents gave him in 1962 because they couldn't afford a DC-8, the next-fastest thing to the Thunderbird they gave him.

I dared not tell my mother I was attempting to get a wheel in front of the Dairy Queen and that's how the dent got there, because of my mother's steadfast belief in never spending an idle penny. To properly scratch off in impressive fashion in front of a group of friends costs about a gallon of gas, I would presume, not to mention all that rubber tread. I am convinced my mother never wasted one penny in her life. She never drove over forty-five miles per hour in order to save gasoline. She would have been OPEC's worst nightmare.

I had a job sacking groceries afternoons, so I paid Buck West four dollars to beat the bumper back in shape on the Pontiac, but I didn't mention I was the one who was responsible for the dent in his trash receptacle. So what we really have here is the fact I lied to my mother, caused property damage at a man's place of business, and blew four dollars of my hard-earned grocery sacking money for what? To impress a woman, that's what.

Things never improved with women after that, and here I am, thirty years later, and I still have a terrible time getting along with them. Maybe that's the way it is with all straight Southern white males. I'm sure that's the way it is with all the straight Southern white males I include as friends. All of us are in our forties and fifties, and none of us have any clue as to what women really want, or how to please them.

One reason for that, I suppose, is we have steadfastly resisted becoming the Sensitive Male they write about in women's magazines and Lifestyle sections of newspapers, which, more and more, are being run by women editors. It used to be women were mostly food editors in the newspaper profession. Not anymore. There are women executive editors, managing editors, and editors of editorial pages. There are women sportswriters, who go into locker rooms of all-male teams and are surprised when big dumb jocks who make so much money they can do just about whatever it is they want to do and get away with it with only a slap on the wrist, walk around with nothing but towels around them and sometimes flash their genitalia at them and make lewd remarks.

Where do they think they are? They are in a place where the machoest of the macho take showers and wash their genitalia. This is where they go to the bathroom and shave and stand around naked. In his book *Ball Four,* Jim Bouton wrote about Yogi Berra standing around naked and when he reached over the table to get some postgame fried chicken, he often dragged his genitalia through the gravy. That's the sort of place a ballplayer's locker room *is*. Female sportswriters say, "We have every right to be able to do our jobs, just as men have." What I'm for is for both men and women sportswriters to stay out of the locker rooms.

I'm digressing terribly here, because I was really about to take on women editors of Lifestyle pages and the Sensitive Male, but I'm running a little hot on this subject, as I often do, so allow me to give you the story that says it all about locker-room quotes.

A man who worked for a large Southern newspaper covered a big-time college-football game. The safety for the winning team had intercepted a pass and ran it back eighty yards in front of ninety-five thousand fans and on national television to win the game. This player played for a school with a pristine image as an academic bastion. The safety was majoring in electrical engineering (or Jumper Cable Management). He also had a distinct problem with the English language. He spoke very little of it.

The sportswriter asked the safety, "Shunanah, what were you thinking as you were running down the field with that interception, heading for a touchdown?"

Shunanah replied, "Nothin."

So get the women sportswriters out of the locker rooms, as well as the males, and let them make up quotes. If you can't write better than most athletes can talk, you should have majored in electrical engineering and sold jumper cables.

Okay, I feel better. Back to where we were. There used not to be anything called Lifestyle sections in newspapers. (They have other names, too—"Living,"

"Today," etc. An old editor friend of mine, forced to hire a woman feature editor in order to be politically correct, called it the "You and Your Vagina" section after she took over.) But one day some idiot with nothing better to do was trying to figure out where to put all the stuff that wasn't news, and figured it would be better if it was all in one section, and that's where Lifestyle sections came from. (I find it interesting that in some newspapers the obituaries may be found in the back of the "Living" sections.)

Other newspapers that had no idea where to put all the stuff that wasn't news started their own Living sections. Then newspapers had to find somebody to edit these sections, and since women had begun resenting being food editors, some became Lifestyle editors.

If you have noticed, as I have, there's been a lot more emphasis on vaginal news in the papers since all that happened. Toxic shock, yeast infections, douching, itching, and various methods of "staying fresh" (this really has to do with odor, but don't tell anybody) have been discussed at length in newspapers. My old editor friend was correct.

But what else began to happen once there were Lifestyle sections and women editors of Lifestyle sections was the women editors of Lifestyle sections decided to go after men. There were a number of reasons for that. First, all women editors of Lifestyle sections read women's magazines.

Women's magazines offer such articles as "Ten Ways to Get Rid of Those Disgusting Fat Thighs with All That Hair on Them" (Step No. 1—Shave all that hair off.) and "Aerobicize Your Way to Larger Breasts" (Put on that teeny-tiny aerobics outfit of yours and go shake your booty and do a lot of pelvic thrusts for a tighter belly in front of a doctor who

might give you a boob job for free), and they also
carry a lot of articles about men.

Before, they were mostly *nice* articles about men:
A sampling of front-cover headlines of a woman's
magazine might go like this:

—What Do Most Men Hate About Women? (I hate
it when they take my credit cards and go charge a
small New England state.)

—What Does It Mean When Your Man Talks in
His Sleep? (It means you cooked that godawful
crap with all the noodles and zucchini and celery
in it again.)

—What Is Your Man's Sexual IQ? ("I promise,
honey, I've never been with no woman named
IQ.")

—How to Tell When Your Husband or Lover
Really Adores You. (He won't moon your Tupperware party.)

—What is a Man's Idea of the Perfect Woman?
(Deaf and dumb and her father owns a liquor
store.)

—How to Keep Your Marriage Sexually Exciting.
(Find a University of Mississippi cheerleader to
stay with him while you're at the fat farm.)

Then the problem changed. I'm not certain when
most women began to hate most men, but it probably had something to do with Jane Fonda.

When Jane Fonda proved that a woman could be
just as outrageous and hateful as she wanted to and
still get away with it because most men simply can't
find it in themselves to physically hurt a woman—a
man should never, ever, hit a woman except if he's
Paul Newman who decked What's-her-name in *The
Verdict* for shitting on him the worst I've ever seen—
because most of us are still bigger than they are.

Jane Fonda got all involved in the antiwar thing

during Vietnam with that pissant-looking ex-husband of hers. Then she went to North Vietnam and aided and abetted the enemy and probably cost more American lives and more suffering for captured American servicemen. She committed an act of treason.

People who commit acts of treason against their countries are supposed to be either hanged or shot. Not Jane Fonda. We allowed her to get away with no punishment whatsoever and go on to ditch Pissant for Ted Turner, who, I am certain, soon will start a twenty-four-hour all–Jane Fonda movie cable station.

Jane Fonda was a traitor to her country and didn't have anything bad happen to her, so women all over the country figured, "If she can do that, I don't have to fix dinner anymore."

Little by little, the resentment, the hatred, began to come out of women for men.

Why hadn't they been allowed to be in Little League and wear those cute uniforms?

Why could men belch in public and get away with it, and they couldn't!

Why couldn't they wear Jockey underwear like men did?

Why did they have to shave their legs and under their arms? Men didn't.

Why couldn't they get a tee time at noon on Saturday at the club? Men could.

Why aren't there cigarettes just for women? (That led to Virginia Slims cigarettes and the Virginia Slims women's tennis tour. Soon the women tennis players started complaining they didn't make as much prize money as the men did. Soon Billie Jean King beat some old man twice her age named Bobby Riggs. Soon after that, we found out Billy Jean was gay and so was Martina Navratilova. Then you throw in women's tennis player Renée Richards, who was a guy before he had his winkie removed and a twinkie put in.)

Why couldn't they kill all the men and take over the entire country and go around with their feet stinking with no makeup on if that's what they wanted to do?

Resentment. And hate. And that's how the women's liberation movement got its start.

So the first thing that happened in the movement of these sisters ("MS.," for short) is women's magazines started giving men a hard time and suggesting to their readers that the goat breath they were living with and sleeping with was insensitive, selfish, uncaring, didn't give a damn about their sexual fulfillment, would rather watch a ball game on television than go on long walks with them, wouldn't engage in long talks about the problems in their relationship, never thought of giving them vibrators on special occasions, was probably responsible for them having PMS and was responsible for the fact they weren't a member of Congress or CEO of a large corporation.

Suddenly, on the covers of women's magazines were headlines like this:

—What Does Your Husband Do When You Say, "We Need To Talk"? (Turns up the volume on the Cubs game.)

—When Is the Last Time He Sexually Satisfied YOU? (November 8, 1971, the day I was going through his workshop and found the Black and Decker power drill with a couple of rather interesting attachments.)

—What Is Your Man's Sexual IQ? (Four years ago, he said, "I quit".)

—When Is the Last Time You Saw a Man Cry?
(When I told my husband I'd run over his dog.)
—What's Wrong with Separate Vacations Once
in a While? (We already have them. He goes
fishing, and I stay in the cabin and keep the
grease hot.)
—Women Who Refuse to Shave Their Legs and
Under Their Arms. (A brief history of the Vir-
ginia Slims tennis tour.)
—How to Tell Your Husband, "I Want to Work,
Too." (Send him a postcard. They pick up the mail
twice a week on the offshore oil rigs.)
—How to Get Out and Stay Out of the Kitchen.
(Set fire to the sucker.)
—How to Spot the Sensitive Male. (He ordered a
salad and white wine when all his buddies or-
dered a cheeseburger and a beer.)

So women started reading articles like that, and
then Phil Donahue got a television show and went
around being sensitive from coast-to-coast five mornings a week, and that led to the era of the Burning of
the Bra.

Women banded in small groups and went outside,
took off their bras, and burned them. This was to
manifest their newfound freedom; not only theirs,
but their breasts' as well. All these years, women
had worn bras so their breasts would stick out more
prominently under a sweater or blouse.

Why had they done that? Because men like pointy
breasts sticking out of sweaters and blouses.

But women showed us. They unleashed those
things and allowed them to go free under their
sweaters and blouses.

What they didn't know is, men don't have to have
pointy breasts all the time. Sometimes, they like to
see roaming breasts (depending on the breasts). If

breasts still retained an angle toward a woman's chin, better to see them under a sweater or blouse than a bra. They look like two Beagle puppies named Biscuit and Rattler fighting in a sack.

The opposite to that, of course, are breasts that point toward Rio de Janeiro rather than at Nova Scotia. Droopers. They look like two watermelons in the bottom of a hefty bag. They cry out for bras.

But women with breasts like that don't care. They refused to wear a bra anyway, which I agree certainly is their right, even if they often frightened young children who thought they were the Incredible Hulk with fallen chest arches.

So what we had then was braless women who all wanted to find a Sensitive Male like Phil Donahue. The problem was, most men thought, and still do, that Phil Donahue either sold out to gain television popularity or was an ex-pissant who probably took home ec in high school.

Didn't matter. Women *insisted* their males be sensitive like Phil, and that has caused a mountain of confusion between men and women.

Here are some of the requirements for being a Sensitive Male:

—He had to bring his woman to a sexual climax seventeen times before it was his turn, regardless of how tired he became and how late he was for the macramé class he agreed to join so they could have something to do together after they got out of bed.

—He had to take her antique shopping and pay seventy-five dollars for an old pee pot in which she could plant flowers.

—He had to cry at weddings, out of happiness, not over the idea that another good soldier had fallen.

—He had to wear an ascot when he took her on

vacation to Paris after fourteen straight years of going to the cabin fishing.

—He had to indulge in open, frank discussion of how their relationship was going and couldn't use the phrase, "Where did you get a crazy idea like that, reading *Redbook*?"

—He had to wear bikini underwear, no matter that he looked more like Yogi Berra than Jim Palmer.

—He had to go for walks, regardless of what game was on television. The fact he'd bet the mortgage and had taken the points didn't hold water either.

—He couldn't belch in public anymore, and if he had to break wind at home, he had to go outside, far away from the house, so it wouldn't scare her cat, Donahue.

—He had to read to her from Omar Khayyám's *Rubáiyát*, instead of from *Sports Illustrated* or *Soldier of Fortune*.

—He could never complain about the fact there were exactly 716 pairs of wet pantyhose hanging over his shower rod.

—He had to spend some time with *her* friends, too, no matter if a couple of them acted like they might be lesbians and had suggested to his wife what she might do to his testicles the next time he asked why she hadn't washed the dishes since Arnold Palmer won a golf tournament.

—He had to suggest, his own self, that her mother come for a weekend visit, despite the fact the last time she came, she tried to smother him with a pillow while he was asleep.

—He had to wear pants with buttons on the fly, not zippers, with no back pockets, that fit too tightly in the crotch and caused him migraine headaches because she'd seen some New York

model dressed like that in a Calvin Klein
cologne ad.

—He had to wear Calvin Klein cologne and throw
away his Old Spice, which men in his family had
been wearing for generations, no matter if the
guys at the club said, "God-damn, who smells like
a French whore?"

—He had to buy her a new Mercedes convertible,
even if it meant taking a night job at a convenience store. (It happened to Pat Buchanan and
ruined his chances at getting the 1992 Republican
presidential nomination.)

—He had to remember flowers on every special
occasion like the anniversary of the first time they
went to a sushi bar together and shared those
scrumptious carp eyeballs. He also couldn't say, "I
remember when we used to call stuff like this,
'bait.' "

—He had to say he would sleep in the wet spot
before she had to say, "You sleep on it, you're the
one that caused it."

—He had to take her to at least one ballet performance, charity auction, dull play, art festival, and
lecture by some tall, ugly female wearing glasses
with a "Dr." in front of her name on "Learning to
share in a relationship" or "Why don't you ever
take *me* to play golf?"

A list like that could go on and on, but the truth of
the matter, at the outset of the formation of the New
Woman, was they wanted their men to become pissants.

Yes, pissants. Do you know how confusing that
became to men, especially men like me with the
background I had?

It became *confusing as hell*, that's how confusing
it became. It was like a large bass that had taken a

bait and was swimming happily off with it when some television fisherman like Orlando Wilson suddenly pulled back on his rod (fishing pole) and set the hook. Suddenly, everything had gone into reverse. Your head is snapped back, your neck pops, and somebody is reeling you in the opposite direction of where you've been going since you slid down a board backward and noticed how impressed the girls on the playground were and figured this is how they want you to be—daring and tough. And one day, you were going down the sliding board on your back and didn't see the rock at the foot of the sliding board and hit the back of your head on it.

The girls all stared at you, and you knew why. They wanted to see if you were going to cry. Blood oozing from the place on the back of your head where it hit the rock. Pain, embarrassment.

But did you cry? Of course not, not until you got home to your mother, of course, the only person a tough guy like you ever felt at ease with when crying.

Now, all that had been turned around on you. Women *wanted* you to cry. They weren't impressed if you slid down the sliding board on your back. They wanted you to go sit down in the grass with them in an exercise that always began with her saying, "Why don't we ever talk?"

It continues when you ask the obvious, innocent question, "Okay, what would you like to talk about?" and she comes back with the inevitable, "If you don't know what we need to talk about, then it's pointless for us to talk."

You think that means you can go back to the sliding board, but it doesn't. It means you are a pig.

"Pig" was the key word in the outset of the women's movement. A woman got up at a session on learning to be more assertive ("Ten Ways to Deliver a Swift Groin Kick") and said, "It's time we taught these pigs a lesson or two."

"What pigs are you referring to?" asked Jeannie Mae Pilkington, recording secretary of her Junior League chapter, whose husband, Harrison, was an attorney, coach of her son's Little League team, and was knocking down a half a million a year, which was the reason she had driven a Mercedes to the assertiveness lecture and was carrying a Gucci pocketbook.

"You poor child," answered the lecturer, Maudine Hurley-Gurley, whose husband was a liberal Democrat and headed last year's drive to fund the local ballet, and was often pummeled atop his bald head by his wife when he slipped and did something like introduce her at a party by saying, "I'd like you to meet my wife . . ." instead of the more politically correct, "I'd like you to meet the person with whom I share a checking account, Ms. Maudine Gurly. The fact she occasionally puts my last name on the end of hers is simply for various legal and social reasons and, God forbid, is no reference whatsoever to the fact she is subservient to me in any way. *Au contraire*. As a matter of fact, she pummels me on the top of my bald head quite often."

Ms. Hurly-Who's-It continued with her answer to Jeannie Mae Pilkington.

"I am referring to men," she began. "*All* men. My husband, your husband, the president of the United States, the king of Prussia. They are pigs, I tell you. Swine! They should all have their testicles torn out with an emery board and then be placed on a leash to walk on all fours behind us."

She was turning red in the face now. Jeannie Mae Pilkington had her mouth open.

"Kill them, I say!" shouted Ms. Hurley-Pigkeeper. "Death to the infidels! Rise up, my sisters! What do we want?"

"Pig nuts!" shouted the group.

"I didn't hear you! What do we want?"

"PIG NUTS!" the group shouted even louder.

"When do we want them?"

"NOW!"

The group, led by Ms. Hurley-Who-Cares-What-His-Last-Name-Is, ran from the room looking for a castration victim.

Jeannie Mae Pilkington went home, punched out her husband, Harrison, breaking his glasses, called him a pig, took back her maiden name, Tushingham, and got a job changing oil in a Jiffy Lube.

"Pig," as a reference to men, later was broadened to "male chauvinist pig," and women all over the country began referring thusly to the male population, although half of them thought "chauvinist" had to do with Nikita Khrushchev in some manner.

And so there were we men.

We were hated, scorned, and we feared for our testicles. Sales on codpieces went up fourfold almost overnight. We slept on so many wet spots many of us began to grow fungi on our hindparts. Actor Bill Bixby had it so bad, he turned into a large green person who oddly resembled Lou Ferrigno.

How to deal with all this wasn't just a problem for us SSWMs. Men all over the country didn't know whether to do No. 2 or go blind. Many of them just closed their eyes and broke wind, which is to say they allowed themselves to be steamrolled into submission and gave in and took their wives to disco-dancing lessons.

I do take a certain amount of pride, however, in the fact I believe a larger percentage of SSWMs resisted than our brothers from other parts of the country. SSWMs tend to be stubborn and don't give up easily. When people from the North move South, they first have to listen to their new neighbor, Harvey Bob, rant and rave about the fact that if Lee hadn't ordered Pickett's charge at Gettysburg, the Civil War would still be going on and he could go get his deer gun and blow their brains out and get a medal, instead of getting arrested. Then they write back up North to tell friends and relatives, "These men down here are the most stubborn people I've ever met. They still think it's 1862 and want to shoot us."

Perhaps SSWMs resisted being run over by the Great Female Cowdozer (saying "Bulldozer" would be politically incorrect) because of the way we were treated by our mothers. I don't know how Northern men are treated by their Northern mothers, because I've never had a Northern mother. But I don't think that many Northern mothers got up at five in the morning to make homemade scratch biscuits for the men in their lives.

My mother was a Southern mother, and despite the fact she held a job teaching first graders how to read and write and how not to pee in their pants, she still awakened my stepfather and me with homemade scratch biscuits on many a morning.

I can recall sitting at the breakfast table and Mama bringing me over a couple of biscuits she'd already buttered for me. One of Mama's great fears was that by the time I got to my biscuit, it would be cold and wouldn't melt the butter.

So she did it for me and always said the same thing when she served them to me, "Here, Son, eat these. I already buttered them while they were hot."

One morning, I was already at the table just as

Mama pulled her biscuits out of the oven. I had eaten biscuits from other ovens, but Mama's were always the best. I asked her that morning, "Why are your biscuits so much better than everybody else's?"

She said, "It's the love I put in them, Son."

Love biscuits. There were a lot of other wonderful and kind things my mother, and likely many other Southern mothers, did for their sons. Here are some more special treatments I got from the lady everybody in town knew as Miss Christine:

—She always let me have the white meat when we had fried chicken for Sunday lunch.

—She cut up my fried eggs until I was twelve.

—For years, I thought when I took off my underwear at night and threw it on the floor, that while I was asleep, it walked to the washing machine, washed itself and then walked back into my bedroom and folded itself in my underwear drawer. My mother was doing that all the time. My mother even ironed my underwear.

—She never made me get out of bed and go to school, when she came to awaken me and I said, "Mama, I can't go to school today. I've had a change in a wart or mole."

—When I left the seat up on the commode, she never complained about it.

—She used to fry corn beef from a can for me and serve it with hand-cut French fries, navy beans, hot, buttered corn bread and ice tea. Whenever I've asked a wife to cook something like that, she's always said, "That's the nastiest-sounding thing I've heard of. Shut up and eat your pasta."

—The summer when I was sixteen, she let me drive the '58 Pontiac to Daytona with three of my friends. She's the only woman I've ever known who trusted me completely. She shouldn't have, but she did.

In a word, Mama *spoiled* me, and that's probably the primary reason I've never been able to get along with women. None ever did for me like my Mama did, and that really surprised me. Remember the song, "I Want a Gal, Just Like the Gal, Who Married Dear Ol' Dad"?

That's the way it's been for me and a lot of other guys. We wanted a cross between Gina Lollobrigida, Betty Crocker, and Mother Teresa. Sadly, there aren't any.

When I was growing up, the best thing people said about husbands were, "He's a real good provider for Janie Lou and the kids."

That's what I thought I was supposed to be, a good provider. I'd go out there and work so we could eat and live somewhere besides a trailer park, and in return, I'd be Head of the Household, the Grand Kaboola, to be cherished and waited upon, the Big Boy to whom my wife would bring homemade apple pie in the living room.

That's what most Southern men thought. But we never considered there would ever be such a thing as the "whomp biscuit," which I think probably started a lot of problems men and women of my generation have experienced. As much as I believe in the Whomp Biscuit Theory, I cannot take credit for developing it myself. The first person I ever heard talk about it was that great American Jerry Clower, of Yazoo City, Mississippi, the Southern storyteller's storyteller and a marvelous philosopher.

Jerry, who married his wife before she had a chance to get ruined, says that a man who gets homemade biscuits every morning for breakfast is very unlikely to stray. Those cute little flat-bellies one might find in some dark drinkery are awfully delicious-looking themselves, but a man getting homemade biscuits would have his priorities in order and go on home to his wife.

But then came the "whomp biscuit." That's a biscuit that comes in a can. In order to get the can open, it's necessary to beat it across the corner of your kitchen counter.

That opens the can, and there sit six of the poorest excuses for biscuits you've ever seen, which likely had been kneaded by some damn machine.

When you beat a can of biscuits on the corner of a kitchen counter, it makes the following sound:

"Whomp!"

Jerry Clower said, "One of the saddest sounds you can hear in the morning is them cans of biscuits going 'whomp' all over the neighborhood."

Jerry Clower contends the whomp biscuit is the primary reason behind the high divorce rate in this country. A man with a shot at a flat-belly isn't going to turn it down with nothing more to look forward to the next morning than "whomp biscuits."

Straight Southern white men like order in their life. They like tradition. They saw how it was with Mama and Daddy, and that's the way they thought it would be when they came of age.

But, no. By the time straight Southern white men of my generation reached thirty-five, all hell had broken loose. There was no order. There was no holding to tradition. Many of us had been divorced at least once by then and figured it was just one of those things and the next woman we married would be the one we were looking for in the first place, the Gina Lollobrigida–Betty Crocker–Mother Teresa woman.

But, as I said, they didn't exist anymore. Women

we met who were our age had been divorced a time
or two themselves and had good jobs driving their
Mercedes and selling real estate and they hated men
in the first place. Women we met who were younger
than we were all had just graduated from law school;
even if they would marry you, they would want to
keep their last name and be known as Ms. Her-
Maiden-Name-Your-Name. Beware of any woman
with a hyphenated last name, especially if she's your
wife's lawyer in your divorce trial.

Younger women who had not just graduated from
law school were aerobics instructors, and weight lift-
ers who had bigger biceps than you did, were vege-
tarians, and thought anybody who would dare eat a
slice of white bread wouldn't live until morning. If
you smoked and didn't drink Perrier, they said,
"When's the funeral?"

And you'd say, "Whose funeral?"

And they'd say, "Yours, Ashtray Breath."

Subservient women who remind us of Mama no
longer existed. Women had decided they didn't want
to be women anymore, and so they basically became
like men always have been—ambitious, greedy,
pushy, want-it-all, want-it-now individuals. And
just like that, all the rules changed. It's suddenly
like they gave you four outs in an inning in baseball.
Like they made footballs round. Like they put the
basket on the floor instead of ten feet in the air in
basketball, and everybody was trying to recruit little short guys. Like in gin rummy you could look
back through the discards.

Now, it was okay for a guy to cry, especially when
some women's libber with a hyphenated last name
had kneed him in the groin for trying to open her
door as she walked into the bank. A friend of mine
actually had that sort of thing happen to him.

He was walking into his bank, and there was a woman behind him. He opened the door and then stepped back to allow her to walk in first.

She turned violent and screamed, "I can open my own door, thank you!" and refused to walk in first.

My friend was too startled to speak. The problem got worse because he was going into the bank to apply for a loan and the woman at the door turned out to be Ms. Hatfield-McCoy, the newly promoted loan director, who got her position after she threatened a lawsuit against the bank for sexual discrimination.

Sexual rules changed dramatically, too. The thing that shocked me the most when the female orgasm was invented by the first members of the women's liberation movement sometime in the mid-to-late '70's, is that women have a thing for male buttocks. I'd never known that, but once I found out, it explained a lot to me.

I was always trying to make my face and hair look attractive to women, get a tan each summer, avoid a beer belly, and keep my nails clipped at all times.

But I never seemed to get anywhere with women based on my looks, no matter how hard I tried. I realize there wasn't a lot of raw material with which to work, but I always tried to keep myself clean and smelling good.

But in my entire life, not a single woman ever walked up to me in a bar and said, "Hey, good-lookin', whatcha got cookin'?", a line from an old Hank Williams song that basically asked the question, "Your place or mine or the nearest Motel Six?"

When I learned about the buttock fetish, I knew the problem immediately.

The women's movement changed forever sexual

relations between men and women, which yet lingers as the sexual choice of most, despite the number of Funts (see Chapter 5) who have come out of the closet.

Women, men soon learned, actually enjoyed sex, too. Previously, a lot of us, including myself, thought it was just something they had to endure so a man could have his jollies. What women got in return was that most men go to sleep soon after sex, and they could lie in bed and do their nails in peace without some man objecting to that awful sound an emery board makes when it is scraped across a fingernail.

But not so. Men came to learn women actually enjoyed sex more than they did. That's because once the women's movement began, women decided it was okay to go ahead and scream their heads off during orgasm. Previously, they would have been embarrassed to do such a thing, afraid it would make the neighbor's dog start howling. Not anymore. They don't care if they violate the city noise ordinance.

Women also were no longer afraid to have multiple orgasms. In fact, some *demand* it. This put even more pressure on the male to avoid premature ejaculation. What men had to do was somehow keep themselves from experiencing an orgasm of their own because even John Holmes, rest his soul, needed a break after his orgasm in order to be able to return to the frolic at hand.

A lot of men learned to turn their minds away from sex altogether, even in the midst of experiencing it. What they did was think of something that was completely asexual, thus delaying their orgasm.

I always think about Harry Truman. I doubt even Bess could have had an orgasm thinking about Give-'em-Hell Harry. Whenever I have sex now, I think about the atom bombs we dropped on the Japanese, the headline DEWEY DEFEATS TRUMAN, the Truman Doctrine, and the fact Truman didn't seek reelection in '52 and Dwight Eisenhower became president and Richard Nixon became vice president. Then I start thinking about Richard Nixon. Anybody who could have an orgasm thinking about him needs immediate treatment.

There was a positive side to the changes in sex that occurred because of the women's movement. There suddenly were more opportunities to have sex with women than before. Women became more sexually aggressive and more likely to agree to sex on the first date, rather than holding out until you married them or you both graduated, whichever came first.

But that soon became more of a pain than a blessing due to cable television. Before there was cable television, there was comparatively precious little sports on television. You might get one baseball game a week, for instance, on one of the networks.

After cable, though, you could get ball games out the wazoo. You could watch the Cubs on WGN, the Mets on WOR, and the Braves on TBS. ESPN started televising every dribble during the college basketball season, and during football-season weekends, you got one game after another. So there you sat, completely engrossed in Miami–FSU, or the Braves–Dodgers, and the woman in your life suddenly went into heat and began chanting, "What do I want?"

And then answering herself, at the top of her lungs, "Sex!"

Continuing with, "When do I want it?"

And, "Now! So cut off that television, big boy, and get your butt to the bedroom."

Before cable, no problem. With cable, a problem. A twofold problem. Once a man is past the age of trying to have sex with every woman on earth as often as possible (most men get past that when they take up golf or get a sexually transmitted disease) his priorities change somewhat.

After being the pursuer for so long, he often becomes the pursuee. The better way to say that is, "Not now, honey, Miami's about to score."

And even if he is dragged to the bedroom screaming, there's the problem of performing sexually when his mind is still on the fact the Braves have the bases loaded and David Justice has a 3–2 count.

I know only one man who has developed a once-unthinkable attitude about sex. We'll call him Pete. He's late forties.

"Sex is overrated," he said to me once.

"I beg your pardon?" I asked back. I'd never heard such a thing.

"You think about it," he said. "First, there's all the hassle you've got to go through to get it. You've got to find a woman, and in most cases, you've got to take her out to dinner at least once. That costs you because she wants to go someplace where they serve fancy, expensive food.

"Throw in a few cocktails and maybe a bottle of wine or two, and you've dropped three big ones. Then, even if she agrees you can go home with her, there's the chance you'll get a DUI on the way home because of the cocktails and the bottle of wine or two.

"Even if you dodge that bullet, your work is far from over. First of all, she'll probably have a couple of cats living in her apartment, and as soon as you assume the position, at least one of the cats will jump onto your bare back and scratch you, not to mention scare you to death.

"And then there's the idea in the back of your head that this person probably has had sex with lots of other guys, which means she'll not only have a lot of other guys with whom to compare you, but also one of those guys could have been Magic Johnson. And you're embarrassed to ask her if she has a condom, and you sure as hell don't have one because you still believe, even in the midst of the AIDS epidemic, wearing a condom during sex is like taking a shower in a raincoat.

"On top of that, you've had the cocktails and the bottle of wine or two, and you know since you passed forty, when you drink too much, sometimes it's impossible to call on your old friend, and what an embarrassment that can be.

"Anyway, so let's say everything works. You latch on to a multiorgasmic whom you can't seem to satisfy. Now, it's two in the morning, your back is beginning to hurt, and you've got an eight-thirty tee time.

"So you finally get to sleep at four, you feel awful when you wake up, you shoot a hundred and four on the golf course, you're out a wad of money, and for what? It's not like you've never done it before.

"I mean, what had been so different about this time and all the other times before? She didn't have a trapeze over her bed or anything. She didn't call up two girlfriends to come over and do a *ménage-à-quatre*.

"You could have stayed home, had a couple of drinks, watched a movie, gone to bed and gotten a good night's sleep and felt good the next day and shot seventy-nine. But, no, for one more notch on your gun, you went through all that trouble and expense. What are you trying to do, break Wilt Chamberlain's record of twenty thousand women? It's no wonder he couldn't shoot free throws. He was too tired.

"I'm telling you there's a lot less pressure on you when you really figure sex for what it is—overrated. You want to spend some money to really feel good? Get a massage. You can call on the telephone, and a woman will come to your house and bring her own massage table. She will put all sorts of creams on you and do things to your back you didn't think were possible. And she'll bring a tape of soft music, or the sound of rain, the wind, or the ocean, and all you've got to do is lay there. It'll cost you forty bucks an hour tops, which is less than you'll spend on a bottle of wine."

"So what you're talking about here," I said to Pete, "is celibacy."

"What I'm talking about here," he replied, "is finally figuring out the screwing you're getting is not worth the screwing you're getting."

I honestly think women's liberation has had a lot to do with men simply saying to themselves, "I don't need this crap. I'm never going to find anybody to treat me like Mama did, so I'll just give up and find me a good dog."

Some men may have even gone the homosexual route once they became so turned off by the new assertiveness of women and the fact that what many of them really want is your testicles in a jar. Those men announce they are leaving their wives and/or girlfriends and are going to Greece, or Daytona Beach, to find themselves.

I have not lost complete interest in sex, and although I admit my libido has gone the way of my once-limber back, I still enjoy sex, as long as it doesn't involve anything that might cause me bodily harm, like whips, chains, and doing it in the rest room of an airliner that has just hit a wind shear.

But no matter how low my interest in heterosexual involvements might become, I'd never run off to Greece or Daytona Beach or anyplace else to find myself. The dog route is infinitely preferable. Your dog won't bring you chicken-noodle soup when you're sick, but neither would your last wife, who probably joined a cult of women who worship Cher.

At least a dog doesn't really care when you get home, where you've been, and what condition you're in. He's just glad to see you. And if you do happen to wind up in bed with a woman after an expensive dinner, he might howl when she goes into an orgasmic seizure, but he won't jump on anybody's back.

We've also got to speak here about sexual harassment in the workplace, which is another new issue they can't stop writing about on the front pages of the Living sections.

Sexual harassment, as it is defined now, is when you walk into your office and make any reference to your secretary looking smartly, and she hauls your butt to court for sexual harassment.

The rules have changed. The Modern Woman doesn't want a compliment. Compliment her and she'll haul you to court.

I have three women in my employ. In the midst of the Anita Hill–Clarence Thomas fiasco, I called all three into my office and said, "Before any of you get any ideas, let me assure you I will never mention anything about your looks. I will never ask your breast size, never mention a porno film I saw or a *Penthouse* letter I read, and I'll also never take any

of you over to the Kennedy estate in Palm Beach
should we happen to meet at the bar.

"If any of you are ever in the Miss Black America
contest in Indianapolis, I won't get any closer to you
than Terre Haute. And if any of you have ever had
sex with Bill Clinton, please tell me so I can have
the scoop."

But didn't our mothers tell us before we went out
on our first dates, "Always compliment a young lady
on her appearance"?

Haven't we heard from thousands of women—
wives, et al.—"You never tell me how pretty I look
anymore"?

But Oleg Cassini used to do that. There would be
a beautiful model, who has just put on some of Oleg's
cosmetics in an old TV commercial.

Oleg would say to her, "You look lovely tonight,
my dear."

And she would respond, "Zank you, Oleg."

If Oleg said something like that today, the model
would respond, "See you in court, Oleg."

But let's go back to the Anita Hill–Clarence
Thomas thing. What was interesting about that is
most straight Southern white guys I know were pulling for Clarence to be confirmed as Supreme Court
justice.

In fact, a friend said, "My granddaddy wouldn't
believe I'm supporting a black man married to a
white woman for a seat on the Supreme Court of the
United States."

I think simply it's a matter of all men, black,
white, or whatever, being terribly confused about
today's woman. They also are tired of them whining
and bitching. That's the thing here. *We can't get in
the men's grill at the country club. We can't get Lee
Iacocca's job with Chrysler. We can't get elected vice*

president, and even if we did, those Neanderthals at Burning Tree wouldn't let us even step on to the grounds, much less play golf on their silly old golf course.

Whine. Whine. Bitch. Bitch.

We want you to take us to see Robin Hood *because there's a scene where you can see Kevin Costner's naked butt, but if you go to a nude dance parlor and put a five-dollar bill in a twenty-year-old's garter belt, you're sick and a sexual deviate.*

Why can't we be members of the Odd Fellows? Why wasn't a woman picked to run Operation Desert Storm? Why do we have to get PMS and you don't?

Make your own god-damn coffee. I'm not your mother. You heat a can of chicken-noodle soup if you're sick. You forgot to give me anything for Valentine's Day, you rotten, selfish S.O.B., and I need new tires for the Mercedes you gave me for Christmas.

Whine. Whine. Bitch. Bitch.

And here was Anita Hill trying to louse up poor Clarence Thomas's life. The guy was born black and into poverty and went out and worked his tail off to make something of himself.

I think George Bush nominated him just to be cute, however. I mean, here was a black guy getting named to the Supreme Court, but because he believed that in the 1990s it was pretty much every man for himself and affirmative action was too much like welfare and had the possibility of draining ambition and curtailing hard work, he was against it.

So the leaders of the brothers had a problem here. He looks black, but he doesn't act black, and that white devil George Bush should never have created this dilemma for us.

As I watched the Thomas hearings, I figured both

Ms. Hill (careful, careful) was telling some truth, a few lies, and so was Clarence Thomas. But I really think she could have left out the part about the pubic hair on the Coke can. Anybody could have put it there. Perhaps Jimmy Swaggart had dropped into the office, and one fell off his jacket from one of his frequent evening ministries.

As for Long Dong Silver, is it sexual harassment on my part if a woman happens to be reading this and I happen to mention the first porno movie I ever saw in a trailer park in Athens, Georgia, during my first year in college? The guy who ran the trailer park always showed porno movies on Friday nights, and you could get in for a dollar. Beer was fifty cents, popcorn was a dime. I went one Friday night and saw my first skin flick. It was entitled, *Tillie Goes to the Dentist for a Filling and Drilling*, but I swear I just threw it in here to make a point, so please don't show up if I'm ever nominated for the Supreme Court and charge me with sexual harassment because you read about Tillie and the dentist in my book.

Nothing in the hearings ever led me to believe Clarence Thomas ever touched Anita Hill, ever threatened her with losing her job if she didn't come across, ever asked her if she happened to be wearing panties and, if so, what color. He never kicked down the door to her apartment at three in the morning and demanded sex and breakfast. Never put his hand on her thigh at lunch, never mentioned to her about the tattoo on his Johnson, an old story that goes:

"Sure, I have a tattoo on my Johnson. When it's sleeping, it says 'Shorty's.' But when I'm around you, it says 'Shorty's Truck Stop, Chattanooga, Tennessee, open 24 hours, All the Fried Catfish You Can Eat, $4.95.'"

Clarence Thomas never did that, did he?

As I said earlier, it was interesting that the male support for Clarence Thomas crossed over racial lines. I was attending a Georgia–Vanderbilt football game in Nashville during the hearings, and I ran into a fellow SSWM, an ol' boy from rural Bowdon, Georgia, who had obviously been studying (Southern for thinking about) the Hill-Thomas affair at great length. One thing I particularly like about SSWMs is they don't sugarcoat a lot of things. They go right to the heart of a matter and then let it be known what they think and to hell with what anybody else thinks.

Bowdon stopped me at the game and said, "Lewis, you know if they just sent ol' Ted Kennedy out to Oklahoma to get that damn woman and drive her back to Washington, none of this would ever have happened."

You get Bowdon's drift. This has nothing whatsoever to do with the women's movement, but if there is anybody on this earth straight Southern white guys hate more than Teddy Kennedy, I don't know who he is, unless it's the president of the Queer Nation.

Teddy Kennedy, Mr. Liberal, Mr. Big Fat Rich Boy, Mr. Don't-Worry-I've-Driven-Over-This-Bridge-Millions-of-Times, was on the Senate panel that considered the Clarence Thomas nomination and had to deal with the sexual-harassment charges by Anita Hill.

Why didn't he decline? Here's a man with more sexual skeletons in his closet than all the television evangelists combined, sitting on a Senate panel in judgment of some black judge who may, or may not, have made some sort of move on Anita Hill.

When they asked Teddy to be on the Senate panel,

he should have declined. He could have said, "Listen, I'd really like to, but I've got some really pressing business on the next satellite we're sending to photograph Neptune."

Instead he showed up on the Senate panel and set a new, indoor record for looking uncomfortable. Hermann Göhring seemed more relaxed at the Nuremberg trials.

I looked at Kennedy being on the Senate panel this way:

1. At least Anita Hill was alive.

2. I didn't care if Clarence Thomas stood on his desk buck naked and read Anita Hill letters from *Penthouse,* he was still a better man than Ted Kennedy.

No sooner had the Clarence Thomas hearings ended than we were treated to live coverage of cousin William Kennedy Smith's rape trial. I don't know about everybody else, but my sensibilities were ruffled a bit by all the discussion of what bodily fluids were found on the alleged victim's panties. What else happened is a lot of men sided with Cousin Willie because of the female prosecutor, who whined and bitched and asked the same questions over and over again and reminded us of our ex-wives. What was this woman's problem? Any sympathy the jury might have had for the victim had to be erased by the prosecutor's nagging. I watched enough *Perry Mason* television episodes to have a certain feeling for prosecutors. Poor Hamilton Burger never won a single case against Perry. He couldn't even get one to go to the jury trial. Every time he met Perry in the courtroom, Perry always got the guilty party to confess. His secretary, Della Street, always made coffee for Perry and his crack private investigator, Paul Drake. Perry was fond of saying, "That Della, we just couldn't do without her around here." Perry also would often come into the office and tell Della about a porno movie he had seen while looking for evidence in a case where his client had been charged with indecent exposure in a theater showing X-rated films, but Della never charged him with sexual harassment.

As far as the public-indecency charge, the defendant at first said he didn't want an attorney because he felt he could get off by himself. But Perry convinced him he'd need a helping hand. The judge threw out the case, ruling the defendant was simply practicing the absolutely safest sort of sex and also ruled that every time Michael Jackson's video was shown, the one where he stood on a car and rubbed his crotch, Perry's client should get a royalty.

The judge also sternly rebuked Lieutenant Tragg for hanging out in the porno movie theater looking for people to arrest, what with all the other serious crime going on.

"I was just trying to make the theater safe from such goings on," Lieutenant Tragg said. "What if a man brought his wife and children there and they saw such a thing taking place?"

The judge said, "Tragg, you're an idiot," and Perry wins again.

Back to the William Kennedy Smith trial. I also think the fact the defendant couldn't recall taking her pantyhose off or what happened to them hurt the case. One certain way not to be taken advantage of sexually is making certain you keep your pantyhose on at all times.

Of course, Teddy was involved in that case, too, and he looked as guilty there as he did on the Thomas hearings.

And what was a man of his age doing out with his

nephew at two in the morning in a Palm Beach bar in the first place? Teddy testified he didn't hear anything and didn't see anything. Where was he, in his bedroom smashing beer cans on his forehead?

I thought with the trials of Clarence Thomas and Willie over, we would get a break from such sexual gore. But I neglected to remember that Mike (Stop Me Before I Fondle Again) Tyson was still on the loose.

Know why Mike Tyson always cries when he makes love? Mace.

Then the presidential campaign began, and we all knew somebody would get nailed with sexual misconduct because of the Gary Hart Rule of Politics, which is also a boxing adage—you can run, but you can't hide.

Sure enough, it was Arkansas Democrat Bill Clinton and the blondes. Ever really look at the wife when a politician gets nailed for fooling around and holds a press conference to say it isn't so? They show up at the press conference and stand next to their tiptoeing husband, who gives it the old "Sure, we've had our problems in our marriage like everybody else, but we've stuck by each other through it all."

What that really means is, "I promised if my wife would show up at the press conference with me and act like it's no big deal with her, if I make it to the White House, I'll buy her a lot of neat clothes like Jackie Kennedy had and let her make all the key decisions during my presidency. Hell, she's made all the key decisions when I was governor/senator anyway. I was too busy on the monkey business."

And the dutiful wife, appropriately bribed, says things like, "We've had a wonderful, strong marriage, we've had our share of problems, but because of our love and dedication to each other, we have been able to get through the trouble spots."

That means, "I'm going to wear the writing off that son of a bitch's credit card when I get to Washington, and if he so much as even mildly questions my decisions on how to run the country, I'll nail his little weenie to his desk in the Oval Office."

Of course, Clinton's wife, Hillary, got into some trouble for talking about standing by her man and then saying, "But I'm no Tammy Wynette."

Tammy Wynette had a big country hit called "Stand by Your Man," although she finally got enough of her husband, George (Possum) Jones to leave him. And I'll have to take Tammy's side on this one. George was bad to drink, and she left him home once and ordered him not to leave the house, which was boozeless. George became extremely angry after she left and took a claw hammer and pried all the heels off her closetful of shoes. It is also legend that George, with no booze in the house and no car keys, which Tammy had taken, took the riding lawn mower to the nearest liquor store.

But Tammy still had a good song in "Stand by Your Man." There was the line ". . . after all, he's just a man," which means we're not infallible, we make awful mistakes, but nobody's perfect and will you hush your nagging and bitching just for a minute?

My Uncle Frank Grizzard had the naggiest wife I ever knew. She was my Aunt Jillie-Willie. I'm not sure if that was her real name, but that's what Uncle Frank called her. Aunt Jillie talked fifty miles an hour with gusts up to seventy. She would get on Uncle Frank, a lawyer, something terrible.

"Frank, Frank, Frank," she would begin, and then light into him with a Gatling gun of verbal abuse.

Uncle Frank would listen for a while and then say, "In the very name of God, woman, can't you just be quiet for five minutes? Five little minutes is all I ask."

But Aunt Jillie-Willie couldn't be quiet for five seconds. She bitched at Uncle Frank in her sleep, which is why Uncle Frank took to sleeping on a cot in the barn where he kept his horse, which he named for his wife—Ol' Nag.

No discussion of women's liberation and the relationship between men and women would be complete without bringing up money. Not every divorce I got, not every relationship that has ended for me, had to do with money. The reason money never entered into my first two divorces was I didn't have any. My first wife took my Naugahyde couch, my stereo, and my dog. My second wife sold the Astroturf I had on the roof of our Chicago apartment complex to a neighbor for fifty dollars before she left and pocketed the money.

By the time I got around to getting my third divorce, I'd accumulated a few shekels. She took her share when she left, and she also took my popcorn popper, the one that you could put a stick of butter in and it would spray butter over each kernel of the popcorn. I loved that popcorn popper dearly because I happen to think one of the greatest rip-offs of all time is buttered popcorn in a movie theater.

"You want some butter on that popcorn?" some kid with terminal acne working behind the concession counter at a movie theater will ask you.

And you take the butter, and the kid charges you another buck. The problem, however, is the popcorn is already in the bag when he sprays the butter on it, and only the top kernels get any butter on them. What they should do is fill the bag a third full with popcorn and spray that with butter. Then put in another third, spray that with butter, etc. I tried to tell a kid with terminal acne, not to mention two earrings, purple hair, and a tattoo on his arm that said "Born to Boogie" that very thing at a movie theater one night, but he replied, *No tengo diaz, Cisso and Pancho conquienda alabama,* which is Spanish for, "Hey, man, I put the butter on like I want to put it on, you dig?"

Anyway, I was in one office with my lawyer, and my third wife was in another office with her lawyer, and my lawyer was going back and forth telling me what her reply had been to a certain offer I had made her in the rite of splitting up what's yours and mine, which is really the woman saying what she will allow you to keep, and you're lucky to get out with your underwear. I even knew of a man who had inherited tickets to the Masters golf tournament from his father. Tickets to the Masters golf tournament are the hardest tickets to come by in sports. There's a waiting list to be on the waiting list. Yup, his wife took them in the divorce.

So the lawyers go back and forth and back and forth, and I'm giving away this and giving away that, and I become frustrated, as well as broke and homeless, so I say, "Listen, just give me my popcorn popper and let her have everything else."

I've been trying to find another popcorn popper like that ever since. My ex-wife decided "everything else" wasn't quite enough.

My favorite line about divorce came from I know not where or whom. I swear I'd give credit for it here if I did. Since I don't, however, I'll just have to say that somewhere in time a man was creamed in a divorce settlement and subsequently was asked, "Think you'll ever get married again?"

To which he replied, "No, every five years or so I'm just going to find a woman I hate and give her a house."

There remains a lot to be said about women and their breasts and how both relate to men. Let us start at the top.

You and your female companion are having dinner, and another woman walks by with large breasts. Naturally, your eyes are going directly to them, and your female companion, naturally, will notice that and say, "They're not real." Women with small breasts always say that when they see women with large ones.

To be quite honest about it, most men don't really care whether or not a woman's breasts are real. It doesn't cut down on their attractiveness, and firmness is always a physical virtue. As I said earlier, breasts do not have to come in jumbo size to be pleasing to me, but if I happen to run into a large pair, it's always a joy. I don't care if they're store-bought or not. I wore a fake Rolex I bought from a guy on the street corner, and it kept perfect time. At least it did before it rusted and sort of flaked away.

I think it's a beneficial thing for a woman to have breast implants if the ones she has are harmful to her self-esteem. Certainly, I also hope there can be a safer way to enlarge breasts surgically than the previous method, but what's the difference between a woman getting new breasts and a man getting a toupee or a penile implant if his Johnson no longer responds when it is called upon?

Better living through science, that's what I say. I draw the line at steroids, of course, because their side effects have been proven to be quite harmful. But, like breast implants, if science can come up with a way a man can bulk up by using a safe drug,

I might even go for such a thing myself. I still have my hair. I admit my Johnson isn't as young as it used to be, but if I'm patient with it . . . well, I'll leave that there.

My physique, however, always has left something to be desired and has caused me my own problems with self-esteem. To be honest again, I'm skinny. Very skinny. Six-one, 165 skinny. I never take off my shirt in public because my chest resembles a washboard with hair on it. I've already discussed the lacking of my butt and legs. So, given the opportunity to bulk up safely and not have to do anything strenuous like lift weights, I'd probably take it and parade around in one of those bikini swim trunks men in Europe all wear, even if they have the bodies of Wally Cox.

Young women would swoon at my sight, and other men would be jealous and say to their female companions, "Well, those muscles aren't real," and their female companions would reply, "We don't care."

A word of caution, however, about women with large breasts. They don't need you as much as you need them, because they know they have large breasts, and as long as they don't start drooping, they can get along just fine without you because finding a replacement for you is a snap.

A woman with large breasts who will wear one of those low-cut things with a short skirt can walk into any place and have her pick of the available men. Even the unavailable ones, for that matter.

So if you are involved with a woman like that and complain because you're supporting her and expect a little gratitude once in a while, she may not say it, but she is thinking, "Who does this bozo think he is? I can have ten more just like him by sundown, or at least until happy hour is over."

Given that, it's probably better to involve one's self with a woman who does not have large breasts. Her alternatives will be greatly diminished compared with large-breasted women, and she will show more gratitude, be more forgiving, and be much more likely to hand-cut her French fries and make you an occasional biscuit from scratch.

It will also make it less likely that other guys will hit on your female companion. Men have very little (or no) scruples when it comes to women with large breasts.

I speak from experience. I once dated a girl who was the most perfectly constructed human being I'd ever seen. She would make the best-looking cheerleader in any number of conferences—Big Ten, Southeastern, Big Eight, you name it—look like a boy. If I took her to a bar and left her to go to the rest room, by the time I returned to our table, she would have had three offers for around-the-world cruises, a Mercedes convertible, a condo in Maui, and six marriage proposals. She was, as the country song goes, a hard dog to keep under the porch.

Naturally, with all these other men offering her the earth, the moon, the stars, and even an occasional part in a movie, she expected me to deliver in the same manner. I couldn't get her a part in the movie, but she did cost me the approximate price of about a half-dozen Stealth bombers with genuine leather upholstery and Jacuzzis in case the pilots needed to relax a bit.

This woman had more blond hair than Trigger, extremely large breasts, the perfect eyes, face, legs, butt, and probably pancreas. She could stop the Indy 500, runaway trains, Broadway plays, and a civil war. She dressed quite provocatively, and often wore no underwear whatsoever.

"You know that all she wants," I heard about ten thousand times, "is your money."

Hey? What's money for?

I admit, however, there are other drawbacks of dating women who look like this and have large breasts.

One of those is, if they don't want to be, they don't have to be on time. For anything.

I never got this woman a part in a movie, but I did take her with me when I appeared on the Carson show. The limo came to pick me up for the five o'clock taping.

"I'll meet you at the studio," she said.

She never showed, which likely was a blessing. She might have earned herself a co-host job if she appeared.

This woman didn't play around when it came to being late. I'd dealt with women's tardiness before, but that normally had to do with minutes.

We're talking hours and *days* with this woman. We were supposed to meet at a resort for a little vacation on Monday. She didn't show up until Thursday.

"Oh, did we say Monday?" was her reply when I asked where she'd been for three days.

I didn't argue with her. How can you argue with a goddess who might not be wearing underwear?

I had tickets for a Broadway play once. She left the hotel to go buy New York and said, "I'll meet you at the box office of the theater."

She arrived just in time to see the bows.

"You mean the show started at eight?" she whispered into my ear just before she put her tongue into it. I didn't even complain when we returned to our room and there was no place to walk because of all the clothes and accessories she had bought with my plastic the previous afternoon.

We finally broke up when my accountant said the words "Chapter Thirteen."

I'm not certain what happened to this young woman after I weaned myself of her, but I would be willing to bet twice what she cost me that there's some poor fool out there right now who is saying to himself, "I know twenty thousand dollars is a lot to spend in one afternoon at Neiman-Marcus, but God, that thong she wore to the beach in Tahiti last week."

I want to make clear here I don't think every woman on this earth has only one purpose, and that is to take every man with whom they come in contact with for every penny they can get. I know at least one who is not like that. In fact, she is half of one of the few married couples I know who are truly happy.

Allow me to tell you about my friends Tim and Roselle Jarvis.

I met Tim when I lived in Chicago and worked for the Chicago *Sun-Times*. We met playing tennis, and we would wind up playing tennis with one another practically every day for the next ten years before both our bodies went bad and we had to take up golf.

I was in Chicago three years, then moved back to Atlanta. Tim was a native Chicagoan and had never been South before. My second ex-wife actually made biscuits one morning when we were in Chicago and asked Tim and his former wife over for breakfast. Tim took one look at the biscuits as Kay was putting them in the stove and said, "So those are grits."

A few weeks after I returned to Atlanta from Chicago without No. 2, Tim came to visit me. It was during May, when Atlanta is breathtaking with its azaleas and dogwoods and wonderful weather. I'd say it's only snowed once in Chicago on May 5.

We played tennis at Pepper Rodgers's house. Pepper was head football coach at Georgia Tech at the time, and he had a beautiful house and tennis court on a lovely lot.

Tim went back to Chicago after three days in Atlanta. Six weeks later, he came back with everything he owned stuffed into a gray Volvo. He came back with everything but his wife. He had fallen in love with Atlanta and wanted no more part of any place where it snows on May 5.

The only problem Tim had in Atlanta was finding a girlfriend. He complained that the young women he met were disappointed because he didn't drive a Mercedes, and the ones his age basically hated men. We've been through that discussion before.

So after five or six years in Atlanta, Tim is reading a magazine and comes across a story about American men taking Asian wives. Tim figured, "What do I have to lose?"

He writes an address given in the article and gets a catalog with the names and pictures of Filipino women interested in meeting American men.

He writes letters to some of the young women, and they write him back. He narrows the list and then narrows it some more. One of the young women is named Roselle. She is a nurse.

Tim has this thing for skinny women. He despises what he calls "thunder thighs." Roselle has written she weighs ninety pounds.

Tim flies to the Philippines. He meets Roselle. He meets her family. He calls me and says, "I'm getting married. How about being my best man?"

Long story shortened:

Tim's family—mother, father, brother, and sister—live in San Jose, California. Roselle and her family fly to San Jose. I fly to San Jose.

I'm standing there with Tim and the minister and Roselle appears in her white wedding gown. She looks like a doll. She's tiny. She's beautiful. Tim's face lights the room. I cry. They get married. I write a column about the whole thing.

Women write me and say, "How can you glorify what's nothing more than an American man taking a mail-order bride?"

They write, "Why would a man go all the way to the Philippines to get a wife when there are so many available American women?"

They write, "This is disgusting. Obviously, all the woman wanted was to get to America. She'll ditch him in six weeks."

Men write, "How can I get a copy of that catalog?"

Gabriella is three now. She has beautiful black hair and big, brown eyes. She is my goddaughter. Tim and Roselle bestowed me with that honor. They actually meant "until death do us part."

··· 8 ···

Last and Final Chapter, Thank God

I NEED TO EXPLAIN MY POLITICS AND EXACTLY WHAT I WOULD do if I were president. You can learn an awful lot why a person says and acts the way he or she says and acts by learning of their politics and exactly what they would do if they were president.

First, my politics. It's like a friend of mine explaining what to do when you are faced with which way to turn. He said, "Always go right. If you go left, you can never go right, and if you go right, you can never go wrong."

Right is where I am on the political spectrum. The only good liberal is one who has been thrown out of office or is up in Alaska somewhere trying to save the whales and isn't around to get on my very last nerve.

You want to know just how right I am? Okay, let's take some key issues of today, and I'll tell you where I stand on them.

In no particular order, then:

Welfare: I'm against it. I explain how to take care of people who are truly needy somewhere else in this book, but I can't remember exactly where.

Immigration: America first, with apologies to one of my heroes, Pat Buchanan.

Trade Barriers: Tell the Japs if they try to sell one more Toyota, we're cranking up the *Enola Gay* again. We need to continue to trade with England, however, because I own a Jaguar and might need some parts. As far as the Germans are concerned, I don't like German wines, and I got rid of my two-seater Mercedes convertible.

I also figure we can make our own vodka, and there's nothing else in Name du Jour (formerly the Soviet Union) worth having. I've been there. Trust me. The same goes for France and their wines. And their food always has too much sauce on it.

As far as Italy is concerned, I do have a certain fondness for Gucci shoes, but I wore Bass Weejuns exclusively for years, and I can go back to them.

And North Korea can just plain kiss my butt, and I wear an American-made watch, so that's it for the Swiss. I could go on, but you should have my bent on this issue by now.

Meanwhile, allow American producers to sell anywhere to whoever'll buy whatever we're selling, which also brings up foreign aid.

Foreign Aid: Give everybody in the world who is starving some food. If one of our friends needs some weapons to battle one of our enemies, we get Schwarzkopf and go in and blow away the enemy of our friends ourselves. Cut out the middleman.

Tax Incentives for the Rich: You saw what happened with the liberals' stupid luxury tax, didn't you? It was a way to get the rich, but it didn't. The luxury tax on boats, for instance, was so high, rich people didn't buy any boats, so the boat industry went to hell and put a lot of people out of work.

We ought to keep the rich as rich as possible, because nobody poor was ever able to afford to give anybody else a job.

Defense: Stay strong. I don't trust anybody.

Quotas: No, but I do wonder why there aren't more black hockey players and so few Jewish country-music singers.

The Environment: Put a tent over Los Angeles so whatever it is they breathe out there doesn't spread to the rest of the country. Close New Jersey. Protect the water. If there is any way to save a tree when bulldozing for a new condominium complex, do it, but don't spend a lot of money trying to save the snail darter. Move the ozone layer over Chicago so the people who live there can warm up for once in their lives. Leave the fishermen alone. We can always eat baloney if we run out of fish.

Capital Punishment: I'm for it. Not a single person ever executed for murder committed another one.

Prayer in the Schools: Bring it back. Just don't paddle a kid for kicking another kid in the shins while the prayer is going on. I wonder if my fifth-grade teacher, Mrs. Covin, still remembers that incident?

All-Male Golf Clubs: Yes, yes!

All-Female Golf Clubs: The holes would be too short for a long hitter like me, so go right ahead, ladies.

All-Anything-Else Country Clubs: I'm big on the right to privacy.

The High Cost of Health Care: Just try not to get sick until somebody thinks of something.

Bumper Sticker I'm Going to Put on My Car:
NUKE THE GAY WHALES FOR JESUS.

So there I was, already past my deadline for this book and my editor was calling me every day and asking, as only editors can ask, "Where's the book? Where's the book?"

Imagine the urgency in one's voice when one is standing outside a public restroom in terrible need of getting inside and asking the person inside, "Are you through yet? Are you through yet?" That is an editor asking an author when in God's name he's finally going to turn in a manuscript. For reasons I don't understand, if a book is to come out in October, they want you to finish it by March.

"Be patient," I said to him. "Be patient. They haven't even started the NBA playoffs yet. We've got plenty of time."

Anyway, I was finally tooling toward the end of this thing when two major news stories occurred. I realized I could not turn in a book that didn't comment on both. I will start with the Rodney King verdict because it came before Murphy Brown had her bastard child on national television (that last comment to preview just where I stood on that issue).

First, one of the best lines to come out of the Rodney King thing was a white guy—I don't know who—saying, "I was so upset by the verdict, I went downtown, knocked out a window in Brooks Brothers and stole a couple of suits. Made me feel much less irate."

Some people take Xanax. Others loot, I suppose, in stressful times.

Then, I heard this one: "Why do you never shoot a looter on a bicycle?"

Answer: "It's probably your bicycle."

And this was big among the politically incorrect bunch of louts I hang out with in Atlanta:

"Did you hear the Braves traded David Justice?"

"Who'd they get?"

"Four cops from L.A. who can hit."

A few things that struck me about the entire Rodney King story, a couple of which the Speech Police, in fact, gave me tickets for:

1. There is a very simple way to keep the cops, just about any cops, from beating the hell out of you.

Do exactly what they say.

If they said, "Okay, slimeball, stand on your head and sing the third verse of 'Amazing Grace'," then you do it.

If you don't know the third verse to "Amazing Grace," you explain that to the police and ask, politely, if you may sing all the words to the theme song to *Wanted Dead or Alive* instead.

If a policeman tells you to lie flat on your belly and remain perfectly still while he puts handcuffs on you, you do that, too.

It doesn't make sense to argue with policemen or to resist them. I heard a comedian point out, "It's crazy to argue with cops. They've got guns and large sticks and they have a telephone number they can call to get *more* guys with guns and large sticks."

Rodney King, of all people, should have known that. He had had, shall we say, intimate dealings with the police before.

So here is what he could have done to have kept from getting sticked:

A. He should have pulled over when he first saw the blue lights behind him.

B. Once apprehended, whatever the police asked him to do, he should have said, "Yes, Mr. Policeman sir," and hit the third verse of "Amazing Grace" if he had been so asked to do.

He should have, in the fewest words possible, gone quietly.

Jimmy Cagney would never go quietly when he played gangsters in movies. He would also say, "You'll never take me alive, you dirty coppers!" and the coppers probably didn't really care one way or the other, so Jimmy Cagney was getting shot all the time.

If Rodney King hadn't tried to outrun the police in his car and then had gone quietly once he was caught, I would be willing to bet everything Steve McQueen in *Wanted Dead or Alive* ever collected as a bounty hunter he could have avoided a great deal of pain and there wouldn't be nearly as many people in South Central Los Angeles with free TVs the next couple of days.

2. I didn't understand the looters.

Why are these people burning their own neighborhoods and killing their own people if they're so mad about the Rodney King verdict?

It would have made a helluva lot more sense to go over to Rodeo Drive and burn and loot there. Or, even better, to have found out where all those white jurors who wouldn't convict the cops lived and go burn them out.

It was like somebody shooting me in the foot and me deciding to shoot myself in the other foot to get even.

3. I saw many photographs in newspapers during the riots showing looters. One, carried in *The Atlanta Constitution*, showed women stealing clothes out of a clothing store. The women were all smiling.

If they were that angry about the Rodney King verdict, why were they smiling? What has committing a felony and smiling while you do it got to do with rage against the justice system?

4. The videotape: "I know what I saw, and I believe it," said some of the angry protestors/burners/killers/looters.

Let me see if I've got this straight. You've seen a short videotape on television taken by an amateur photographer at night, and you are convinced you know everything that happened before, during, and after the incident?

Do you realize that during the filming of *My Three Sons* all those years it ran on television, Fred Mac-Murray wasn't on the set with everybody else? No, he did his part alone and they then cut him into scenes with the rest of the cast. And the show was filmed under very bright lights and by professioanl filmmakers. But you never knew the difference, did you? Of course, you didn't.

But Rodney King, you believe all that. You didn't see the entire videotape like the jury did. You didn't see it in slow motion like the jury did. You didn't hear every movement made on the tape analyzed like the jury did.

What you saw was a black man trying to get up off the pavement and a bunch of white cops beating him back down each time.

So let's go burn, loot, and kill. I read an article by a legal expert who dared to say, "Maybe the Simi Valley jury was right." Then, he explained why he thought that and also said he knew he was taking a chance voicing his opinion because his friends would all think he was a racist.

He said, "The L.A. policemen," referring to the description the officer gave of the black man trying to stand erect, etc., "might have just gotten on the wrong side of a metaphor."

5. What now: A colleague, who is white, said to me a few weeks after the violence, "I was hoping they wouldn't find the black guys who beat up the white truck driver."

"Why on earth?" I asked him. "He was nearly killed."

"Imagine," he answered, "what's going to happen if a jury finds them guilty?"

I've been thinking about moving back to Moreland, so I can be near the fallout shelter my stepfather built in 1962, the year of the Cuban Missile Crisis.

Okay, now for Murphy Brown.

I know Dan Quayle has said a lot of stupid things during his term as vice president, and I know he can't spell "potato."

But what he said about Murphy Brown made perfectly good sense to me.

What he said was it is typical of Hollywood to look past traditional values and glorify a woman having a baby out of wedlock.

He wasn't taking a blast at single mothers, per se. My mother was a single mother until she remarried after she divorced my father. A lot of women become single mothers for a lot of reasons that have nothing to do with morals or values. Through no fault of their own, they wind up there.

Dan Quayle was saying, "Good God, we're in enough mess here without letting go of the idea that people ought to be married first before they have children."

And I might add that if women have little boys and they don't bother with a father, those little boys might never know how to throw a baseball correctly and get it from other little boys in their schools whose fathers taught them correctly, and sure enough, those kids will be branded "pissants" by the time they're in the third grade.

So Murphy Brown is fictional. So is Santa Claus, and who'll get knocked up next?

Tinkerbell?

I probably just hit the highlights of current political issues, and I did leave out at least two because, believe it or not, there are at least two in regard to which I don't have a strict right-wing opinion.

I'll start with gun control:

I'm for it. I know that might be a shock after what I've written here before, but I do believe guns kill people, and if there were a lot fewer guns, a lot fewer people would get shot by them.

One idea would be to ban bullets. That way, the gun nuts could keep their guns, but to kill anybody with them, they would have to chase their targets down and beat them over the head with their guns.

That's a lot more trouble and takes a lot more time than simply pointing a gun at somebody and pulling the trigger. Of course, there would be bumper stickers that said, OUTLAW BULLETS AND ONLY OUTLAWS WILL HAVE BULLETS.

I'll give you that, but at least people who aren't outlaws might not have to go through the horrible experience of one of their children finding the household gun and shooting himself or a playmate.

But I don't hold to the theory that some sort of sane, intelligent form of gun control necessarily would lead to a total end to the right to bear arms. I simply don't think when the Founding Fathers put in that right, they had any inkling there would ever be anything like Uzis and drive-by shootings. In those days, the only guns were those that took a half hour to load, and you could load only one shot at a time. We have guns now that will fire the same amount of bullets in about eight minutes that were fired in the entire Revolutionary War.

Do you think Benjamin Franklin ever considered Saturday-night specials and liquor-store holdup killings? Of course not. Thomas Jefferson didn't either.

I'll bet if Benjamin Franklin had said to Thomas Jefferson when they were discussing the right to bear arms, "Hey, maybe we'd better temper this a little in case two hundred years from now drug dealers have bazookas," Tom would have agreed with him.

The gun nuts with the National Rifle Association, whose motto is "Shoot first, make a rational decision later," claim that any form of gun control eventually will lead to a total ban on firearms, and people won't be able to have a gun in the house for protection, to go hunting, trap shooting, or enjoy a little target practice.

That's like saying when the speed limit was lowered, which I was against, incidentally, eventually we wouldn't be able to drive at all.

What I want is some form of gun control that keeps guns out of the hands of people who might shoot other people. It's not possible to establish a foolproof method here, but it is possible to make it a lot more difficult for some nut who has decided to shoot up a cafeteria filled with people to get his hands on firearms.

I think before you can buy a gun in this country, you ought to be made to go before a gun board. Get a minister or two on there, a teacher, a Scoutmaster, and maybe a couple of people who have been shot when somebody tried to rob their places of business.

You go and plead your case to the gun board.

You have to have recommendations from former

employers, no past criminal record, no history of mental illness, and you must explain in detail why you want the gun in the first place.

BOARD MEMBER: So, Mr. Barrow, why do you want this gun?

MR. BARROW: Me and my honey Bonnie are going out and rob a lot of banks.

BOARD MEMBER: Request denied.

But if somebody comes before the board who has a clean record, doesn't have a tattoo that reads "Born to Kill," and wants a gun in his convenience store because people keep coming in to rob him, the board agrees to the purchase.

The board obviously will screw up occasionally, as every board does. But if its hit-and-miss rate is 50 percent, it would cut out at least half the crazies who want to shoot somebody.

What else I would do is not let anybody have any sort of gun that could shoot up an entire apartment complex in eight seconds. Make automatic weapons illegal for everybody who isn't about to go into war.

I mean, if you want to own a gun that fires multiple rounds per second, it's not likely you want that gun to go into the woods and shoot Bambi. You can do that with one bullet. With an Uzi, Bambi would be filled with holes, there wouldn't be enough big parts left to tie on your car and drive through the neighborhood to impress everybody with your hunting prowess.

If a person came in and wanted a handgun because this person lived in a bad area and people were always breaking in, the board would okay it, as long as this person met the aforementioned requirements.

However, the board would also tell this person, "Hide this gun so no kids can find it."

If a kid did find it and shot himself or herself or somebody else, then the person who went before the board to get the gun in the first place would be charged with all sorts of crimes. That would make adults be a lot more careful about putting their guns in places their children couldn't get their hands on them. If I owned a gun, which I don't, and had children, which I don't, I would put my gun in the safest place I could think of, and each time I left the house, I'd take all the bullets out and carry them with me, just in case.

I've been hunting only once in my life, so I admit I don't give one hoot about it. My grandfather and my uncle made me go hunting with them on Thanksgiving afternoon. I didn't want to go hunting, and I hid in the pump house, but they found me anyway and said, "If you don't go hunting, it means you're a pissant."

So I went. They both had shotguns. They gave me a .22 rifle. We were going to hunt rabbits.

My uncle said, "You can't hit a rabbit with a .22 when it's running, but maybe you can find one sitting in his bed."

That's just what I wanted to do, shoot some harmless rabbit in its bed. I prayed I didn't find one, and I didn't.

It was also cold and wet in the woods, the gun became heavy, and I got tangled up in a lot of briers. I decided at that point if not going hunting meant I was a pissant, I'd just have to be one. The next Thanksgiving afternoon, I ate six pieces of pumpkin pie so I would throw up and couldn't go hunting. It worked, and I've never been hunting again. I've also never eaten any more pumpkin pie, but that was a welcome price to pay.

Hunt if you want to, but if I had anything to do with it, I'd change the hunting rules a bit.

First, I would make it against the law to say you were going hunting in order to do whatever it is you're hunting a favor.

Deer hunters say, "If we don't kill the deer and keep the population down, they'll run out of food and starve to death."

If one is that concerned over animals starving, why doesn't one simply go into the woods every day and leave a lot of food?

If I'm a deer, I just couldn't think of getting blown away as the hunter doing me a favor.

I also think it's unfair that deer don't have guns so they can shoot back. Okay, so deer couldn't be taught to shoot a gun. Then how about this? Hunters all have to go into the woods and hunt naked. The deer are naked, too, after all. So you get something rather tender tangled up in the briers? It's simply the price you pay in order to give the deer a better chance.

I'm also a little skeptical when I hear deer hunters say, "What's the difference in me shooting a deer to eat and farmers sending all those cows to slaughter?"

That's a good point, but I just can't make myself believe any modern-day hunter goes hunting for the primary purpose of feeding his face. He goes to see the deer fall when he shoots it.

So I would make another rule that if you killed a deer, you had to eat the whole thing before you could go back into the woods and shoot another one. I would have game wardens do surprise freezer checks, and if they found out you still had some deer in there, but you were still going out hunting for another, you would be heavily fined and made to wear antlers and a target on your butt to go hunting again.

None of this, of course, fits with the usual stereotyping of the conservative, and neither does my stance on abortion.

I'm for it. Sort of. I don't mean to waffle here, but I figure if it's my body, I've got a right to do with it what I want. It's why I still smoke after trying to give it up 417 times, and will continue to eat real hamburgers even when they come out with soybean burgers that are supposed to taste the same. I'll know it's not a real hamburger, and that's enough for me, no matter how it tastes.

The "sort-of" part here, however, is very few women ever get pregnant by accident. I mean, a jar of sperm doesn't fall over somewhere, and some of those little devils don't crawl into an unsuspecting womb.

So I figure one of the ways to cool off the abortion debate is for women who don't want to become pregnant not to have sex. That, as is the case with AIDS, is a surefire solution. There hasn't been one other single report of a virgin birth for nearly two thousand years now.

Contraceptives work. We know that. But not always. We know that, too. So if you are a woman and you don't want to get pregnant, abstinence is the way to assure yourself you won't.

Just to be on the safe side, however, another idea is always to wear pantyhose and, in any situation whatsoever, refuse to take them off. Pantyhose are the modern version of the chastity belt. As long as your pantyhose are on, you're safe from getting pregnant.

If women who didn't want to get pregnant would follow this advice, there wouldn't be a need for so many abortions, and people could stop fighting one another on the streets over this issue.

So if a woman came to an abortion clinic and asked for one, she'd have to fill out a questionnaire swearing her pantyhose suddenly disintegrated when somebody like Mike Tyson took them off her. Otherwise, she'd have to pay the fiddler, and not get the abortion.

There are instances when I think abortions are absolutely necessary. One is, of course, if having the baby would endanger the mother's life. Another is if a rape has occurred, or it's a twelve-year-old girl whose parents had refused to let her take sex-education classes.

I'm against welfare, but as long as we have it, I'd stop it for any welfare mother with nine children already who gets pregnant again. I would say, "No more welfare unless you get an abortion, and don't give me this 'I-didn't-mean-to-get-pregnant-again' look. If nothing else, here's a dime. Make certain you hold this sucker between your knees at all times, and we won't have to go through this messy little situation over and over again."

With some issues, there must be compromise, and this is one of them. What I think is happening, however, is this is an issue activists can really have some fun with.

Pro life gets on one side of the street, and pro choice gets on the other. Everybody carries a sign, and everybody chants. Then they argue with each other, and some even duke it out.

This, of course, then appears on the evening news, and everybody's suddenly a TV star, and what was that joke about Dan Quayle being asked about *Roe* v. *Wade?* Did he say, "Wade by a knockout in the sixth"?

Animal rights? I'm for them in most instances because I don't like to see anybody harm a dog. But I still want to eat steak and barbecue.

I don't own a single fur anything, however, and if animals were protected against becoming coats and hats, it would save men a lot of money because their wives wouldn't ask for such expensive clothing.

How about lizard boots?

I've never owned anything from lizards, but I do remember a story from that great American Jerry Clower, the storyteller.

Jerry said he was on a talk show in California and was wearing his lizard boots. One of the show's producers saw his boots and began to lecture him about the fact a little animal had to die for him to have those boots.

Jerry replied, "No, ma'am. The lizard they used to make these boots had done been run over by a Greyhound bus and the bootmaker found him in the road."

He also added, "Some people are educated way beyond their intelligence level," which says one helluva lot.

I feel the real problem we have with the hottest issues of the day is this: It comes down to too much either/or. Nobody is willing to compromise, because fighting and screaming and getting on TV is a lot more fun than sitting down to take it point by point.

I mentioned earlier, I would explain what I would do if I were president. I'd put the speed limit back to seventy on the interstates and arrest anybody who got into the passing lane and went forty-five.

I'd make whining against the law, too, and I'd also order the Seattle Mariners moved to Washington and sold to the highest American bidder.

Let the Japs get their hands in American baseball

and pretty soon Tommy Lasorda will be bowing to umpires while he tells them what effing idiots they are.

I would make sure not a single dime of tax money went to any sort of art exhibit where there was any sort of image showing a naked man with a bullwhip in his rectum. Anybody who violated this would have to read and memorize every speech Senator Jesse Helms ever made.

If anybody wanted to ride around on a motorcycle without wearing a helmet, I'd let him. We wouldn't have nearly as much trouble with bikers if we did that.

I would order the airlines to seal off a space in all their planes for smokers, as long as they promised to return their seat backs to their original upright and locked position for takeoff and landing. And in the unlikely event of cabin depressurization, I would expect them to stop smoking, but I would allow them to have a drink during takeoffs and landings, which is the time I need a drink the most while flying.

I'd make members of Congress pay for everything in cash and travel on Amtrak. Coach. I'm very angry at Congress and probably would become even angrier if I were president and had to deal with it.

I would put any television evangelist who isn't already in jail behind bars if he cried when begging for donations.

I would order any television commercials barred that had to do with keeping a female "fresh." Same for anything a woman wears in case she pees in her pants.

I'd ask the Israelis to get rid of Saddam Hussein and Mu'ammar Qaddafi. They would be glad to. I'd impose a fine on any athlete who said "you know" more than five times in any single interview. I would tell Magic Johnson to stick a basketball in it the next time he complained about what my administration was doing about AIDS. If Magic had kept his jockstrap on, well . . .

I would put an immediate cap on television talk shows, like *Donahue, Geraldo,* and *Oprah Winfrey.* I also wouldn't allow any more programs like *Hard Copy* or *Current Affair.* The president is sick and tired of all those shows and would rather watch old black-and-white movies.

There are also a few things I'd do if I were president regarding the form of government we have now.

Speaking of Ben Franklin, Thomas Jefferson, and the boys, wasn't it their idea that the federal government be weak and stay the hell out of our lives for the most part?

It was. When Ben said to Tom, "Do you think the federal government should have anything to do with anything like public television, getting involved in the arts, or taxing people out the wazoo to pay for 17 septmillion government programs," I think Tom would have said, "My, Ben, but I think you've tarried a bit too long in the grape again."

Here is what I would do if somebody asked me to take charge of all the problems we have in this country:

I'd basically do away with the federal government and allow the states to figure things out on their own.

The only thing I think the federal government should be involved in is making sure we have a strong defense to fight foreigners in case that ever became necessary. We would elect a president to be simply commander in chief of our armed forces. He would say whom we were going to bomb and when.

This idea came to me when I was watching the news and somebody said if Congress didn't vote to give out the money it takes to run the federal government by such-and-such a date, "all nonessential governmental services will be shut down."

I asked myself, "If they're nonessential, then why the hell am I paying taxes to keep them going?"

What really *is* essential? The post office? We've got Fed Ex and all those other companies. Manning national parks? Give them back to the bears. They were there first anyway. The space program? Hey, we sent a man to the moon, and all we got was a few stupid rocks. If there's life on Uranus, they'll get in touch with us sooner or later.

Amtrak? Let Disney build a railroad hooking up Disneyland and Disney World with the rest of the country, since that's where most people are going to these days anyway.

Grants? No more grants. To study anything. Especially things like "How porcupines can sleep on their backs with all those pricks." They can do it because God *wanted* it that way! So there's no reason to spend a lot of money to study it.

We don't need all those people who work in the Smithsonian and the other points of interest in Washington on the federal payroll. No. Make Washington, D.C., a state and let it pay for all that.

What you do first is to disband Congress. Make 'em all go back home and get a real job. Once a year, all the state governors will have a convention and discuss anything they need done on a national basis, which shouldn't be one helluva lot if the states ran themselves, free of federal interference.

If they want to build a road between Spokane and Tacoma, fine. Let the people in Washington pay for it. If Georgia needs a new bridge over the Oconee River near Athens, Georgia can pay for it.

And if Texas and Oklahoma get into some sort of dispute and go to war with each other, fine. The rest of us will watch it on CNN.

If there were no longer a huge federal government, I realize all those bureaucrats would be out of a job. Tough titty. Go back to Alabama and open up a bait-and-beer store.

Maybe we would have to pay more state taxes, but that's okay. I think I would be able to keep up with where my taxes went if the state, not some monolith called the federal government, had control of them.

With no federal government, we'd save billions and trillions. The states could run their own schools, build their own roads and bridges, decide for themselves what to do about their environments, make their own laws about sodomy, and simply mind their own businesses.

How simple that would be. How clean that would be. That's what the Founding Fathers had in mind in the first place. If they'd known the federal government was going to grow to the size it is today, they probably would have said, "Hell, we might as well let the British stay. Maybe they don't have as many lawyers."

No, I wouldn't kill all the lawyers. I'd let the states decide for themselves what to do about their own lawyers. In Georgia, I would hope we could cut it down to about one per thousand citizens, instead of a thousand lawyers per one citizen.

Now, you can start throwing specifics at me, so go ahead.

What would happen if one state, say, Iowa, decided it didn't want anybody from another state moving in?

You want to live in Iowa? Where do you live now,

New Jersey? That's the only reason I could think of anybody would want to move to Iowa. But that would be Iowa's business.

What if a state like Florida made you pay an entry fee when you went to Disney World?

Been to Orlando and seen all the traffic there lately? I think such an idea would help Florida a lot and make a lot of slow-driving Yankees who move there to retire to consider staying in Pennsylvania.

What if the South got together and decided to secede again?

The first thing I would do as president of the New Confederacy is try to take Hilton Head Island, South Carolina, back from the Yankees.

What if one state attacked another?

I mentioned that already. A war between Oklahoma and Texas would be a lot of fun to watch on TV, I think.

If commander in chief was his only duty, would the president wear a military uniform?

Sure. Think how Ronald Reagan would have looked decked out in a great-looking military outfit we'd have had somebody like Bill Blass design for him.

What if one of the states ran into some trouble, economic or whatever. Who would help it?

The other forty-nine. We would all pitch in and say, "South Dakota is one of our neighbors. We can't let it down in its time of need."

What would we do about federal protection for the wetlands?

Aren't you paying attention? If Louisiana didn't want any condos built in the bayou, that's its business.

What if several states ganged up on another state because they didn't like some of the things the other state was doing? Who would step in to handle that?

Look, I haven't worked out every tiny little point yet. Off the top of my head, however, I'd say there was something called "keeping the domestic tranquillity" in our forefathers' idea of what our union would be. Perhaps there could come a time when the commander in chief would be asked to send in a few troops for that purpose, but I don't see this happening very much. If each state had to deal with all the things the feds used to do for them, they'd probably be too damn busy to worry about what was going on in a neighboring state.

Have you ever tried marijuana?

Yes, when I was a Roads Scholar. They told me if my grades didn't pick up, I could hit the road. But I didn't light it.

Speaking of drugs, how could we continue the war on drugs with no strong central government?

Again, it would be up to the individual states. But what I think each should do is legalize drugs, since liquor is legal and it kills more people annually than cocaine.

We tried Prohibition with alcohol, and that didn't work. We've tried to keep people from using drugs, too, and *that* hasn't worked. They will find a way.

Legalize drugs. Then each state can pass laws that will help keep them out of the hands of at least some minors. It's easier to control minors' usage if the way you get drugs is over the counter in a convenience store, not from some dealer in a back alley.

Drugs aren't going to disappear. People aren't going to stop using them. Think of the money that would be saved if we didn't have to pay federal agents for beating their heads against the wall trying to control the uncontrollable.

There always has been too much of an effort on

the part of government to legislate morality. It's the Lifestyle Police. It's time to kick them out and decriminalize activities that don't fall under the category of a moral no-nos for everybody. Murder is a moral no-no. However, if you don't want to go to the horse track and lose money, then don't—but I enjoy it, and if I want to toss away ten bucks on a 30–1 longshot, that's my business.

If I were governor of my state, I'd fight any laws against nude-dancing clubs, too. It's still a pretty good idea not to let any of the customers touch any of the dancers, though, which every place I've ever been in enforces to the hilt. But if I want to go and see some of God's best handiwork, I don't think there should be a law against me doing that.

The victimless crimes need to go. That would allow the cops to concentrate on crimes like murder, rape, theft, and swindling folks on a driveway-paving deal, instead of staking out an adult movie theater to see whom they can catch whacking off. It would also free up our jails and courts, and, as I mentioned earlier, isn't whacking off the safest sex of all in the first place?

I fully realize, after all that, however, the chances of my idea of dismantling about 98 percent of the federal government has no chance of actually happening. It's too radical. And it makes too much sense.

But there is one thing I think we can do that could be adapted rather easily.

Under our present system, there is no way to really monitor the performance of the Congresspersons we send to Washington. Goofballs, polecats, swindlers, thieves, do-nothings, and check-kiters keep getting in. Some stay in office for a long time and continue to goof off, stink up the place, swindle, steal, do nothing, and write 888 bad checks.

First, we go to a one-term limit on members of Congress. Let's say six years for a senator, four for a representative.

I'm convinced Congress is where everything goes wrong in Washington. The president is just one person, and the opposition party can keep him from enacting any sort of sweeping reforms, such as the radical idea of not allowing the government to spend money it doesn't have.

Okay, we go to a one-term limit. But that's not all we do. We've got to make the people elected to Congress, even for just one term, realize they can't screw around with us and not have to pay a penalty. They are there to serve the people who elected them, not lobbyists and special-interest groups.

So each state also elects somebody to sit on a panel with a representative from all the other states. This panel could be called the Congressional Review Board. I like that.

States would elect people who had never been politicians before and had no political ambition. But good people. Successful people.

In North Carolina, they could elect the Reverend Dr. Billy Graham, the only televangelist I trust. In Texas, they could elect former University of Texas football coach Darrell Royal, for instance. I think it was Darrell who said, "There's only three things that can happen when you pass the ball, and two of them are bad."

I like a man with deductive powers like that.

In California, they could elect Gregory Peck to the Congressional Review Board. Ever since I saw *To Kill a Mockingbird,* I've trusted Gregory Peck.

In Oklahoma, I don't care who they elect, as long as it's not Oral Roberts or his son.

I live in Georgia. We could elect television anchorperson Monica Kaufman, whom I've always admired for not giggling a lot when she is giving the news. Too many local TV people giggle and engage in repartee with the weather or sports guy to suit me.

Anyway, when a senator or a representative had served his six or four years, this person would go before the Congressional Review Board, who would have been given a record of this person's activities while in office—the voting record, the absentee record, how many checks he or she kited, how many DUIs there were, how many affairs took place, all that sort of stuff.

The member of Congress would be allowed to plead his or her case before the board. Then the board would vote on whether this person did a good job or a bad job while in office. If the vote said, "good job," this person would be allowed to live. If not, this scoundrel would go before a National Rifle Association firing squad.

I realize that sounds terribly harsh, but it's time for a little harshness. Anybody who wanted to run for Congress would be warned ahead of time about the board and the firing squad, and I think that would weed out a lot of pretenders from seeking political office.

But you may be asking, "Who would review the board?"

I haven't figured that out yet, either, but if Bear Bryant were still alive, I would think he would be a good choice.

So that's my politics, and those are my plans. As I said earlier, one should not rest one's case as long as one still thinks one has finished his say.

Well, that pretty much does it, and if I forget anything, I still have one book left on my current contract, so there's always next year.

But at least I've had my say, and at least there was still somebody around who would let me have it. Freedom of expression certainly is being hindered, but I managed to get these thoughts through.

I thank my publisher for that, and I thank my editor, who said to me, "I don't agree with a lot of this, but I think you ought to be able to say it."

My editor's name is Peter, by the way. He is one of the few Yankee liberal cat-lovers I deeply care about, and I think if he hangs around me enough, he really has a good chance to come to his senses.

So, what next? Well, it's April 1992 as I type this. By the time the book is out, the presidential election will be over or will be near. I predict Bush will be reelected. But I was for Buchanan first, and I can't wait to see if Ross Perot gets in the middle of it all.

It will also be football season again when this book is released. At Georgia, we have a great sophomore quarterback named Eric Zeier. Oh, to see him cast once more at the defensive secondary.

Grand Canyon was the worst movie I have seen in 1992. *Fried Green Tomatoes* was the best. The Atlanta Braves are off to an awful start, but Otis Nixon is back with the team after getting kicked off because of drugs.

I stand ready now to take the fire of the Speech Police, the Thought Police, and the Lifestyle Police. I've already picked out a hiding place in case I have to do a quick Salman Rushdie. By the way, I've always wanted to write a book about my operations and hospital stays called *Satanic Nurses,* but know I'll probably have to have another operation and go back into the hospital someday, and nurses are the ones who are in charge of the pain medicine.

So I leave you now, the same as I started—still a confused, often-bewildered heterosexual Southern white male.

My hair is turning gray, and I'm having trouble getting off the tee with my driver. But I still haven't married again, and I had Fred Couples in a Masters pool.

I think what I will do is put on a Willie Nelson tape, call Catfish over beside me, put my feet up on the coffee table, and have myself a cold beer.

God bless America, and how 'bout them Dawgs.

If laughter is the best medicine, then

LEWIS GRIZZARD

is recommended by 9 out of 10 doctors

to cure what ails you.

Published by Ballantine Books.